WHY ANIMAL EXPERIMENTATION MATTERS

SOCIAL PHILOSOPHY AND
POLICY FOUNDATION

WHY ANIMAL EXPERIMENTATION MATTERS

The Use of Animals in Medical Research

Edited by Ellen Frankel Paul and Jeffrey Paul

transaction

Transaction Publishers
New Brunswick (USA) and London (UK)

Published by the Social Philosophy and Policy Foundation and by Transaction
Publishers 2001

Library of Congress Cataloging-in-Publication Data

Why animal experimentation matters : the use of animals in medical research /
edited by Ellen Frankel Paul, Jeffrey Paul.
      p. cm—(New studies in social policy ; 2)
    Includes bibliographical references and index.
    ISBN 0-7658-0025-X (cloth)—ISBN 0-7658-0685-1 (paper)

    1. Animal experimentation—Moral and ethical aspects. 2. Animal models
in research—Moral and ethical aspects. 3. Medicine—Research—Moral
and ethical aspects. 4. Animals—Treatment—Moral and ethical aspects.
I. Paul, Ellen Frankel. II. Paul, Jeffrey. III. Series.
R853.A53.W47 2001
174′.28—dc21

                                      99-047844

Cover Design: Kathy Horn
Cover Image Credits: Patient in bed—© Blair Seitz/Stock Connection
                    Mouse on vials—www.comstock.com

*To the brave and inquisitive scientists who advance
medical knowledge and better the human condition*

Series Editor: Ellen Frankel Paul
Series Managing Editor: Matthew Buckley

The Social Philosophy and Policy Foundation, an independent 501(c)(3) tax-exempt corporation, was established in 1985 to promote advanced research in political philosophy and in the philosophical analysis of public policy questions.

Contents

Acknowledgments

The editors would like to acknowledge several individuals at the Social Philosophy and Policy Center, Bowling Green State University, who provided invaluable assistance in the preparation of this volume. They include Mary Dilsaver, Terrie Weaver, Carrie-Ann Biondi, and Pamela Phillips.

The editors would also like to thank Publication Specialist Tamara Sharp, for attending to innumerable details of the book's day-to-day preparation, and Managing Editor Matthew Buckley, for providing dedicated assistance throughout the editorial and production process.

Introduction

A teenager is rushed from an after-prom party to the nearest emergency room with head and neck trauma from a diving board accident. His neck is broken, and the prognosis is grim. The youngster will in all likelihood be a quadriplegic, with little prospect of ever recovering the use of his limbs. For fulfilling the simplest of life's functions, he will be dependent upon the assistance of caregivers. This scenario is all too familiar, and immensely frustrating for the attending physicians, who can offer scant hope of recovery because severed or severely damaged spinal cord nerves cannot be naturally regenerated by the body. Whether from an automobile accident or hijinks gone wrong at the local swimming pool, injuries of this sort are justly categorized as catastrophic, both for the patient and for his family. It is shocking to our sensibilities that a life can be turned around so ruinously in a fraction of a second.

Where does hope lie for this teenager and for those who will surely follow him? Cutting-edge research on regenerating damaged nerves may one day unlock the secret, and ER doctors will then be able to offer many of these victims a brighter future than a life of severe impairment of major bodily functions. Less than one month into the new millennium, newspapers carried stories about the identification by three research teams of a gene, named Nogo, that produces a protein that apparently blocks spinal cord and brain nerves from regenerating. This may be a first step toward the development of a drug that could block the protein, and thus allow these damaged nerves to repair themselves. However, as in all things scientific, the whole process is highly speculative, and many promising beginnings in spinal cord regeneration have led down blind alleys. While nerves in other parts of the body do repair themselves, spinal cord and brain research is aimed at unlocking one of the human body's most mysterious defense systems.

Breakthroughs in treating spinal cord injuries, like practically all medical advances, depend upon experimentation on animals. In the studies involving the Nogo gene, rats were the experimental animals of choice. Rats whose spinal cords had been partly paralyzed experienced some restoration of function to their legs after treatment with a Nogo antibody. This success provided researchers with confirmation that they were at least pursuing a potentially viable course of investigation. This was a much more revealing finding than the Nogo protein's ability to thwart the normal nerve growth of other types of nerves

1

in vitro; thus, there was no adequate substitute for experimentation on animals. The members of one of the research teams, from the University of Zurich, who achieved the nerve regeneration in rats hope that their discovery will lead to a drug that can be tested in humans suffering from spinal cord injuries. Stroke and multiple sclerosis sufferers may also benefit from this same genetic discovery.

In addition to the innate difficulty of spinal cord research, there is another impediment to progress, one that is perhaps even more frustrating. This impediment is posed by the many highly vocal activists, philosophers, and even some scientists who oppose all scientific experimentation on animals—rats, birds, and mice included. More extreme elements within this antivivisection* movement wish to end animal research immediately. Animal rights activists have attacked laboratories, threatened scientists, and, in Great Britain, even posted on the Internet a list of ten researchers targeted for assassination. Other, more moderate animal rights advocates wish to severely curtail experimentation on animals beyond measures already in place for many years in Europe and the United States, with the ultimate goal of ending all such research.

Although the case for animal experimentation is a strong one, animal rights advocates have thus far been much more successful in stating their case to the public. Most people in advanced industrial societies have little contact with animals, for most are generations removed from the farm. Animals are our furry children, spoiled and doted upon as our beloved pets. The slaughter of farm animals is not within our repertoire. It is very easy, then, for animal rights activists to tug at our emotions with pictures of laboratory cats and dogs suffering the aftereffects of disfiguring surgeries. It is difficult for us to think of medical advances and the furtherance of human knowledge when we imagine the visage of our family pet on the laboratory animal's body.

This lopsided emotional factor favoring the animal rights position is the principal reason why we thought it desirable to assemble a cast of leading research scientists to express their thoughts and feelings about what they do in their laboratories, the benefits that their research produces, and how their work is perceived by activists and the public. Accompanied by philosophers and historians who, to varying degrees, share the scientists' appreciation of the necessity of animal research, this collection represents one side in the debate, the side that has typically gone about its business, neither seeking nor receiving much in the way of sympathetic publicity. Thus, this collection, by design, does not represent the work of those who wish to end animal research. Rather, it is dedicated to furthering the public's understanding of what research scientists do in their laboratories, and of how vital their work is to the health and welfare of all of us, especially to our children and their children.

Vivisection is dissection or surgery performed on animals for scientific purposes.

This volume had its origins in a working group that brought together all of the authors to discuss and critique each other's preliminary arguments. As someone who works decidedly outside of the scientific community—as a political philosopher—what struck me the most about the scientists was their dedication to the advancement of human knowledge and their hope that their lifetimes spent in the laboratory will one day banish the genetic and infectious diseases that blight so many human lives. Cynicism, an occupational hazard among many academics, was not present among these scientists; they were optimists all, determined to make their contribution to the welfare of their fellows. Their only regrets were expressed over the misunderstandings of their enterprise that they believe the animal rights advocates have spread so effectively among the public. Some expressed outrage, but not fear, against the extremists who have carried out acts of violence against their labs and those of their colleagues.

The scientists repeatedly took me aside and implored me to craft an introduction to their essays that would make readers understand what is at stake in the activists' campaign to end or drastically curtail animal experimentation. I promised to do my best. The stakes are, indeed, high. Despite the claims to the contrary by animal rights activists, for most vital medical research there is at this time no sufficient substitute for animals. A ban on experimentation—or the implementation of a vastly more restrictive regime than the one that the government presently enforces—would leave the population vulnerable to the next deadly AIDS or Ebola virus that suddenly appears. Antibiotics that are now nearing the end of their utility in combating many deadly bacteria could not be replaced by next-generation drugs of greater efficacy. People afflicted with genetic or communicable diseases, or suffering from catastrophic accidents, would be denied hope of future discoveries that might palliate or remedy their afflictions. Life does not stand still, and neither do the threats to human life in the form of pathogens as yet unknown. We ought not hobble our ingenious, dedicated, and compassionate research scientists who want to advance human knowledge so that future threats to life, organic and otherwise, are manageable, rather than mysterious and calamitous.

I. Past, Present, and Future:
The Contribution of Animals to Human Health

A perusal of the list of research projects that have received the Nobel Prize in medicine since its inception in 1901 reveals just how critical animal experimentation has been to the understanding of biological functions, pathogens, genetic diseases, and their treatment. Mice and other rodents contributed to the 1984 recipients' development of the technique of forming monoclonal antibodies,[1] a discovery that led to new tools for fighting some types of cancers.

Mice also played a part in the 1996 winner's understanding of how the immune system detects cells infected with viruses. Earlier, mice were instrumental in the understanding of penicillin's role in fighting bacterial infections, a contribution that garnered a Nobel Prize in 1945. Perhaps most memorably, mice contributed to the development of the vaccine that eradicated polio. Cows and sheep were the subjects of experiments that led to the 1905 prize for discoveries involving the pathogenesis of tuberculosis, while work with pigeons led to a 1902 award for unraveling the life cycle of malaria. Antibiotics depended for their development, and still do, on animal experimentation, with the 1952 prize for the discovery of streptomycin as one example of how the guinea pig advanced the treatment of infectious diseases. The recipient in 1964 experimented on rats to understand how our bodies metabolize cholesterol and other fats that clog our arteries and lead to heart attacks, strokes, and coronary diseases that shorten the lives of millions and leave others in a debilitated condition. Dogs and cats made immensely useful contributions of their own: organ transplantation techniques developed in dogs garnered a Nobel Prize in 1990, and work on dogs also contributed to the 1924 prize winner's development of the electrocardiogram, which has become the routine screening device for cardiovascular disease. Cats aided our understanding of how nerve transmitters function (the subject of the 1970 prize), how visual information is stored in the brain (1981), and how the brain organizes itself to coordinate internal organs of the body (1949). Today, nonhuman primates constitute 0.3 percent of laboratory animals, and their use is among the most controversial. Yet in the past, their use has led to many discoveries that greatly augmented our ability to treat disease: experimentation on monkeys led to the development of a vaccine for yellow fever (1951); monkeys also played a part in the 1975 prize for the study of the interaction between tumor viruses and genetic material. This account is necessarily selective because an overwhelming majority of Nobel Prizes awarded in medicine over the years depended upon animal experimentation.[2] It is also selective in a wider sense because the experiments that received Nobel Prizes are the tip of a vastly larger iceberg of research.

Animal rights advocates respond to these inventories of accomplishment in several ways: some moderates acknowledge that using animals was necessary in the past, but maintain that such use is no longer justified because other experimental modalities exist that are equally effective. More extreme advocates advance an animal rights argument that trumps any list of discoveries that benefit humans—past, present, and future. (I shall discuss the more extreme position in the following section, and the moderate position here.)

The moderates recognize that animal experimentation brought about advances such as penicillin and all of the other antibiotics; vaccines for polio, smallpox, diphtheria, and other formerly fearsome scourges; blood transfusions that save the lives of hemophiliacs, trauma victims, and surgical patients; insulin, which improves and prolongs the lives of diabetics; and anesthetics, which make life-saving surgeries possible. It is controversy over the present and the future that sets them at odds with research scientists. Cures for AIDS, Alzheimer's disease, cystic fibrosis, cancer, Parkinson's disease, and countless other devastating conditions are the present targets of researchers,[3] yet activists argue that animal research should be banned or so severely restricted that most experimentation would be brought to an end. Is their case a reasonable one? Are there viable alternatives to the use of animals? The vast majority of scientists respond in the negative to both questions.

Why, then, do most scientists maintain that animal experimentation is still necessary? Although alternatives to animals exist and are used by scientists when appropriate, the fact is that in most cases there are no good substitutes for animals as experimental subjects, as proxies for how the human body may react to new drugs and chemical substances, and as subjects for new medical devices and surgical techniques.

There are many techniques that researchers utilize to minimize the use of animals: cell extracts; tissue and organ studies *in vitro*; computer-assisted mathematical modeling; graphical tools that model biological and pharmacological actions; humans who have consented to noninvasive and nonhazardous procedures; and the substitution of plants, invertebrates, and microorganisms as predictors of vertebrate function.[4] But these and other techniques cannot serve as complete substitutes for animals, as the animal rights advocates contend. New drugs, medical devices, and procedures need to be tested on animals whose systems function in ways similar to our own before researchers proceed to human trials. The law requires such testing in order to reveal unanticipated dangers that otherwise would afflict human trial subjects. Drugs that appear promising *in vitro* may be ineffective or even dangerous when instilled in a functioning biological system, whether animal or human. Nazi atrocities in human experimentation led to the Nuremberg Codes,[5] which insisted upon animal experimentation before human exposure. Subsequent international agreements, such as the Declaration of Helsinki in 1964 by the Eighteenth World Medical Assembly,[6] reinforced that message. It is grotesque to imagine human trials being performed without some assurance that the drugs, medical devices, or surgical techniques involved are presumptively safe. Even with extensive animal testing and human testing, sometimes drugs come to market that when taken by millions, rather than the hundreds or a few thousand who typically participate in human trials, are found to cause significant damage. Fortunately, these tragic surprises occur with only a tiny fraction of newly marketed drugs. Examples of such surprises include the off-label prescribing problem that emerged when Pondimin and Redux, two similar diet drugs, turned out to cause heart-valve irregularities when either one was taken in combination with another drug, phentermine, to form the popular "fen-phen." A pain reliever, Duract, was voluntarily withdrawn from the market by its manufacturer because its use was linked to liver damage and some deaths. Posicor, an antihypertensive and antianginal medication, was removed from the market voluntarily by Roche Laboratories because of the potential for dangerous drug interactions. If federal law did not require that all drugs must be tested on animals before they go into human trials and then general distribution, these occasional disasters would be everyday occurrences, with thousands if not millions of lives in jeopardy. Alternatively, new drugs would cease to be produced, at least in this country, for fear of class action product liability suits.

As science has become more sophisticated since vivisection became prevalent in the late nineteenth century, alternatives to animal use have, in fact, become better substitutes in some situations. In the early stages of drug development, for instance, cell cultures can rule out toxic or ineffective substances and lead researchers to substances that work *in vitro*. However, at our present state of knowledge, these and other alternative techniques cannot replace a complete biological system—an animal—in facilitating our understanding of how a substance acts upon cells, tissues, and organs in their complicated interplay in a living organism. Yet over the last three decades of the twentieth century, the use of animals in research has dramatically decreased, with the use of cats, for example, dropping by 66 percent since 1967. Although estimates of the number of animals used in laboratories vary widely, with government estimates being much lower than those offered by animal rights activists, the trend has been one of a dramatic decrease, especially among primates, dogs, and cats. The U.S. Department of Agriculture's *Animal Welfare Enforcement Report for Fiscal Year 1997* reported that 1,267,828 dogs, cats, primates, guinea pigs, hamsters, rabbits, and farm animals were the subjects of laboratory experiments in registered facilities.[7] Dogs and cats now comprise less than 1 percent of U.S. laboratory animals, while mice, rats, and other rodents represent 80 to 90 percent.

For the foreseeable future, then, animals as research subjects are our best hope for understanding and combating incapacitating or deadly human diseases and conditions. Treatments for AIDS, diabetes, and toxoplasmosis; organ transplants; the training of emergency room physicians in trauma techniques; life-saving heart and lung surgeries; the study of neurological diseases such as amyotrophic lateral sclerosis (ALS or Lou Gehrig's disease); the study of gene therapies to fight cancer—these and countless other methods of treating diseases and educating medical personnel depend upon experimentation on animals. Most of the time, these goals simply require the use of rodents, but sometimes, out of necessity, higher animals must be used as well.

Interestingly, it is not just humans who have benefited and will benefit in the future from animal experimentation. Discoveries that led to human advances have also been used in veterinary practice to improve the lives of animals. Studies in dogs, for example, led to treatments for ills that canines suffer, including medicines for diabetes, pacemakers for heart irregularities, hip and joint replacements for degenerative conditions, chemotherapy for cancer, and vaccines against rabies and other illnesses.[8] Cats, too, have benefited from research on their species, and over a thirty-year span the life expectancy for domesticated cats has been increased by six to eight years.[9]

II. Animal Rights Philosophy

Although antivivisectionists have condemned animal experimentation since the early nineteenth century, and vegetarians opposed to the human consumption of animals have advanced their arguments since ancient times,[10] the modern animal rights movement drew its inspiration from a more recent source: a forcefully argued book written by philosopher Peter Singer. Published in 1975, *Animal Liberation: A New Ethics for Our Treatment of Animals* formulated arguments that would dictate the direction of the debate over animal experimentation to this day.[11] Singer, a confirmed utilitarian, drew his moral framework from the work of Jeremy Bentham (1748–1832), utilitarianism's founder. Bentham argued that morality ought to be based upon the capacity of individuals to experience pain and pleasure, a characteristic that all individuals share equally. From this beginning he derived the greatest happiness principle: that society ought to aim at the greatest happiness for the greatest number. Most importantly for Singer, Bentham argued that each individual ought to count for one and not for more than one, that is, each should count equally in our moral calculations.

In Singer, this utilitarian principle is extended beyond humans, an extension that he found foreshadowed in Bentham. Other sentient (conscious) creatures are capable of experiencing suffering and happiness, Singer points out, and given this, he finds no basis for limiting moral consideration to humans. Not all entities, however, deserve consideration, and Singer draws the line at sentience, the salient characteristic in his mind. Stones have no interest in not being kicked along the street by a schoolboy, he argues, but a mouse does, because the mouse can suffer. The capacity of other sentient creatures to suffer leads Singer to his principle of equality: all sentient creatures must be given equal consideration, irrespective of their abilities or other qualities. What does "equal consideration" require? It does not require, Singer argues, equal outcomes. He illustrates this point with an example: concern for a child would require that we teach the child how to read, while concern for a pig might require that we leave it among other pigs, free to roam, and in the proximity of adequate food. "But the basic element—the taking into account of the interests of the being, whatever those interests may be—must, according to the principle of equality, be extended to all beings, black or white, masculine or feminine, human or nonhuman," Singer concludes.[12]

Perhaps Singer's most influential argument is his equation of 'speciesism' with racism and sexism. He defines speciesism as "a prejudice or attitude of bias toward the interests of members of one's own species and against those of members of other species."[13] Equality for him is not a factual allegation that individuals are actually equal in their intelligence, moral capacity, physical strength, or other salient qualities—all features that other philosophers have identified as the foundations of their own egalitarian arguments. Nor does he base his argument on a factual claim that the races or sexes are equal, on average, in every salient feature, as others have argued. Rather, "[e]quality is a moral idea, not an assertion of fact."[14] By forswearing facts, Singer intends to immunize his version of equality from countervailing factual arguments that might, for example, identify genetic disparities in intelligence or other qualities that differ by sex or race. The moral, as opposed to factual, grounding of equality is also advantageous for Singer because it provides an easy transition to his contention that there is no essential difference between humans and animals that would delimit moral consideration just to humans. Contemporary debates about whether animal experimentation on healthy animals can be justified if we refuse to experiment on severely disabled people can be traced back to Singer's claim that there is no essential difference between humans and animals.

For the animal liberation movement, which largely built its case upon Singer's arguments, his equation of 'speciesism' with racism and sexism proved auspicious. When married to speciesism, racism and sexism—the two most despicable "isms" of the late twentieth century—provided the animal rights movement with a marketing stratagem of no mean proportions. Singer equated all three of these "isms" by asserting that each rests on violations of the principle of equality. The "racist violates the principle of equality by giving greater weight to the interests of members of his own race," Singer wrote. "The sexist violates the principle of equality by favoring the interests of his own sex. Similarly the speciesist allows the interests of his own species to override the greater interests of members of other species. The pattern is identical in each case."[15]

Over the years, Singer has become a very controversial figure. Particularly contentious was his appointment in 1999 as a professor of bioethics at Princeton University's Center for Human Values. This appointment was opposed by religious fundamentalists as well as advocates for the disabled. Critics objected to his claim, stated in various writings over thirty years, that it would be morally permissible to kill a disabled infant if that would result in the birth of a healthy infant, thereby augmenting the total amount of happiness in the world. Disability advocates saw this as a threat to the existence of people with disabilities. Religious activists objected to Singer's frequently outrageous statements in support of infanticide and euthanasia.

Tom Regan, another prominent moral philosopher, has also influenced the animal rights movement. His book, *The Case for Animal Rights,* published in 1983, argues for animal rights based not on a utilitarian moral framework, as in Singer, but on a "rights view."[16] Regan believes that all individuals have inherent value, and they have that value equally, "regardless of their sex, race, religion, [or] birthplace. . . . The genius and the retarded child, the prince and the pauper, the brain surgeon and the fruit vendor, Mother Teresa and the most unscrupulous used-car salesman—all have inherent value, all possess it equally, and have an equal right to be treated with respect, to be treated in ways that do not reduce them to the status of things, as if they existed as resources for others."[17] Just as each human is "the experiencing subject of a life, a conscious creature having an individual welfare,"[18] so is each animal. For Regan, animals have inherent value and, therefore, rights. Several criteria have been advanced to distinguish humans from other animals, in an attempt to rebut this assumption of inherent value and rights for animals; Regan considers these criteria and rejects them. *Lack of reason* is rejected because many impaired humans are in the same straits, and they are still considered to have rights. *Animals' nonmembership in the species Homo sapiens* is rejected because accepting this would amount to blatant speciesism. The *absence in animals of an immortal soul* is rejected because this criterion would add a controversial metaphysical assumption to an already contentious debate. Regan concludes that "*[a]ll* who have inherent value have it *equally,* whether they be human animals or not."[19] The practical result for Regan of his rights view is to declare himself an "abolitionist": all commercial animal agriculture should be terminated, as should all scientific experimentation on animals. Commercial agriculture exploits animals as a renewable resource for mankind, and must be abolished along with hunting and trapping for sport or commercial purposes. Similarly, laboratory animals are not treated as ends in themselves, as beings with inherent value, but as servants to the needs of mankind, and so their rights are "systematically violated" and animal experimentation must end.

Singer and Regan differ in the philosophical underpinning of their animal rights positions, but they concur in their abolitionist conclusions. Also, despite the divergence in their moral frameworks—one is a utilitarian, the other a rights theorist—their manner of disputing opponents is very similar. Both claim that factual differences between individuals, whether animal or human, do not matter morally. Both charge their opponents with a failure to identify a criterion that would distinguish humans from other animals and permit sacrificing the latter to the interests of the former.

Critics have responded to Singer's and Regan's arguments in a number of ways. Some invoke the traditional Judeo-Christian argument that places humans, because they have a soul and are God's preferred creatures, above the animals. On this view, animals are put on earth for man's use, including those uses that aim at the advancement of human knowledge and the remediation of human diseases. Others attack the duo on weak points in their arguments. The notion that moral equality reaches beyond the human species to encompass all sentient creatures is vulnerable because it is difficult to see how creatures who cannot reason or speak can take part in the moral community, can be the possessors of rights (in Regan's case), or can merit equal treatment with humans simply because they experience pain and pleasure (in Singer's). Animals who cannot refrain from violating the rights of humans—say by attacking humans— are incapable of understanding or respecting the sorts of rights and duties that comprise any moral system. Singer and Regan are also vulnerable on the ground that they reject the claim that any facts might differentiate humans from animals; as noted above, they think all facts are irrelevant to their arguments, which are morality-based. Yet if humans were to refrain from using animals as means to their ends, they would be the only creatures so restrained, since all others—lacking reason—are incapable of such restraint. Rationality, then, looks like a factual difference that should make a difference in their arguments, despite their claims that no factual differences between humans and animals can matter. Animal rights theorists have proposed various ways around this criticism, but their arguments still seem vulnerable on this point. Several essays in this volume will address various weaknesses in the arguments of the animal rights philosophers and propose alternative moral frameworks that justify animal experimentation and even, some will argue, make it morally obligatory given our current state of scientific knowledge.

III. Animal Rights Activism

Animal rights groups, both old and new, have flourished in recent decades, their memberships fed by readers of the works of Singer, Regan, and other animal rights theorists. The most prominent of the new wave of activist groups is People for the Ethical Treatment of Animals (PETA), founded in 1980 and frequently the beneficiary of Hollywood fundraising extravaganzas. PETA is dedicated to convincing the public that animal experimentation is a "sadistic scandal," that alternative means are available to scientists if they would only use them, and that these alternative means are actually more efficacious. PETA also opposes the testing of cosmetics and household products on animals, advocates vegetarianism, campaigns for the termination of the fur trade, calls for the extinction of circuses for their alleged cruelty to animals, and organizes activist chapters on college campuses.[20]

Since the early 1980s, the more extreme wing of the animal rights movement has engaged in assaults on laboratories and threatened the lives of scientists engaged in animal research. Although PETA itself forswears such terrorist methods, it is loath to reproach this extremist element. One of the groups representing this element is the Animal Liberation Front (ALF), an organization founded in Britain in 1976. ALF has since spread to the United States, where it carries out assaults on laboratories, causing millions of dollars in property damage, freeing experimental animals, and jeopardizing years of research. PETA has offered the following comment on ALF's violent activities:

> Throughout history some people have felt the need to break the law to fight injustice. The Underground Railroad and the French Resistance are both examples of people breaking the law in order to answer to a higher morality.
>
> "The ALF" . . . breaks inanimate objects . . . in order to save lives. It burns empty buildings in which animals are tortured and killed. ALF "raids" have given us proof of horrific cruelty that would not have been discovered or believed otherwise. . . .[21]

Meg Turville-Heitz reported in *Scientific American* that in 1999 eighty scientists received letters booby-trapped with razor blades. At the University of Wisconsin-Madison, eight such letters were received, and the director of the Wisconsin Regional Primate Research Center fled town with his family after protesters held vigils in front of his home, shouted insults, and wrote denunciations on his sidewalk.[22] An animal rights group allied with ALF, the Justice Department, which had operated primarily in Britain and Canada, claimed credit for the letters, which threatened further unspecified violence if the researchers did not cease vivisection by the fall of 2000.[23] Other attacks have caused damage to laboratories and intimidated researchers, including some raids for which ALF has publicly taken credit: one assault at the University of Minnesota caused three-quarters of a million dollars in damage and set back work on a vaccine against brain cancer; another assault at the University of California at San Francisco damaged data aimed, ironically, at developing alternatives to research on animals.[24] In November 1999, ALF broke into a research lab at Washington State University, destroying equipment, damaging the building, and pouring acids on the floors. In taking credit for the raid, ALF noted that it was its second assault on a research facility in Washington State in that month.[25]

In a study conducted by *The Oregonian* in 1999, the newspaper investigated one hundred major acts of "eco-terrorism" that had occurred in the eleven contiguous western states since 1980.[26] Damages from these acts amounted to $42.8 million. The four years preceding the study accounted for $28.8 million of that total, indicating that eco-terrorists—a group that includes animal rights extremists as well as those who attack logging companies and ski resorts in the name of protecting Earth from development and curbing the recreational use of the wilderness—are a growing menace. The article recounted ALF's acknowledged link between itself and the Earth Liberation Front, an underground group dedicated to a full range of eco-terrorist exploits, targeting developers, loggers, gas stations, aerial herbicide spraying, motorcyclists, and other symbols of industrialization. One of their joint exploits was a 1996 Columbus Day weekend raid against gas stations and fast-food restaurants along Oregon's Interstate 5.

The report also documented a 1987 raid by ALF on the University of California at Davis, which caused $3.5 million in arson damage to a laboratory working on the diagnosis of diseases in veterinary animals.

In England, where the first animal welfare organization was established in 1824, some three thousand such groups are now in existence. The most notorious extremist groups—ALF, for example—were born there, and some English groups are not reticent about threatening and committing acts of physical violence against scientists. Many targets of their outrage have been forced to lead lives of seclusion and fear, ensconced in their homes behind antiterrorist barricades of security fences, alarms, and tripwire lights. Colin Blakemore, a physiologist at Oxford University who works on advances for the treatment of infants and children with vision problems, is one of ten British scientists who has been put on an assassination list by ALF, the Justice Department, and their allies. Activists threatened that when one of their members who was engaged in a hunger strike died, they would kill the ten scientists. (In response to activism of this sort, the British government had already banned animal testing for cosmetics, alcohol, and tobacco.) The hunger strike was eventually called off, but the fear persists. In the mid-1990s, police intercepted a package masquerading as a Christmas gift for Professor Blakemore's daughter; the "gift" actually contained explosives. The professor's family has endured thirteen years of harassment from animal rights activists, including two letter bombs, razor blades in envelopes, and an attack by a mob that succeeded in breaking into their house. In February 2000, one protestor, who had used a megaphone outside Blakemore's house since 1994 to denounce him as a cat torturer, was found guilty of harassment. Cynthia O'Neill, the protestor, was tried under a new antiharassment law. Police protection for Professor Blakemore is at the same level of intensity as that afforded targets of the Irish Republican Army, yet he remains an outspoken defender of animal research and opponent of the extremists.[27]

In November 1999, Niel Hansen, chairman of Britain's National Anti-Hunting Campaign, targeted shareholders of Huntingdon Life Sciences (HLS), a laboratory that tests the safety of new drugs on animals. Hansen threatened that those who did not divest their shares would face round-the-clock protests in front of their homes. (Testing drugs on animals is, in fact, a legal requirement in Britain.) Using the alias of the BUAV Reform Group, in March 2000 Hansen sent personal letters containing an ultimatum with a date by which shareholders had to divest. Many of the 1,700 shareholders were so intimidated by the threats that they called for police protection, and the managing director of the company demanded that a national crime squad be formed to monitor the activists.[28]

There are many animal-welfare groups that forswear extremist measures, to be sure, but the groups that grab the headlines—and, in that way, shape the public agenda—are not inhibited by concern for property rights nor, in some cases, concern for human life. For a movement dedicated to extending rights beyond human beings to all sentient beings, it is surprising that for some of its constituent groups, on some occasions, human rights and human welfare seem to count for so little.

IV. Legislative and Regulatory Control over Animal Research

While animal rights activism has a longer history in Britain than it does in the United States, and the British movement's extremist element is more robust than its American counterpart, the welfare of laboratory animals has in fact been a concern of the British government since it passed the Cruelty to Animals Act in 1876. It would be almost a century before American federal legislation addressed animal experimentation via the Animal Welfare Act of 1966 (AWA), an act that has been amended frequently since its passage. Current British law governing animal experimentation is shaped by the Animals (Scientific Procedures) Act of 1986, which has as its purpose ensuring that research using protected animals is justified by the potential benefits that it might secure. Approved research must be conducted with the least possible suffering, and it must minimize the number of animals used. Researchers must secure a license to do particular experiments. Securing this license requires approval by an ethical review panel, based on the so-called "3 Rs"—refinement, reduction, and replacement—criteria designed to minimize animal use.[29]

The U.S. regulatory scheme is more fragmented than Britain's, as the former depends on several federal regulatory agencies for its implementation and enforcement. The AWA and its various amendments established standards for the care and treatment of laboratory animals, excluding rats, mice, and birds. The original impetus for passage of the act was a media-generated frenzy among the public that dogs were being stolen from backyards for sale to laboratories. The act's coverage extended beyond dogs, and its principal purpose remains the protection of cats, dogs, and primates. Under the AWA, laboratories using animals must register with and be inspected by the Animal and Plant Health Inspection Service (APHIS), an enforcement agency of the U.S. Department of Agriculture. The act also mandates that animals must be anesthetized during painful procedures unless the objective of the experiment would be thwarted, that they receive postoperative care, and that they experience only one major procedure. Since the passage of amendments to the AWA in 1985,[30] an Institutional Animal Care and Use Committee (IACUC) must be established in each institution that conducts animal research; these committees are responsible for approving all experiments and ensuring the safety and conditions of the animals at their respective institutions. Committees must include at least two members not affiliated with the institution, one of whom must be a veterinarian.

In addition to regulation by the Department of Agriculture, another regulatory layer is afforded by the Public Health Service (PHS), which provides most of the funding for animal experimentation in the United States. The Health Research Extension Act of 1985 mandated that the Public Health Service draw up guidelines to which all grantees must adhere.[31] As this law requires, the *Public Health Service Policy on Humane Care and Use of Laboratory Animals* provides guidelines on presurgical and postsurgical care; veterinary and nursing care; and the use of analgesics, tranquilizers, and anesthetics.[32] PHS guidelines also cover the responsibilities and membership requirements of IACUCs. The Office for Protection from Research Risks (OPRR), an office within the PHS and located at the National Institutes of Health (NIH), has implementation and oversight responsibility for the PHS *Policy,* which covers all live, vertebrate animals, including rats and mice. The OPRR negotiates with all PHS-supported laboratories for their Animal Welfare Assurances (a document outlining compliance with the PHS *Policy*). To further complicate the regulatory landscape, the PHS *Policy* endorses and implements another set of guidelines established by an Interagency Research Animal Committee, the "U.S. Government Principles for the Utilization and Care of Vertebrate Animals Used in Research."[33] The White House Office of Science and Technology adopted the nine principles endorsed in this document in 1985, during the Reagan Administration. The "Principles" stress humane care, diminution of pain, and species-appropriate living conditions. Still another document guides research institutions that must comply with the PHS *Policy.* This document is the *Guide for the Care and Use of Laboratory Animals,* which dates back to 1963 and has been frequently revised.[34] The latest revision (in 1996) was written by the Institute for Laboratory Animal Research of the National Academy of Sciences, and was funded by the NIH and the Departments of Agriculture and Veterans Affairs. The PHS *Policy* also mandates compliance with the Animal Welfare Act. Nongovernmental organizations also play a role in overseeing animal experimentation. For example, the NIH encourages labs to join the Association for Assessment and Accreditation of Laboratory Animal Care International (AAALAC), a nonprofit organization that monitors laboratories and conducts on-site inspections.

Exponents of animal rights find this regulatory scheme in the U.S. deficient. More moderate forces wish to extend the AWA's coverage to rats, birds, and mice, which together comprise 80 to 90 percent of laboratory animals. More extreme elements desire to go far beyond regulation—to abolishing animal experimentation altogether. In the essays that follow, you will find many dispassionate arguments about the necessity of using animals for the advancement of human knowledge and the discovery of new therapies that can alleviate dreaded diseases that afflict mankind. You will also encounter the more personal reflections of researchers who have brought to their essays the passion of a lifetime dedicated to scientific advancement.

V. The Essays

Our first essay, "Experimental Animals in Medical Research: A History," by Kenneth F. Kiple and Kriemhild Coneè Ornelas chronicles the history of experimentation on animals, demonstrating its early and continuing importance. Animal experimentation played a vital role in advancing medical knowledge during two periods of great intellectual fervor: during Greco-Roman times and later in the Renaissance. In the nineteenth and twentieth centuries, with refinements to the scientific method, advances proceeded at a remarkable pace by historical standards. Animal experimentation contributed to the development of germ theory, to the discovery of the role of various vitamins in forestalling disease, as well as to the creation of a vaccine for yellow fever. After discussing these historical developments, Kiple and Ornelas turn to one of the most important medical problems facing the twenty-first century: the rise of various viral plagues. These diseases, which include the Ebola virus and HIV, are some of the most potent killers ever to have attacked the human race. Even more distressing, they may represent only a fraction of the potential danger posed by viral diseases, for continued human encroachment into remote areas may uncover equally virulent viruses. Discovering the sources and treating these diseases will only be possible if modern science has the best tools at its disposal, including animal experimentation. Kiple and Ornelas conclude with some sobering thoughts on the animal rights movement, arguing that Singer's and Regan's positions reflect at root a fundamental disapproval of the medical advances made possible by animal use.

The animal rights movement receives a more extensive treatment in "Making Choices in the Laboratory." In this essay, Adrian R. Morrison gives a broad overview of the zealous nature of the animal rights movement. Morrison sounds a theme that will be echoed by other authors in this collection: that the moral claims advanced by the animal rights movement lack a coherent foundation. This is not to say that humans have no responsibilities to animals used in research: Morrison thinks we must treat them as humanely as possible. However, this side-constraint does not entail a far-reaching ban on animal experimentation. Drawing on his experiences both as a researcher and as an active participant in the debates over the medical use of animals, Morrison moves from an analysis of the arguments of animal rights activists to a troubling assessment of their tactics. Blatant intimidation, including attacks on laboratories and threats against researchers, is combined with misleading "evidence" designed to distort the public's perception of the scientific establishment. Activists argue that medical advances achieved through animal experimentation could have been secured by other research methods. Morrison shows, to the contrary, that there is simply no substitute for the use of laboratory animals. Animal rights advocates also skew historical facts, Morrison contends, twisting scholars' research to make it seem as if their conclusions supported the animal rights agenda. Morrison ends his essay by recounting recent developments in his field, neurology, that would have been impossible without animal experimentation. These advances offer the hope that someday soon spinal nerves may be regenerated, an outcome once thought to be impossible. If animal rights activists succeed in limiting or even banning animal experimentation, Morrison warns, this and other cutting-edge advances will be put in jeopardy.

A distinction between "basic" research and "applied" research plays a significant role in the arguments of some animal-rightists. In "Basic Research, Applied Research, Animal Ethics, and an Animal Model of Human Amnesia," Stuart Zola shows that this distinction is problematic. On its face, the distinction seems plausible: basic research is performed solely for the advancement of knowledge, while applied research is directed at solving particular real-world problems. Some in the animal rights movement concede that applied research aimed at carefully and narrowly targeted practical objectives might be justifiable, but basic research, because it lacks such immediate relevance, should be prohibited. This distinction is only viable if research can be neatly bifurcated in this way. Zola contends that it cannot. At times, it may seem as though "applied" research produced a medical advance, but in reality, "basic" research played a key role in grounding and guiding its "applied" cousin. In fact, Zola argues, much research consists of both elements so intermingled as to be nearly inseparable. Zola offers a case in point: the development of an animal model of human amnesia. Several studies showed that monkeys with lesions on various parts of their brains exhibited certain distinct types of memory loss. These studies were undertaken with a specific purpose in mind, for the treatment of memory loss in humans is of obvious practical value. Yet the studies also yielded a wealth of basic neuroanatomical information. For instance, they helped show that memory in monkeys involves the medial temporal lobe system of the brain. This suggested that the same lobe system plays an analogous role in humans. A sharp basic/applied distinction between permissible "applied" research and impermissible "basic" research would have precluded these vital studies.

Jerrold Tannenbaum sees threats to research coming not only from the animal rights movement, but from some internal critics who have been influenced by that movement. In "The Paradigm Shift toward Animal Happiness: What It Is, Why It Is Happening, and What It Portends for Medical Research," he identifies the source of this threat as a change in how some researchers want to measure animal welfare. Under the traditional approach, animal welfare involves concern about the infliction of unpleasant mental states: pain, discomfort, etc. Use of animals is considered ethically acceptable even if it may cause such unpleasant states; the approach merely stresses that animals not be subjected to such states *unnecessarily* or *unjustifiably*. U.S. laws that regulate animal research reflect this traditional approach. However, a new conception of animal welfare has recently attracted a significant following. Under this emerging approach, researchers' duties to animals would extend beyond sparing them unnecessary pain. The new approach demands that animals be provided with pleasurable and satisfying experiences in order to ensure that they have happy lives. Tannenbaum warns that this approach suffers from serious problems. First, it requires the use of a variety of concepts whose meanings cannot be clearly defined nor practically applied to particular species. A second, related worry is that the emerging approach is simply impractical. The costs of adopting the new approach, in terms of both research possibilities denied and increased financial outlays, is likely to be extremely large. Finally, Tannenbaum argues, the emerging approach will cause dramatic changes in how we view research animals. Rather than treating them as objects of study, we will inexorably be drawn into treating them as our friends. The end result, he fears, will be the elimination of animal experimentation altogether.

In "Defending Animal Research: An International Perspective," Baruch A. Brody examines European laws on animal experimentation and finds them to be less wedded to the traditional approach than are U.S. laws. U.S. laws reflect a commitment to giving the interests of humans lexical priority over those of research animals, while European laws give the interests of animals significant weight, forcing European researchers to balance the benefits that a particular experiment would provide to humans against the costs that it would impose on animals. Contemplating the European approach, Brody poses an intriguing question: how should one balance human and animal interests? On the one hand, one could assign human and animal interests equal significance; this is the view of many animal rights activists. On the other hand, one could move toward the other extreme of giving human interests an almost lexical priority. Between these two poles lies a wide spectrum of possible positions in which animal interests are discounted to various degrees. Brody argues that the discounting approach provides a coherent way of allowing significant amounts of research, while at the same time providing reasonable safeguards for animals. First, Brody refutes one of the major arguments against the discounting approach by arguing that cross-species comparisons of human and animal interests are possible. Second, he notes that while U.S. laws seem to reflect the lexical-priority position, deeper consideration shows that the actual policies implemented under these laws involve precisely the sort of interest-balancing demanded by the discounting approach. Brody finds the discounting approach compatible with the generally accepted moral position that individuals are not required to treat everyone equally, that people have special obligations and personal prerogatives that require or allow them to treat various people differently. This compatibility should reassure us of the soundness of the balancing approach.

Evolutionary biology has become an increasingly important part of debates over ethical issues, and in "A Darwinian View of the Issues Associated with the Use of Animals in Biomedical Research," Charles S. Nicoll and Sharon M. Russell use this evolutionary perspective to defend animal experimentation. Like all other organisms, humans have evolved over time as a result of adaptive advantages. For humans, the relevant advantage is a larger brain. This advantage has two major consequences. First, the relative size of the human brain makes humans different from other animals in a way that has moral consequences. Humans use language and have other intellectual abilities that are clearly superior to those of other species. As a result, Nicoll and Russell maintain, humans can be members of the "moral community" in a way that other animals cannot. Because the possession of rights depends on belonging to the moral community, the upshot of animals' relative lack of intelligence is that they cannot have rights. A second consequence of humans' superior brain is that we have a uniquely powerful ability to process and utilize knowledge about the outside world. Humans will naturally use this ability to help themselves survive challenges posed by their environment, such as the threats created by microbes, parasites, and insects that destroy crops and carry diseases. In practical terms, dealing with these challenges will require the acquisition of medical and agricultural knowledge, which in turn will necessitate the use of animals as research subjects. Hence, Nicoll and Russell argue, a moral justification for animal experimentation is in an important sense unnecessary: to disallow such experimentation would be to adopt a maladaptive strategy, one that might endanger human survival.

The claim that it is humans alone who possess moral status recurs in "Animals: Their Right to Be Used," by H. Tristram Engelhardt, Jr. Engelhardt maintains that humans are the only animals who can engage in the practice of morality, and that this unique role gives humans the right to put other animals in their "moral place," namely, a position of subordination to man. He justifies these claims with three separate arguments. First, only moral agents can properly assess the moral standing of animals, and because humans are the only beings who can balance competing moral claims, humans are the only animals that can be moral agents. The fact that humans embody the fullest representation of the moral life makes it plausible, Engelhardt says, that human interests are of a higher priority than those of animals. The second argument for the unique status of humans involves man's capacity for cultural life. As self-conscious, rational agents, humans embed certain behaviors and practices within a cultural context. This allows humans to appreciate experiences in a far deeper way than animals can. In particular, practices like hunting, domestication, and culinary preparation— all of which depend upon the use of animals—are of deep satisfaction to many individuals. Because we live in a pluralistic society, Engelhardt argues, individuals must be given the liberty to use animals in various ways if they are to be able to perfect themselves as beings within a culture. Engelhardt's third argument rests on the recognition that only humans can view themselves as praiseworthy or blameworthy. This means that the domain of rights and obligations is meaningful only to humans. Engelhardt, consequently, draws a conclusion similar to that of Nicoll and Russell: animals themselves cannot have rights. For Engelhardt, man's use of animals is nearly always justified, and any practice that jeopardizes human concerns for the sake of animals is inherently morally suspect.

In R. G. Frey's "Justifying Animal Experimentation: The Starting Point," the author explores a puzzle in the standard defense of animal experimentation that compels him to conclude that a full philosophical defense has yet to be made. Frey begins by pointing out that all justifications of animal experimentation are ultimately based on the argument from benefit, the consequentialist view that research on animals has benefits for humans that outweigh the costs imposed on animals. But there is a problem with the benefit argument: experimentation on humans could provide enormous benefits as well, but such research is almost universally held to be impermissible. If one advocates animal experimentation on the basis of the argument from benefit, one must explain why experimentation on humans should be treated differently: this is the puzzle. If one tries to solve the puzzle by identifying a characteristic that separates humans from animals, Frey counters that for any characteristic that one identifies, there will be humans who either lack that characteristic or exhibit it to a lesser degree than do many animals. If, for example, cognitive capability is the characteristic of choice, how will we justify the common intuition that experimentation on Alzheimer's victims or anencephalic infants is unacceptable? They have a cognitive capacity that is clearly inferior to that of many animals. Another strategy would be to abandon a characteristics-based argument by proclaiming that the ability of humans to have a quality of life is what separates them from animals. Yet we measure quality of life by assessing a life's experiential content, and while animals are not as sophisticated as humans, they are nevertheless experiential creatures. Hence, Frey suggests, animals can have a quality of life in the same way that humans do, and arguments to the contrary will therefore be insufficient to distinguish humans from animals. Frey emphasizes that he is not an opponent of animal experimentation. On the contrary, he believes that the benefits achieved through animal experimentation clearly justify such research. It is just that he is troubled by the lack of a definitive argument for animal use.

We hope that these essays will advance public debate on this vital issue, and underscore just how important it is to all of us and to generations to come that the acquisition of knowledge not be thwarted, so that future scourges, the successors of AIDS, will find a vibrant scientific community willing and able to mount an effective counterattack. This community is being threatened by animal rights extremists. Discouragement and the abandonment of scientific careers by the best and brightest, which has already begun in Britain, is a worrisome prospect for the United States. The debate between animal rights advocates and research scientists is a high-stakes battle. Human lives—our lives as well as the lives of our parents and our children—will be the price of an abolitionist victory.

Ellen Frankel Paul
August 2000

NOTES

1. Progress has been made in recent years in providing substitutes for animals in the production of monoclonal antibodies (MABs). MABs are used widely in medical research and in laboratory tests. Switzerland, Germany, and the Netherlands have banned the use of mice for the production of MABs, and the American Anti-Vivisection Society (AAVS), an animal rights organization, has petitioned the U.S. Department of Agriculture and the National Institutes of Health to do the same. American Anti-Vivisection Society, "Antibodies without Animals Campaign: An Historic Opportunity," April 1997, available at http://www.aavs.org/Docs/awa.htm.

   However, the use of mice to produce human antibodies has already led to the development of new drugs to fight two of the most feared types of cancer: breast cancer (Herceptin) and lymphoma (Rituxin). These drugs still depend upon a small percentage of mouse antibodies, which is a problem, since mouse antibodies can trigger rejection in the human body. This is why the early promise in the 1980s and early 1990s for drugs based on monoclonal antibodies did not come to fruition. Recently, two biotechnology companies, Abgenix and Medarex, have developed genetically altered mice (transgenic mice) that produce human antibodies for various cancers and other human diseases. These mice should speed up drug development and negate the rejection problem that plagued the early years of monoclonal-antibody research. This type of research is in its infancy, and holds great promise for the future. Associated Press, "Mighty Mouse: Genetically Altered Mice Fight Disease Like Humans and Help Scientists Make Antibody-Based Drugs," *Orlando Sentinel,* April 2, 2000, A6; Bethany McLean, "Why These Biotechs Are as Hot as Net Stocks," *Fortune,* January 10, 2000, 132.

2. See the Foundation for Biomedical Research (FBR), "The Payoff from Animal Research," at http://www.fbresearch.org/nobels.html, where a list is available of the sixty-five years in which Nobel Prizes in medicine were awarded for experiments on animals; the list notes the animals experimented upon in each case, and the nature of each discovery. Between 1901 and 1999, the prize was awarded ninety times (excluding 1921 and 1925 as well as the war years of 1915–18 and 1940–42). A comparison of the complete list of Nobel Prize winners in medicine with the FBR list reveals that 72 percent of prizes were awarded for discoveries that involved animal experimentation. (This calculation does not take into account some years in which multiple awards were made for similar work.) The complete list of winners is available at Nobel Prize Internet Archive, "Nobel Prize in Physiology or

Medicine Winners, 1999–1901," available at http://nobelprizes.com/nobel/medicine/medicine.html.

3. These examples are drawn from the Laboratory Animal Science Association's *LASA Newsletter*. See "RDS Campaign Challenging the Antivivisectionists," *LASA Newsletter,* Summer 1996, 12; and Les Ward, "Keynote Conference Speech," *LASA Newsletter,* Spring 1997, 6.

4. See B. R. Howard, "Alternatives—What Alternatives?" *LASA Newsletter,* Summer 1996, 6–7, for a discussion of these alternatives, their utility, and their inadequacy for many purposes.

5. The Nuremburg Codes (enacted August 19, 1947) are available at http://www.princeton.edu:80/dipowell/Nuremberg.html.

6. World Medical Association, "Recommendations Guiding Physicians in Biomedical Research Involving Human Subjects" (adopted in 1964 by the Eighteenth World Medical Assembly; revised in 1975, 1983, 1989, and 1996), available at http://business.virgin.net/cdss.com/Declaration.htm.

7. USDA figures do not include rats and mice, which comprise the vast majority of animals used, because the U.S.'s Animal Welfare Act does not protect these species (nor does it protect birds). The Office of Technology Assessment estimated in 1986 that the USDA figure represented approximately 10 percent of the total number of animals used in research. Foundation for Biomedical Research, "Figures on Animal Research (Fiscal Year 1997)," available at http://www.fbresearch.org/amres96.htm. Figures on research animals would also be significantly increased if mice used in the production of transgenic mice were counted, since many generations of mice are required to produce those with the desired genetic traits (derived from other animals or humans) necessary to conduct a particular experiment. For example, research on mad cow disease was greatly facilitated by the creation of mice with the relevant genetic characteristics of cows—these mice develop the disease much more quickly than do cows.

8. Foundation for Biomedical Research, "Dogs and Research," available at http://www.fbresearch.org/dogsf.html.

9. Foundation for Biomedical Research, "Cats and Research," available at http://www.fbresearch.org/catsf.html.

10. Ancient vegetarianism was of religious origins, but the modern vegetarian movement also dates from the nineteenth century.

11. Peter Singer, *Animal Liberation: A New Ethics for Our Treatment of Animals* (New York: A New York Review Book, 1975).

12. Ibid., 6.

13. Ibid., 7.

14. Ibid., 5.

15. Ibid., 9.

16. Tom Regan, *The Case for Animal Rights* (Berkeley: University of California Press, 1983).

17. Tom Regan, "Why the System is Fundamentally Wrong," in Andrew Harnack, ed., *Animal Rights: Opposing Viewpoints* (San Diego, CA: Greenhaven Press, 1996), 37.

18. Ibid.
19. Ibid., 38.
20. For more information on PETA's positions, see their website, http://www.peta-on-line.org.
21. PETA, "Frequently Asked Questions and Comments," available at http://www.peta-online.org/faq/index.html.
22. Meg Turville-Heitz, "Violent Opposition: Escalating Protests May Be Driving Away Some Researchers," *Scientific American* 282, no. 2 (February 2000): 32, also available at http://www.scientificamerican.com/2000/0200issue/0200techbus1.htm.
23. The threat was posted to the Animal Liberation Frontline Information website. See Americans for Medical Progress, "Latest News," available at http://ampef.org/news/index.htm. (The AMP is a group dedicated to defending animal research.) The story's byline date is October 25, 1999.
24. Turville-Heitz, "Violent Opposition," 32.
25. AMP, "Latest News." This story's byline date is November 20, 1999.
26. Bryan Denson and James Long, "Eco-Terrorism Sweeps the American West," *The Oregonian,* September 26, 1999, available at http://www.ampef.org/articles/ter-art4.htm.
27. Warren Hoge, "British Researchers on Animal Rights Death List," *New York Times,* January 10, 1999, 8; Richard Ford, "Terrorism Law to Cover Animal Militants," *Times* (London), November 15, 1999; Valerie Grove, " 'Cruelty? They Just Have No Idea,' " *Times* (London), February 26, 2000. Articles from the London *Times* can be found on the *Times*'s online database, available at http://www.sunday-times.co.uk/news/pages/resources/library1.n.html.
28. Valerie Elliott and Elizabeth Judge, "Lab Investors Told: Sell Shares, or Else," *Times* (London), March 29, 2000.
29. Ronald W. James, "LASA's Reply to the Review of the Animals (Scientific Procedures) Act, 1986," *LASA Newsletter,* Summer 1996, 4–5; Ward, "Keynote Conference Speech."
30. *Animal Welfare Act of 1985,* Pub. L. No. 99–198, 99 Stat. 1645 (1985) (codified at 7 U.S.C. sec. 2131 [2000]).
31. *Health Research Extension Act of 1985,* Pub. L. No. 99–158, 99 Stat. 820 (1985) (codified in scattered sections of 42 U.S.C. [2000]).
32. National Institutes of Health—Office of Protection from Research Risks (NIH-OPRR), *Public Health Service Policy on Humane Care and Use of Laboratory Animals* (Bethesda, MD: NIH-OPRR, 1986).
33. "U.S. Government Principles for the Utilization and Care of Vertebrate Animals Used in Research," available at http://grants.nih.gov/grants/olaw/tutorial/relevant.htm#2b.
34. National Research Council and Institute for Laboratory Animal Resources, *A Guide for the Care and Use of Laboratory Animals,* 7th ed. (Washington, DC: National Academy Press, 1996).

Experimental Animals in
Medical Research: A History

Kenneth F. Kiple and Kriemhild Coneè Ornelas

[T]here can be no doubt that any useful knowledge in medicine or surgery
is abundantly worth the lives of the animals destroyed to obtain it.[1]

—*John Call Dalton, 1875*

I. Introduction: Animal Experimentation
and the History of Modern Medicine

Books, anthologies, and articles abound that center on the controversies surrounding the use of animals in biomedical research and teaching. A couple of
these on our desk at the moment promise moral edification with titles such as
Animal Research and Ethical Conflict[2] and *Animal Experimentation: The Moral
Issues*.[3] A third, whose author is disturbed by opposition to the use of animals
in medical research, elegantly wonders "Whither Goest Vivisection?"[4] The title
of a fourth work is equally intriguing. It expresses its authors' outrage that animals are employed in medical research by proposing *Reinventing Biology*.[5]

Interestingly—especially to those of us who make our living as historians
while lamenting that the only thing we learn from history is that we do not learn
from history—the main positions on the use of animals in medical research
were already staked out well over a century ago. In 1875, American physician
John Call Dalton began a defense of such use in *Experimentation on Animals
as a Means of Knowledge in Physiology, Pathology, and Practical Medicine.*
Seven years later, he rolled a boulder down on the opponents of animal experimentation in the form of a book entitled *The Experimental Method in Medical
Science*.[6] However, as he and others were framing the issue as one of objectiv-
ity versus emotion, reason versus passion, and the like, they only encouraged a

"hardening of the categories"; they changed few minds. In addition, it became apparent that those making a case for the use of animals in medical research could be as emotional as those who deplored it. For example, "speciesism"— the devaluing of animals because they are not human—is at least as much an emotional construct as it is a rational one. Furthermore, in the world of Christianity, where the entire order of plants and animals has been viewed as subordinate to human control (and as lacking moral standing), there has long existed a powerful theological rationale for the employment of animals in any number of unpleasant ways.

Yet animal experimentation took place long before the advent of Christianity. Paleolithic hunters who carved up their kills must have been curious about the functions of the organs they exposed and the networks of arteries, veins, and nerves they uncovered, as well as the bones, and bodily architecture in general. To discuss the individual routinely credited as the first to methodically dissect animals, however, we need to jump forward hundreds of millennia, to ancient Greece and to Aristotle (384–322 B.C.). (Note that we have skipped over Hippocrates [460–379 (?) B.C.], whose works indicate that he did little or no animal experimentation.) Aristotle's studies of the "history," "gait," "parts," and "motion" of animals, all done with an eye toward determining internal differences, became the first animal physiology.[7]

We must travel a little further forward in time to discover the person recorded as the first to employ live animals in research: Erasistratus of Ceos (304–258 B.C.). A physician in the third century B.C., Erasistratus studied at Aristotle's Peripatetic school in Athens before going to Alexandria. There, he began the work that earned him the title "the Father of Physiology," awarded to him by later medical historians because of his studies of the nervous and circulatory systems of animals as well as humans. Indeed, because he correctly identified the heart as the distributor of blood, he is thought to have come tantalizingly close to anticipating William Harvey's discovery of the circulation of blood, a discovery that came about almost two thousand years later.[8]

Celsus (ca. 25 B.C.–A.D. 50) is sometimes thought of as the first important medical historian because of his De Medicina. This account of Roman medicine sheds light on the state of medical knowledge between the time of Greek medicine as reflected in the Hippocratic corpus (the fifty to seventy books attributed to Hippocrates that were drawn together in the third century B.C.) and that of Roman medicine at the time of Galen of Pergamum (ca. A.D. 130–200). But Celsus was also very involved in comparative anatomy and experimental physiology, and his research depended heavily on dissection and vivisection (the practice of cutting into live bodies) of both animals and humans—the latter were often criminals turned over to him by the prisons.[9]

By the time of Galen, however, dissection of the human body was illegal; Galen thus had to rely solely on animals for his anatomical observations—a hardship he got around, to some extent, by using a variety of animal subjects. He put pigs, sheep, cattle, dogs, cats, bears, mice, monkeys, and even an elephant all under his knife; in doing so (and we are quoting here), he "put animal research on the map, not only for his contemporaries but also for the next fifteen centuries."[10]

The trouble with this quotation is that for the next fifteen centuries, hardly anybody associated with European medicine read that map. After Galen, the Greek tradition in medicine (as carried forward in the Roman Empire) lapsed into sterility; following the fall of Rome, it regressed even further, to what we may call "medieval" levels. During the so-called Dark Ages, this meant monastic medicine, because monasteries increasingly became the last bastions of learning. However, after the Church Council of Clermont prohibited monks from practicing medicine in 1130 (because it was deemed too disruptive for monkish "orderly" life), its practice shifted to the secular clergy (in other words, to the priests) and to Scholastic medicine. Unfortunately, the latter consisted mostly of a sterile adherence to classic authorities, even though there was much to learn from medicine in the Arab world, where practitioners had remained intellectually alive.

Although Galen was foremost among the authorities that Scholastic medicine relied upon, its practitioners had a pronounced aversion to anatomical studies, indeed to any sort of experimentation. Just in case there had been any lingering interest in anatomy, the pronouncement of "*Ecclesia abhorret a sanguine*" ("the Church abhors bloodshed") by the Council of Tours in 1163 took surgery out of the hands of physicians, which is to say the hands of the clergy, leaving the field to "barbers, bath-keepers, hangmen, sow gelders . . . and quacks of every description."[11]

Interest in both anatomy and medical experimentation returned, however, with the revival of learning engendered by the Renaissance — a time when intellectual curiosity began breaking free of the grip of the Church. The experiments of Andreas Vesalius (1514–64) at Padua employed dogs and pigs to challenge some of Galen's observations and, presumably, they helped in his creation of the first modern anatomy text. It was this basic anatomical knowledge, much of it gleaned from animal experimentation, that would undergird the growth of the scientific revolution in the seventeenth and eighteenth centuries.

William Harvey's (1578–1657) discovery that blood circulates through the body, a discovery that has been called "[t]he greatest physiological advance of the seventeenth century, and perhaps of all time,"[12] was based almost exclusively on animal experiments. Indeed, Harvey vivisected everything from sheep (to measure the mass of blood passing through the heart at any given time) to snakes (to discover the effects of ligature on the veins and arteries of the heart). In contrast, English clergyman Stephen Hales (1677–1761) used only a mare to develop techniques for measuring blood pressure and the capacity of the heart.

He did this by inserting a long glass tube into one of the horse's arteries and, with each heartbeat, measuring the rise and fall of blood in the tube.[13]

At about this time, French surgeons such as François Pourfour du Petit (1664–1741) and, later, Nicolas Saucerotte (1741–1814) employed animal experiments to shed light on problems in neurosurgery. Pourfour, for example, discovered the vasomotor nerves and, by cutting the intercostal nerves in the necks of animals, disproved earlier theories of these nerves' cerebral origin. British physician John Hunter (1728–93), a tireless dissector, used experimental animals to take medicine long strides forward in pathological and comparative anatomy with his celebrated studies on disorders of the vascular system and his *Observations on Certain Parts of the Animal Oeconomy* (1786).[14] Such important breakthroughs were continued in the nineteenth century—especially in France, where François Magendie (1783–1855) and his student Claude Bernard (1813–78) pioneered in experimental physiology. Bernard's physiological study, for example, contains his classic work on the functions of the pancreas, the liver, and the gastric glands—all knowledge both obtained and confirmed by animal experimentation.[15]

Not coincidentally, it was also in the nineteenth century that France became the country most closely associated with animal experimentation aimed at the unravelling of disease etiologies; this work brought about germ theory. Germ theory, the understanding that it is microorganisms that cause disease and infection—not witches, or God's will, or the weather—opened the door to the scientific medicine that has followed.

This is not to dismiss the roles of English and German scientists in the elaboration of germ theory. In the former country, William Jenner experimented with cowpox, a disease of cattle, and perhaps horsepox, a now-extinct disease of horses; this work led, in 1798, to Jenner's demonstration of the efficacy of vaccination against smallpox, and thus to one of the greatest of all contributions of medicine to public health. At the same time, John Hunter, Jenner's close friend and teacher, who counted rabies among his numerous interests, summed up what was known of the disease and made some explicit suggestions for animal experiments that would further improve understanding of it.[16]

As it turned out, the study of the zoonoses rabies and anthrax (and consequently of the animals that hosted them) contributed enormously to the validation of the scientific method; it did so by permitting the testing of hypotheses with observation and experimentation. Of course, it was the scientific method that ushered in germ theory. In Germany, the scientific method guided Robert Koch's research on anthrax, which he published in 1876. For the first time, a specific microorganism was linked to the production of a particular disease in animals, especially in cattle and sheep, for which anthrax is especially deadly.[17]

Meanwhile, the following year in France saw Louis Pasteur turn his attention to the diseases of humans and the higher animals, and to the elaboration of preventive vaccines. Together with his brilliant students Émile Roux, Charles Chamberland, and Louis Thuillier, he launched a series of experiments that resulted first in a vaccine for chicken cholera—an economically devastating disease that wiped out whole flocks. Next, Pasteur succeeded in attenuating the infective agent of anthrax—an even more economically damaging disease. In a public demonstration on May 5, 1881 (and a brilliant exercise in the use of the scientific method), Pasteur vaccinated twenty-four sheep, one goat, and six cows. He left a similar number of "control" animals unvaccinated and, on May 31, gave all of the animals an injection of a virulent anthrax culture. By June 2, the control sheep and goat had died, and the control cows were bloated. The vaccinated animals had no symptoms. The experiment was spectacularly successful, as were those Pasteur conducted to counteract rabies.

In working with dogs, guinea pigs, monkeys, and especially rabbits, Pasteur had by 1885 created a vaccine that could be used to cure people already infected with the rabies virus. In doing so, he tamed an illness that is among the oldest of the documented diseases of humankind—one whose horrible symptoms and invariably fatal outcome had made it among the most dreaded.[18] As the twentieth century dawned, the sort of experimental approach Pasteur used, based largely on animal experiments, had swept the West into "The Golden Age of Scientific Medicine."[19]

II. Animal Experimentation and Nutrition

Animal experiments were useful for more than just the study of diseases transmitted by pathogens. They also played a vital role in our understanding of human nutrition. In the nineteenth century, dogs figured prominently in investigations by French and German researchers that worked out the principles of energy and protein metabolism.[20] In the twentieth century, the rat was the animal that contributed most to the discovery of vitamins and the deficiency diseases brought on by their dietary absence, although guinea pigs, pigeons, pigs, mice, dogs, and chickens were also important subjects.

In fact, the story of the role of animals in the discovery of vitamins might be said to have begun with chickens in 1890, when Christiaan Eijkman, a prison medical officer in Java, the Dutch East Indies, noticed that a paralytic disease could be induced in these fowl by feeding them polished rice. A decade later, he and his successor Gerrit Grijns discovered that the disease could also be cured in chickens by feeding them rice bran. The disease was beriberi—caused in both animals and humans by a dietary lack of thiamine.

Beriberi has been especially prevalent among people whose diets center too closely on polished rice; this is because the polishing or milling process strips away the rice's bran, which contains thiamine. The disease is characterized by both paralytic and cardiac symptoms in humans, and these were especially widespread in the Philippines, where, in 1910, Edward Vedder, a U.S. Army medical officer, began the successful treatment of human beriberi cases with an extract of rice bran. It was not until 1933 that thiamine was discovered to be the anti-beriberi factor, but by then, thanks to the animal model worked out by Eijkman and Grijns, the disease had been successfully treated for almost two decades, and thousands of lives had been saved.[21]

Meanwhile, at the University of Christiana (in Oslo, Norway), scientist Axel Holst was working on "ship beriberi," a disease we know as scurvy. He had visited Eijkman's laboratory in Java to learn more about his pioneering use of chickens, but back in Norway, Holst utilized pigeons (because they were cheaper and smaller) to repeat Eijkman's studies. Not satisfied that he was closing in on ship beriberi, Holst decided to experiment with a mammalian species. Fortunately—perhaps even incredibly—he chose guinea pigs, which constitute one of the few species other than humans that cannot synthesize their own vitamin C: this means that guinea pigs can, and do, develop scurvy.

After switching from fowl (which do synthesize their own vitamin C), Holst was rewarded with the discovery that the diet that produced beriberi in fowl provoked scurvy in his guinea pigs. Following his report of these results in 1907, it began to seem even more clear that scurvy, a disease that had killed more than one million sailors between 1600 and 1800—one that had generated more deaths among them than had shipwrecks, naval warfare, and all other diseases combined—was definitely caused by some deficiency in the diet.[22] The nature of that deficiency was later made apparent with the isolation (in 1927) and synthesis (in 1932) of vitamin C, achievements that emerged from a series of animal experiments begun during World War I at the Lister Institute in London.

The discovery of the individual vitamins might be dated to 1906, when researcher Frederick G. Hopkins embarked on his famous nutritional studies using rats. Working at the University of Cambridge, he elaborated his concept of "accessory foodstuffs" (later called vitamins) after learning that young rats stopped growing when fed only purified protein, fat, carbohydrate, and minerals, but quickly began growing again when small amounts of bovine milk were added to this diet. In 1912, Casimir Funk, at the Lister Institute named these as yet unknown accessory foodstuffs "vitamines" (later changed to "vitamins") when he made the startling proposal that scurvy, beriberi, pellagra, and rickets were all the result of dietary deficiencies of factors he called "vital amines."[23]

The isolation of the complex organic substances known today as vitamins A through K quickly followed. Elmer Verner McCollum, a biochemist at the University of Wisconsin, looked over the literature of experiments using mice that had been fed restricted diets such as those Hopkins had employed, and set about discovering what caused the animals' inability to grow (or, in some cases, their rapid decline and death). Like Hopkins, McCollum decided to use rats in his experiments. However, he got no encouragement from the dean of the university's College of Agriculture, who refused to provide the money to purchase the rats; at the time, though guinea pigs and even mice were regarded as cute, furry creatures, rats were perceived to be vicious and dangerous disease-carriers. Consequently, McCollum allegedly wound up personally catching his first seventeen rats in a horse barn at the Wisconsin Experiment Station Farm.[24] In fact, he got little financial help at all with his rats for fully six years, during which he devoted much of his own time to his rat colony and was assisted only by an unpaid volunteer. This situation changed, however, after he noticed that even on whole-cereal diets, his rats required something else for survival. That "something else" seemed to be provided by butterfat, but not by lard or olive oil. When McCollum announced the discovery of vitamin A and explained his experiments, the dean brightened considerably. The news, in 1913, that McCollum's rats had proven butter to be superior to lard and olive oil was also warmly received by Wisconsin's dairy farmers (who doubtless collectively wished that oleomargarine had also been included in the experiment and shown to be an inferior food).[25]

Three years later, McCollum's rats pointed the way to the discovery of vitamin B; the following year, McCollum moved to Johns Hopkins, taking his rat colony with him. There he followed up on experiments by English physiologist Edward Mellanby, who had used puppies to provide the first convincing evidence that rickets was a deficiency disease.[26] The result of McCollum's follow-up work was the discovery of vitamin D; the large-scale elimination of rickets soon followed.

These are but a few of the highlights of the early years of research that employed animals in the service of human nutrition. Such experimentation (which focused on minerals as well as vitamins) not only led to an alleviation of much human misery; it also cleared the way for still more research. Breakthroughs in vitamin research helped to demolish the prevailing notion, generated by germ theory, that all disease was the result of microbial action.[27] As a consequence of such breakthroughs, the field of nutrition became attractive to more and more investigators. Researchers in the field soon broke vitamin B down into different elements; others discovered vitamins C, E, and K. Animals figured prominently in all of these achievements. In the case of vitamin K, the dietary production of a bleeding condition in chicks pointed the way for the biochemists Henrik Dam of the University of Copenhagen and Edward Adelbert Doisy of St. Louis University to jointly announce the discovery of the vitamin in the mid-1930s.[28]

III. Conquering Yellow Fever

Turning from nutrition back to the history of employing animals to eradicate infectious diseases, we might first note that between 1835 and 1935, animal research played a major role in most of the discoveries of the causes of fifty major human diseases.[29] In fact, such research was fundamental in investigating diseases that are intimately bound up with animals; these include rabies and anthrax, both noted above, as well as dengue fever, trichinosis, schistosomiasis, filariasis, glanders, brucellosis, bubonic plague, sleeping sickness, tick-borne relapsing fever, influenza, Rocky Mountain spotted fever, typhus, leptospirosis, and yellow fever.

Of these animal-related illnesses, yellow fever kindles symptoms at least as appalling as any of the rest, and it joins smallpox and bubonic plague as one of the most lethal epidemic killers of all time. Spread by mosquitoes, yellow fever is an illness whose etiology involves monkeys. Although monkeys had been used on occasion in nutritional and medical research (especially notable was Austrian immunologist Karl Landsteiner's successful transmission of poliomyelitis to monkeys in 1908, and his isolation of the virus the following year[30]), it was during the Rockefeller Foundation's effort to eradicate yellow fever that monkeys became key to an understanding of an illness.

Interestingly, however, in the initial yellow fever research, monkeys showed how animal experiments can mislead experimenters. Beginning with the Reed Commission in Cuba, and continuing with the Rockefeller Foundation-sponsored efforts in Africa at the start of the 1920s, investigators, unable to find an appropriate animal model, had in their frustration either voluntarily or involuntarily become experimental subjects themselves, sometimes with fatal results.[31] One says "appropriate" because although the researchers had plenty of monkeys at hand, and monkeys, as primates, were regarded as the best experimental subjects aside from humans, all attempts to induce yellow fever in African monkeys failed, convincing investigators that these primates simply could not host the disease.

It was only after rhesus monkeys—brought to Africa from India in 1927—proved extraordinarily susceptible to yellow fever that it dawned on Rockefeller investigators that African monkeys were immune to the disease because they had already hosted and survived it. With the use of the susceptible rhesus monkeys, researchers were quickly able to confirm that the yellow fever pathogen was a *filtrable virus* (an ultramicroscopic agent able to pass through filters that would retain the smallest known bacteria), and that it could be transmitted from monkey to monkey directly through inoculation or via the *Aedes aegypti* mosquito vector.[32]

About three years after research using the rhesus monkey had begun, microbiologist Max Theiler, working at Harvard in 1930, discovered that white mice could also be employed to study yellow fever; as mice were considerably more convenient for laboratory purposes, they joined monkeys in the effort. Next, Theiler demonstrated that if the virus was transmitted from mouse to mouse, it could be weakened and used to immunize monkeys against yellow fever, thereby providing a realistic hope of finding a vaccine for humans.[33] The employment of mice in yellow fever research also led to the development, by the Rockefeller Foundation's laboratory, of the "mouse protection test" whereby blood samples from humans could be tested for their ability to protect mice from injections of the yellow fever virus. This test made it possible for researchers in the field to "map" human populations that had hosted the disease and to thereby determine regions of yellow fever's endemicity.[34]

Monkeys, however, continued to figure prominently in the study of yellow fever, for the very good reason that yellow fever turned out to be a disease of monkeys.[35] There were several clues to this, such as the African monkeys' immunity to yellow fever in areas where the disease was endemic, the extreme susceptibility of the rhesus monkeys from India (an area that had always been free of yellow fever), and the susceptibility of New World monkeys (which helped convince epidemiologists that the cradle of yellow fever was in Africa). However, it was not until the mid-1930s that Rockefeller researchers in Brazil came to the realization that the yellow fever virus was very much alive in the bodies of monkeys in the jungle treetops of South America, and that humans were not needed to perpetuate it.[36]

Finding the virus in these monkeys led researchers to the understanding that yellow fever could not be eradicated after all. Fortunately, by the late 1930s, Theiler and his coworkers had managed to attenuate the virus by successively passing it through chick embryo tissues to the point where it could serve as a vaccine for humans. Called the 17D *Valline strain,* this vaccine, which has afforded yellow fever immunity to millions of people in Africa and the Americas, derives from a blood specimen taken in 1927 from a West African native. From that native, the vaccine has been "carried down . . . from one laboratory animal to another, through repeated tissue cultures and enormous multiplication," to our present day, in which we now produce it in embryonated chicken eggs.[37]

Despite the enduring endemic presence of jungle yellow fever, success in eradicating the *Aedes aegypti* mosquito vector (by destroying its eggs) made it seem that at least epidemic yellow fever had been eradicated. After the turn of the twentieth century, mosquito control meant that the virus no longer leapfrogged across the Caribbean and into U.S. coastal cities, where, from 1693 to 1905, it had caused upwards of 150,000 deaths.[38] In 1954, however, there was an epidemic in Trinidad, and howler and cebus monkeys native to the island were called into medical service by investigators, who slaughtered selected bands of the animals and then conducted systematic serological studies that indicated that a large proportion of the monkeys had developed immunity to yellow fever. Clearly, the virus was present in the island, a fact documented by its reappearance in 1959, and again in 1979–80, among portions of the population that had not been vaccinated against it. Monkeys were subsequently employed in Trinidad as sentinels to warn humans of the approach of yellow fever, just as they had been used by Rockefeller researchers in Brazil after the discovery of the jungle form of the disease.[39]

IV. Viral Plagues—Present and Future

Primate and rodent sentinels have also been pressed into service to isolate "the backlog of viruses still unstudied plus [the] continuing annual influx of several dozen 'new' viruses from around the world[.]" In 1982, this situation was pronounced "an embarrassment" by virologist Wilbur Downs, then the director of the Yale Arbovirus Laboratory.[40] By this he meant that medicine had become relatively complacent about bacterial diseases because of antibiotics, and had even become complacent about viral diseases after the Salk and Sabin vaccines stopped polio (at least in the developed world). Investigators had turned away from focusing on infectious diseases to focusing on chronic illnesses like heart-related diseases and cancer. Medicine, however, was urgently reminded of the danger of viral ailments with the emergence of such killers as the Marburg virus in 1967, the Lassa virus in 1969, and the Ebola virus in 1976. Even as Downs wrote, the human immunodeficiency viruses HIV-1 and HIV-2, which cause the acquired immune deficiency syndrome (AIDS), were about to burst upon the world.[41]

Because at least two of these new plagues—the Marburg and Ebola virus diseases—were, like yellow fever, associated with monkeys (later, the AIDS viruses would be similarly associated), monkeys assumed a position of enormous importance in laboratory investigations aimed at controlling the viruses. But, as in the case of yellow fever research, such experimentation can prove risky. In fact, monkey research was responsible for the 1967 unleashing of the "Marburg" virus in a laboratory in Marburg, Germany, where the kidneys of vervet (African green) monkeys were being removed for preparation of cell culture. Of the 25 laboratory workers infected, all fell gravely ill, and 7 died with horrible hemorrhagic symptoms, yielding a case-mortality rate of 28 percent.

At the same time, an epidemic of what came to be called "Marburg virus disease" broke out among three batches of monkeys that had been delivered to a laboratory in Belgrade, Yugoslavia; one-third of the monkeys died. It was learned that the monkeys had all originated in Uganda, and investigations showed that as many as a third of some monkey groups there carried the virus. Almost eight years passed, however, without another sign of the virus in humans. Then, in 1975, an Australian couple visiting Rhodesia (now Zimbabwe) became the first known human cases of Marburg virus disease in Africa. One died, and the autopsy supplied proof that this pestilence had not vanished after all; other human cases subsequently reported in Africa have continued to confirm the presence there of a Marburg virus "reservoir." Moreover, in the laboratory, baboons and chimpanzees have been shown to have the virus, as have guinea pigs (an American animal long acclimated to Africa); alarmingly, experimental infection of New World primates with the Marburg virus has proven 100 percent fatal.[42] Nevertheless, to this day, investigators have no idea where and how the disease originated. Not surprisingly, the Marburg virus is now viewed as a potential time bomb and has compelled much in the way of field and laboratory research, although animals used in such research are now (understandably) treated with extreme caution.

Lassa fever was the second virus that, previously unknown to medical science, emerged to shake medical complacency. Its first documented outbreak came in 1969 among nurses at a hospital in Lassa, Nigeria. By 1978, there had been 16 additional episodes reported, with 386 cases and 105 deaths (again with the most gruesome of symptoms), yielding an overall case-fatality rate of about 27 percent. Laboratory research with various experimental animals revealed that the illness was a zoonosis; originally a disease of small rodents in Africa, it had managed to jump the species barrier. That research—much of it conducted with laboratory mice—also revealed that Lassa fever could be acquired by inhaling viral particles from infected humans or animals, by contact with contaminated urine, and by contact with the blood of an infected person.[43] Clearly, here was a second potential time bomb.

A third virus, which appeared in 1976, was the most frightening of all. It erupted in towns along the Ebola River in Central Africa. The first reported outbreak, in Sudan, killed 151 of 284 individuals known to have been infected, for a case-fatality rate of 53 percent. The second outbreak, in Zaire, was even more ferocious, killing 288 of 318 known cases, which meant that it had generated an incredible case-fatality rate of almost 91 percent.[44] Again, hemorrhagic manifestations were frequently observed, vomiting was common (often with red blood), and jaundice was seen in the dying because the virus produces lesions in almost all organs. Death could occur as early as the fourth day after infection, but generally the patients suffered for an average of eight or nine days before expiring.[45]

At first it was believed that the disease was the work of the yellow fever virus, but gradually it became clear that this horrible and incredibly fatal illness—soon to be named "Ebola virus disease"—was yet another new virus. Over three thousand animals from some one hundred different species, ranging from snakes to chimpanzees, were tested for the virus; monkeys, baboons, and guinea pigs were used in experiments aimed at developing a treatment, but to no avail. It has been learned, however, that the Ebola virus is related to the Marburg virus. Both have a bizarre morphology (or structure) that seems to make them unique among viruses, and for both pathogens the animal (or animals) in which they originated remains a mystery.[46]

As already noted, however, these sorts of illnesses have been associated with monkeys, and monkeys are high on the list of suspected sources for the Ebola and Marburg viruses. Indeed, in 1989, monkeys managed to dispel any notion that the wealthy nations of the West, far away from Africa, were safe from Ebola virus disease. This revelation occurred when an epidemic broke out among 100 monkeys, 60 of which died, at a Virginia laboratory near Washington, D.C.; the monkeys had reached Virginia from the Philippines via Amsterdam and J. F. K. International Airport. Although no human cases developed, a collective shudder passed through the world's community of viral researchers.[47]

In addition to these three lethal pathogens that have so rudely seized the attention of medicine, there are also those many other viruses that were new or newly discovered when Downs had found the situation to be so embarrassing. Among them are the arboviruses (that is, arthropod-borne-viruses) Chikungunya, Congo-Crimean hemorrhagic fever, O'Nyong-Nyong fever, Rift Valley fever, and West Nile fever. To these one can add the arenaviruses (most of which have rodents somewhere in their etiology as vectors) Amapari, Araguari, Flexal, Johnston Atoll, Junin, Latino, Machupo, Mobala, Mopeia, Parana, Pichinde, and Tamiami. Most of the arenaviruses are New World pathogens, hosted by a variety of animals ranging from rodents and bats to birds and opossums. All have infected humans and many are deadly, Biosafety Level 4 germs for which there are no vaccines and no cures. Good examples of Level 4 arenaviruses include Junin (Argentine hemorrhagic fever) and Machupo (Bolivian hemorrhagic fever), which have generated case-fatality rates of around 25 percent during epidemics.[48]

Yet so far, the most lethal of the new viral diseases has, of course, been AIDS, which in the 1980s was viewed as a modern version of the "Black Death,"[49] and as a plague that was predicted—despite an uncertain term of latency—to sooner or later generate 100 percent case-mortality rates. It was in June of 1981 that U.S. physicians first read in the Centers for Disease Control (CDC) *Morbidity and Mortality Weekly Report* (*MMWR*) of this novel illness, which a bit later was named GRID (Gay-Related Immunodeficiency syndrome) because the disease seemed mainly to occur among homosexuals.[50] It was next found among drug users; neither they nor homosexuals elicited much sympathy in the Reagan administration, whose most "avid constituency was composed of right-wing religious moralists."[51] As a consequence, the heavy guns of U.S. medical research institutions were slow to be trained on the problem, even though it seemed for the moment that this new viral disease was strictly a U.S. concern.[52]

But then the virus was discovered in Haiti, adding race to the political stew that this new illness had set to bubbling. When, in 1983, Ebola researchers in Central Africa began to report astronomical rates of AIDS infection there that were the result of heterosexual rather than homosexual activity, the health advisors of the Reagan administration reportedly refused to believe it for over a year, with the result that even more valuable time was lost.[53] Yet although AIDS research attracted little funding at first, knowledge of the disease began to accumulate nonetheless.

At the beginning of the epidemic, the most obvious approach to studying the disease was to inject blood samples of AIDS patients into laboratory monkeys to make certain that the virus was in their blood. But the CDC initially had no budget for more primate research, and thus a couple of its researchers had to begin by injecting and studying just four marmoset monkeys. Months passed, during which the monkeys remained well. Other laboratories, however, began the same kind of research, and when, in 1983, there were outbreaks of what seemed to be AIDS among laboratory monkeys in California and Massachusetts, some investigators began to wonder if the AIDS virus that was killing humans had come originally from monkeys. As in the case of yellow fever, although some monkeys were clearly susceptible to AIDS, others, like the first four experimented upon by CDC researchers, seemed immune.[54] Then, in 1985, Max Essex of the Harvard School of Public Health reported that he had isolated a retrovirus in wild African green monkeys that was very similar to the AIDS virus. (A *retrovirus* is an RNA virus that, after gaining entry to cells, makes a reverse mirror-image copy of its RNA in order to produce a DNA version of its genes.) The monkeys carried this retrovirus without any apparent ill-effects.[55]

It was at about this point (in 1985) that the potential ramifications of the AIDS epidemic became evident. As a result of this awareness, Congressional approval for research began to rise significantly, the National Academy of Sciences issued a consensus report on the disease, and the World Health Organization (WHO) established a global program to monitor it. Thus, both money and monkeys were finally mobilized for a crusade against AIDS, a mobilization also galvanized by data in the CDC's *MMWR* (and, later, other data reported from Africa) that the AIDS epidemic was also causing a resurgence of tuberculosis (TB)—a disease that medicine had believed was under control, at least in the developed world.[56] In July 1990, the WHO estimated that some eight million AIDS cases existed worldwide; the following year, that estimate was raised to between ten and twelve million.

By 1998, despite the campaign against AIDS, the number of cases had increased to between fourteen and fifteen million, and the WHO warned that the figure would probably increase to somewhere between twenty and thirty million by the year 2000.[57] With the number of cases accelerating wildly throughout the 1990s, and with no vaccine or cure in sight, it seemed to some onlookers that hundreds of millions of dollars were being wasted. It also appeared that those in charge at the WHO (which in 1993 had spent nearly a third of its enormous budget on AIDS research) had lost their collective mind. Furthermore, it seemed to some as if AIDS research institutions were staffed mostly by incompetents.[58]

In Africa, however, more research had uncovered the fact that primates other than green monkeys carried the disease, and that AIDS, like Lassa, Marburg, and Ebola, was an African illness. That some monkey groups were immune to the virus raised expectations for vaccine development. Though a vaccine has not yet been found, azidothymidine (AZT), shown in 1986 to prolong the period of HIV latency, has, along with the new drug lamivudine, been improved to the point that AIDS patients (in the wealthier nations, at least) now have some reasonable hope of living out a normal life span.[59]

For this new lease on life, AIDS patients owe a large debt to the experimental animals that have made possible the testing of medications as well as the unsnarling of the etiology of AIDS. Moreover, it seems now that the question is not *if* a vaccine will become available, but rather *when*. When it does, we will owe even more of a debt to experimental animals, precisely as we owe them for every vaccine from that of Jenner against smallpox in the eighteenth century, through those of Salk and Sabin against polio in the mid-twentieth century, to the fin de siècle vaccine against Lyme disease approved by the U.S. Food and Drug Administration in 1999.

We should also note that experimental animals have been in the forefront of the fight against cancer and heart-related diseases, and are being used in a variety of ways: to examine the role of trypsin inhibitors in pancreatic cancer; to promote a fuller understanding of the atherosclerotic process in humans; and to aid in the discovery, development, and toxicity-testing of drugs for chronic illnesses.[60] Indeed, the breakthroughs achieved in combating chronic illnesses, just like advances dealing with the infectious plagues, have invariably involved experimental animals.

Let us fast-forward to the future and its pathogenic perils for just a moment. At the turn of the twenty-first century, AIDS is dramatically demonstrating that the developed world can no longer afford to ignore any of the new or newly discovered diseases in the developing world. AIDS, for example, arose in nonhuman bodies and only assumed a uniformly virulent form in humans, all of which suggests that because the so-called human immunodeficiency viruses and groups of nonhuman African primates are so well-adapted to one another, AIDS must not be a new virus after all—it is just new for humans.[61]

Today, such "new" diseases cannot be easily contained. Sailing ships took weeks, and steamships days, to cross oceans that jet planes now traverse in hours. In 1960, sub-Saharan Africa had no cities with a million or more people; now there are close to a dozen. As populations swell, the pressure on rain forests squeezes out more and more viruses, which find their natural habitat there. In short, most of the so-called "new" diseases have probably been around for centuries and escaped detection because they smoldered in remote regions, either in animal hosts or in little-studied human populations. Like AIDS, many of these diseases only come to be recognized as disease entities when they make contact with people in the middle latitudes, as opposed to tropical populations.[62] In view of this, AIDS may represent only the proverbial tip of a viral iceberg, and medical science needs to be both alert and agile to confront the plagues to come. However, the state of this alertness and agility—and, consequently, of the lives of millions of humans—will depend to a great extent on the ability of biomedical researchers to use experimental animals.

V. The Opposition to Animal Experimentation

Yet a look at the history of opposition to experimental animal use suggests that, at least in Great Britain and the United States, there will be no lessening of efforts to hamstring such researchers. In fact, just as Western scientists were closing in on germ theory during the nineteenth century with the help of experimental animals, agitation began in Britain (though not in France, or in Germany, for that matter) for stopping their use. Some see the contrast between British and French attitudes toward experimental animals as beginning with the conflict between British anatomist Charles Bell and the aforementioned François Magendie. The latter's discovery, in 1822, of the motor and sensory nature of the anterior and posterior spinal roots triggered a bitter controversy with Bell over who made the discovery first; this dispute "took on an international character that was to endure for over a century."[63] Magendie had conducted his experiments on various animals decades before ether, chloroform, cocaine, or any other effective means of pain control came into common usage at the end of the nineteenth century; thus, his experiments surely caused the animals intense pain. Indeed, Bell claimed that, although he was entitled to much of the credit given to Magendie, he had failed to carry out as complete a series of experiments as the French physiologist because of the "protracted cruelty" of exposing the spinal marrow.[64]

As the century progressed, French investigators such as Claude Bernard, a student of Magendie, were relentless in the employment of experimental animals, as was Bernard's student, the American John Call Dalton. As such, these researchers were representatives of a new experimental method that would carry us into a modern age of medicine. By contrast, British medical journals began to proclaim the increasing reluctance of their physicians to vivisect; as a consequence, the achievement of germ theory was probably dominated more by Continental scientists than it might otherwise have been.[65]

Great Britain was fertile soil for antivivisection activity, and in 1824 participants in such activity organized as the Royal Society for the Prevention of Cruelty to Animals. By mid-century, the society was aggressively opposing animal experimentation, and by 1870 the antivivisection movement in England was white-hot: public demonstrations against animal experimentation were on the increase, bills opposing vivisection were read in Parliament, and the press was in a frenzy. The British Association for the Advancement of Science developed guidelines for physiological experiments; those it established had the effect of discouraging much of the animal experimentation that was still ongoing. Furthermore, in 1876 the Cruelty to Animals Act was passed to regulate (and oversee) such experimentation.[66] Henceforth, persons wishing to perform experiments on animals had to be licensed. Experiments on dogs, cats, horses, mules, and asses required special certification, as did experiments not aimed at the alleviation of human suffering (e.g., those used to illustrate medical lectures). Although the Act was watered down and certainly did not satisfy the antivivisectionists, this British experience nonetheless showed that animal protection groups could raise the consciousness of biomedical investigators, and that investigators would cooperate to ensure the continuance of animal research, albeit presumably by treating animals more humanely.

The British experience was somewhat paralleled in the United States. Although the Humane Society was founded in 1866 to prevent cruelty to animals in the cities, its members were of varying opinions about animal experimentation. In 1883, the American Anti-Vivisection Society was established in Philadelphia, and between 1896 and 1900, important confrontations took place between its members and those who defended the use of animals in research.[67] During this period, antivivisection activities and bills were vigorously opposed by physicians and scientists, and the American Medical Association (AMA) was able to prevent passage of the Gallinger bill, which would have regulated the use of animals in medical research and teaching throughout the District of Columbia.

The Gallinger bill's model was the British Cruelty to Animals Act, and one fear of those who opposed the bill was that it had the potential to be even more restrictive than the British act had proven to be. An even more important fear, of course, was that such a bill, if passed, would become a precedent for similar legislation in the states as well as for the federal government.[68] However, defeat of the Gallinger bill did not prevent legislative initiatives at the state level; as these proved unsuccessful, infuriated extremists began breaking into laboratories and threatening the lives of scientists.[69]

All this transpired just as nutritional research using animals was accelerating. In 1908, antivivisection activism prompted a reaction by researchers who formed the Council on Defense of Medical Research (CDMR) within the AMA. The CDMR was especially effective in denying legislative victories to the opposition, and in 1945 it was strengthened by the formation of the National Society for Medical Research (NSMR), organized by a committee of the Association of American Medical Colleges.[70]

Nonetheless, despite a half-century in which the use of experimental animals was successfully defended, the massive expansion of the country's biomedical research between the end of the Second World War and the 1960s finally led to legislation in the form of the Laboratory Animal Welfare Act (AWA) of 1966, which, among other things, regulated the sale and transportation of experimental animals by dealers.[71] The legislation was the result, at least in part, of a public relations effort by animal rights activists that convinced much of the nation, and therefore Congress, that household pets were being kidnapped and sold for research purposes.[72] In 1970, 1976, and 1985, the provisions of the act were extended to ensure that laboratory animals were treated humanely and that those who used them had training to ensure that the animals would be employed for appropriate purposes. As the AWA provisions were extended, the Association for Biomedical Research was organized in 1979 and merged with the NSMR to oppose any further restrictions regarding experimental animals.

Meanwhile, almost in anticipation of the massive biomedical research efforts that AIDS would precipitate, the animal-welfare movement was galvanized by the work of academic philosophers, beginning with Peter Singer's 1975 book entitled *Animal Liberation: A New Ethics for Our Treatment of Animals*. Singer urged activists in movements for the liberation of blacks and women to also support the liberation of animals who could not speak for themselves.[73] Such support, in Singer's view, meant practicing vegetarianism; ending the exploitation of animals for meat, furs, and other products; and prohibiting the use of animals for experiments in science and industry.

This opening salvo was followed the next year with an anthology edited by Singer and Tom Regan, *Animal Rights and Human Obligations,*[74] and, in 1981 (just as the AIDS epidemic was beginning), by Bernard E. Rollin's *Animal Rights and Human Morality*.[75] Singer's book in particular, however, became "the philosophic base" of the animal rights movement, which drew (as Singer had called for) a wide variety of activists to its standard.[76] The movement also discovered a number of ancestors, such as philosopher Henry Salt, whose 1892 *Animals' Rights Considered in Relation to Social Progress* (reissued in 1980) not only made a strong moral case for vegetarianism but also cited a number of authors who had preceded him in arguing for animal rights.[77]

In 1983, Regan (whom Singer has called "[t]he leading defender of the rights of animals"[78]) set forth the goals of the animal rights movement: the total abolition of the use of animals in science; the dissolution of commercial animal agriculture; and an end to hunting and trapping, both for sport and commercial purposes.[79] Increasingly, however, the latter two goals seemed to give way to the one issue that was clearly the most compelling for the activists: the use of animals in scientific—and especially biomedical—research. Opposition to that use increased in intensity to the point where a violent wing of the animal rights movement—organizations called the Animal Liberation Front and the Animal Rights Militia—began assaulting laboratories, freeing animals, and threatening medical schools and their faculties (not to mention the occasional public official) in the United States, Canada, France, and the United Kingdom.[80]

Passions have not abated a quarter of a century after the appearance of Singer's pivotal book. "The Nazi Treatment of Animals and People," for example, is the title of a recent animal rights essay that points out that the Nazis were kind to animals and cruel to people.[81] Although this is hardly fresh news and is not very relevant to the questions at hand, the essay does illustrate something of the emotionalism of the animal rights movement, as well as its durability. It also shows, by insisting on the equal value of animals and people, the seemingly unbridgeable chasm that separates biomedical investigators from these organized champions of animal rights. In the words of Regan, "[t]he fundamental wrong is the system that allows us to view animals as *our resources,* here for *us*—to be eaten, or surgically manipulated, or exploited for sport or money."[82]

Doubtless because of this chasm, those who oppose the use of animals in medical research must even deplore the myriad contributions animals have made over the ages to human health in preventive and clinical medicine as well as nutrition and epidemiology. Often such disparagement is done on Regan's uncompromising grounds, but it is also done on the somewhat more flexible ground that such contributions to medicine have mostly benefited people at the expense of animals. The latter argument, however, ignores the extent to which animals have benefited from such research, as their own plagues—from anthrax and brucellosis to a host of other zoonotic diseases—have been eliminated or brought under control. It also ignores the creation of the field of veterinary medicine and the establishment of an entire field of laboratory-animal medicine, a field that aims to ensure humane treatment for laboratory animals.[83] Finally, it ignores the fact that the study of living creatures is basic to biology—a science that cannot progress without such scientific inquiry.[84]

The danger posed by animal rights activities, now as in the past, is that they may prove successful to the point of summoning the kind of regulation that will seriously impede medical research. A more oblique—and therefore more troubling—effort toward that end has very recently appeared in a book entitled *Brute Science: Dilemmas of Animal Experimentation.*[85] The book is troubling because its authors, philosophers Hugh LaFollette and Niall Shanks, give the appearance of steering a course between those who favor and those who oppose the employment of animals in experimentation. Indeed, they concede that humans have benefited in the past from the use of animals in biomedical investigations. Yet the thrust of the book is that those benefits have not been as great as the public believes them to be, and are much smaller than researchers have claimed. In other words, the authors claim that the ends have not proven sufficient to justify the means—all of which makes us wonder if perhaps it is true that the only thing we learn from history is that we do not learn from history.

VI. Conclusion

The basic point of this essay has been that, at least since the ancient Greeks, experimental animals have been vital to our understanding of the biological processes that make life possible on the one hand and threaten it on the other. The compilation of this knowledge was slow at first. Indeed, it took some two millennia of observation and tinkering with the bodies of experimental animals, as well as those of humans, to cobble together the understanding of human anatomy and, then, physiology that let Harvey publish his 1628 treatise on the circulation of blood.

After Harvey's discovery, it took a mere two hundred years before scientists began the research that, with the use of animal models, resulted by the end of the nineteenth century in the establishment of germ theory. Then, with the beginning of the twentieth century, medical research using experimental animals shifted into high gear on a number of fronts—among them that of nutrition. Animals helped to unravel the etiologies of a number of heretofore elusive diseases that turned out to be caused by nutritional deficiencies; animals were thus instrumental in the discovery of the various vitamins and minerals.

Moving back to infectious diseases, germ theory shed light on the causes and courses of illnesses triggered by most known microparasites, save the viruses; yellow fever research, with its wholesale employment of monkeys and countless other experimental animals, represented the beginning of an endeavor aimed at discovering the etiologies of viral diseases, many of which have tropical and subtropical origins. The yellow fever work represented a major success; however, efforts in discovering the origins and sources of a host of other mysterious viral killers that have confronted us more recently have thus far proven unsuccessful. The Marburg, Lassa, Ebola, and (of course) HIV viruses are the most prominent, but there are a good many more for which there are, as yet, no vaccines and no cures. What all of these viruses seem to share is that they are hosted by a variety of animals, ranging from monkeys to rodents and bats to birds, which means that experimental animals will be absolutely indispensable to understanding and, hopefully, conquering these viruses in the new century.

In a world with a population now standing at six billion individuals, the inevitable globalization of business, science, agriculture, and even cuisines has also meant globalization of disease environments. AIDS serves as a nasty reminder of the new perils posed by pathogenic propinquity and underscores the importance of scientific research to head off, or at least tame, the plagues that seem sure to follow in the wake of AIDS.

Of course, animals are equally indispensable to the study of chronic diseases such as heart disease and cancer, and despite jokes that everything these animals are exposed to either gives them cancer or elevates their lipids, such research is paying huge dividends. It was not all that long ago that cancers and "hardening of the arteries" were viewed as death sentences. Now such conditions (at least in the developed world) are routinely cured, reversed, and treated, so that patients can resume a normal life.

Finally, in the matter of cuisines, their globalization demands successful research in areas such as food biotechnology, food additives, substitute foods and ingredients, and food toxins and poisons. Success in such research is now—and will continue to be—greatly determined by laboratory animals.

It is probably no accident that over the course of close to two centuries, upsurges in the activities of animal rights activists have tended to coincide with upsurges in crucial scientific investigations that have employed experimental animals. Fortunately, the activists' efforts—thus far—do not seem to have significantly slowed the progress of biomedical and pharmacologic research, with the result that today humans in the developed world enjoy unparalleled health and longevity. However, in nature, little remains static, and the relationship of humans with their epidemiological and nutritional environments most certainly does not. Consequently, in a world growing more complex daily, laboratory animals are needed more than ever to help in the discovery of vaccines and cures for the plagues of today and those to come, not to mention in both alleviating the burden of chronic diseases and ensuring humans a safe food supply.

To oppose the use of these animals seems benighted in the face of so many epidemiological and nutritional challenges. We live in a world in which people should be as concerned about what nature can do to them as they are about what people can do to them through crime, terrorism, government regulations, and aggressive military action. This makes any agenda aimed at shutting down—or even hindering—the use of animals in biomedical and biotechnological research seem fanatical, even suicidal.

NOTES

1. John Call Dalton, *Experimentation on Animals as a Means of Knowledge in Physiology, Pathology, and Practical Medicine* (1875), reprinted in Dalton, *John Call Dalton on Experimental Method* (New York: Arno Press, 1980), 11.
2. Mary T. Phillips and Jeri A. Sechzer, *Animal Research and Ethical Conflict: An Analysis of the Scientific Literature: 1966–1986* (New York: Springer-Verlag, 1989).
3. Robert M. Baird and Stuart E. Rosenbaum, eds., *Animal Experimentation: The Moral Issues* (Buffalo, NY: Prometheus Books, 1991).

4. Rivers Singleton, Jr., "Whither Goest Vivisection? Legislative and Regulatory Perspectives," *Perspectives in Biology and Medicine* 38, no. 1 (Autumn 1994): 41–57.

5. Lynda Birke and Ruth Hubbard, eds., *Reinventing Biology: Respect for Life and the Creation of Knowledge* (Bloomington: Indiana University Press, 1995).

6. Both of these works are reprinted in *John Call Dalton on Experimental Method.*

7. Questions of "firsts" are often murky and misleading, let alone naive, especially when a "first" is spied through the mists of time. Medical historians seem to enjoy them nonetheless. Dissection, for example, may or may not be indicated from time to time in the Hippocratic corpus; see Lise Wilkinson, *Animals and Disease: An Introduction to the History of Comparative Medicine* (Cambridge: Cambridge University Press, 1992), 55. However, there is nothing ambiguous about Aristotle's work on experimental animals. His *De Historia Animalium* and *De Partibus Animalium,* both in his *De Animalibus,* ed. Ludovicus Podocatharus, trans. Theodore Gaza (Venice: Johannes de Colonia and Johannes Manthen, 1476), were unquestionably the first animal physiology.

8. Bennett J. Cohen and Franklin M. Loew, "Laboratory Animal Medicine: Historical Perspectives," in James G. Fox, Bennett J. Cohen, and Franklin M. Loew, eds., *Laboratory Animal Medicine* (Orlando, FL: Academic Press, 1984), 2; Ralph Jackson, *Doctors and Diseases in the Roman Empire* (Norman: University of Oklahoma Press, 1988), 27–30.

9. Wilkinson, *Animals and Disease,* 7–8.

10. Andrew N. Rowan, *Of Mice, Models, and Men: A Critical Evaluation of Animal Research* (Albany: State University of New York Press, 1984), 42.

11. Erwin H. Ackerknecht, *A Short History of Medicine,* rev. ed. (Baltimore, MD: Johns Hopkins University Press, 1982), 89. See also 79–93.

12. Ibid., 115.

13. F. C. Bing, "Nutrition Research and Education in the Age of Franklin: A Bicentennial Study," *Journal of the American Dietetic Association* 68, no. 1 (January 1976): 18.

14. John Hunter, *Observations on Certain Parts of the Animal Oeconomy* (London: Longman, 1786). See also Ackerknecht, *Short History of Medicine,* 133; Wilkinson, *Animals and Disease,* 79–80; and Leslie T. Morton, *Morton's Medical Bibliography: An Annotated Check-List of Texts Illustrating the History of Medicine,* ed. Jeremy M. Norman, 5th. ed. (Aldershot, UK: Scolar Press, 1991), 63.

15. Claude Bernard, *Leçons de Physiologie Expérimentale Appliquée à la Médecine,* 2 vols. (Paris: J. B. Baillière, 1855–56).

16. Wilkinson, *Animals and Disease,* 79–80.

17. Robert Koch, *Gesammelte Werke,* 2 vols. (Leipzig, Germany: Georg Thieme, 1912).

18. Roderick E. McGrew, "Immunology," in Roderick E. McGrew, ed., *Encyclopedia of Medical History* (New York: McGraw-Hill, 1985), 147; Guenter B. Risse, "History of Western Medicine from Hippocrates to Germ Theory" and K. David Patterson, "Rabies," both in Kenneth F. Kiple, ed., *The Cambridge World History of Human Disease* (Cambridge: Cambridge University Press, 1993), 11–19, 962–66, respectively.

19. Cohen and Loew, "Laboratory Animal Medicine," 2.

20. Elsie M. Widdowson, "1985 E. V. McCollum International Lectureship in Nutrition: Animals in the Service of Human Nutrition," *Nutrition Reviews* 44, no. 7 (July 1986): 221–27; Kenneth J. Carpenter, *Protein and Energy: A Study of Changing Ideas in Nutrition* (Cambridge: Cambridge University Press, 1994), 28–32, 91–92, 119–20; Peter Pellet, "Protein and Energy Metabolism," in Kenneth F. Kiple and Kriemhild Coneè Ornelas, eds., *The Cambridge World History of Food* (Cambridge: Cambridge University Press, 2000).

21. Melinda S. Meade, "Beriberi," in Kiple, ed., *The Cambridge World History of Human Disease,* 606–11; Robert R. Williams, *Toward the Conquest of Beriberi* (Cambridge, MA: Harvard University Press, 1961).

22. Kenneth J. Carpenter, *The History of Scurvy and Vitamin C* (Cambridge: Cambridge University Press, 1986), 173–79; Stephen V. Beck, "Scurvy: Citrus and Sailors," in Kenneth F. Kiple, ed., *Plague, Pox, and Pestilence* (London: Weidenfeld and Nicolson, 1997), 68–73.

23. Carpenter, *History of Scurvy and Vitamin C,* 178; Ackerknecht, *Short History of Medicine,* 230.

24. Widdowson, "Animals in the Service of Human Nutrition," 223.

25. Ibid., 224.

26. Edward Mellanby, "The Part Played by an 'Accessory Factor' in the Production of Experimental Rickets," *Journal of Physiology* 52 (1918–19): xi–xii, liii–liv.

27. Ackerknecht, *Short History of Medicine,* 230.

28. Myrtle Thierry-Palmer, "Vitamin K and Vitamin K-Dependent Proteins," in Kiple and Ornelas, eds., *The Cambridge World History of Food*. According to Thomas H. Jukes, Herman Almquist (at the University of California at Berkeley) should have shared in the Nobel Prize that was awarded to Dam and Doisy for the discovery of vitamin K; see Jukes, "Herman James Almquist (1903–): Biographical Sketch," *Journal of Nutrition* 117, no. 3 (March 1987): 409–15.

29. Andrew Cliff, Peter Haggett, and Matthew Smallman-Raynor, *Deciphering Global Epidemics: Analytical Approaches to the Disease Records of World Cities, 1888–1912* (Cambridge: Cambridge University Press, 1998), 22–23.

30. Wilkinson, *Animals and Disease,* 212; J. N. Hays, *The Burdens of Disease: Epidemics and Human Response in Western History* (New Brunswick, NJ: Rutgers University Press, 1998).

31. In Africa, in their "laboratories on the edge of the jungle," Drs. Hideyo Noguchi, Adrian Stokes, William Alexander Young, and Theodore B. Hayne all succumbed to yellow fever during the first "heroic" years of the Rockefeller Commission's presence at Lagos, Nigeria. Donald B. Cooper and Kenneth F. Kiple, "Yellow Fever," in Kiple, ed., *The Cambridge World History of Human Disease,* 1105. Other investigators who gave their lives in the very dangerous business of yellow fever research were Paul Lewis, Howard B. Cross, and Jesse Lazear. Wilbur G. Downs, "The Story of Yellow Fever since Walter Reed," *Bulletin of the New York Academy of Medicine,* 2d. ser., 44, no. 6 (June 1968): 727.

32. Cooper and Kiple, "Yellow Fever," 1105; Downs, "The Story of Yellow Fever," 723.

33. Cooper and Kiple, "Yellow Fever," 1106; Downs, "The Story of Yellow Fever," 724.

34. Max Theiler, "Nobel Lecture: The Development of Vaccines against Yellow Fever," in *Nobel Lectures: Physiology or Medicine, 1942–1962* (New York: Elsevier Publishing, 1961), 351–52.

35. This is somewhat misleading because other wild forest creatures may also serve as hosts for the disease, and the mosquitoes that act as vectors remain infective for life. Cooper and Kiple, "Yellow Fever," 1106; George K. Strode, ed., *Yellow Fever* (New York: McGraw-Hill, 1951), 532.

36. Strode, *Yellow Fever*, 532; Downs, "Story of Yellow Fever," 725. It is strange that in the correspondence of Rockefeller investigators among themselves and with their New York headquarters, there is little mention of the suspicion of earlier physicians such as A. Balfour, who wrote "The Wild Monkey as a Reservoir for the Virus of Yellow Fever," *Lancet* 2 (April 25, 1914): 1176–78. See, for example, the January 30, 1934 letter of Fred L. Soper (who was just about to become the discoverer of jungle yellow fever) from the Rockefeller Foundation office in Rio de Janeiro to Wilbur A. Sawyer at the Rockefeller headquarters in New York. He writes: "[A]lthough there is always the possibility that yellow fever may have natural animal hosts and insect vectors, other than the Aëdes aegypti, capable of maintaining permanent endemicity in the region . . . we have yet no proof of this." This correspondence is now housed in the Rockefeller Archive Center (hereinafter RAC) in Pontico Hills, North Tarrytown, New York. Soper's letter is located in the International Health Board (hereinafter IHB), series 305, box 22, folder 173.

37. Theiler, "The Development of Vaccines against Yellow Fever," 351–61; Raymond B. Fosdick, *The Story of the Rockefeller Foundation* (New York: Harper, 1952), 69; Wilbur G. Downs, "History of Epidemiological Aspects of Yellow Fever," *Yale Journal of Biology and Medicine* 55, nos. 3–4 (May–August 1982): 181, 184. Mice were used by the French to develop a mouse-brain vaccine that has now been almost completely eclipsed by the attenuated 17D vaccine.

38. K. David Patterson, "Yellow Fever Epidemics and Mortality in the United States, 1693–1905," *Social Science Medicine* 34, no. 8 (April 1992): 855–65.

39. Wilbur G. Downs, "The Known and the Unknown in Yellow Fever Ecology and Epidemiology," *Ecology of Disease* 1, nos. 2–3 (1982): 103–10; RAC, IHB, Fred L. Soper to Wilbur A. Sawyer, 305/1/1.

40. Wilbur G. Downs, "The Rockefeller Foundation Virus Program: 1951–1971 with Update to 1981," *Annual Reviews of Medicine* 33 (1982): 27.

41. Wilbur G. Downs, "Ebola Virus Disease" and Allan M. Brandt, "Acquired Immune Deficiency Syndrome," both in Kiple, ed., *The Cambridge World History of Human Disease*, 699–702 and 547–51, respectively.

42. John C. N. Westwood, *The Hazard from Dangerous Exotic Diseases* (London: Macmillan, 1980), 107–17; Wilbur G. Downs, "Marburg Virus Disease," in Kiple, ed., *The Cambridge World History of Human Disease*, 682–85.

43. Wilbur G. Downs, "Lassa Fever," in Kiple, ed., *The Cambridge World History of Human Disease*, 817–19; Laurie Garrett, *The Coming Plague: Newly Emerging Diseases in a World Out of Balance* (New York: Penguin, 1994), 83.

44. Westwood, *The Hazard from Dangerous Exotic Diseases*, 118–39.

45. E. T. W. Bowen, "Ebola Virus Disease," in G. Thomas Strickland, ed., *Hunter's Tropical Medicine*, 6th ed. (Philadelphia: Saunders, 1984), 193.

46. Westwood, *The Hazard from Dangerous Exotic Diseases,* 135; Downs, "Ebola Virus Disease," 700; Garrett, *The Coming Plague,* 147.

47. Downs, "Ebola Virus Disease," 699–700; D'Vera Cohn, "Deadly Ebola Virus Found in Va. Laboratory Monkey," *Washington Post,* December 1, 1989, 1A; and "Deadly Virus Discovered in Laboratory Monkeys," *New York Times,* (December 3, 1989), sec. 1, p. 41.

48. Wilbur G. Downs, "Arenaviruses," in Kiple, ed., *The Cambridge World History of Human Disease,* 595–98. This is but a partial list of the newly identified viral illnesses. To it we could easily add another thirty, including the very recently identified Venezuelan hemorrhagic fever. See Arno Karlen, *Man and Microbes: Disease and Plagues in History and Modern Times* (New York: Putnam, 1995), 6, 163.

49. For some people, HIV/AIDS is in fact proving to be another such epidemiological catastrophe. With the lifetime risk of dying of AIDS approaching 60 to even 90 percent in some African populations, "this means that many countries in Southern and East Africa are facing the kind of excess adult mortality levels that the Black Death brought to Europe in the fourteenth century. . . ." John C. Caldwell, "Reasons for Limited Sexual Behavior Change in the Sub-Saharan African AIDS Epidemic, and Possible Future Intervention Strategies," in John C. Caldwell et al., eds. *Resistances to Behavioural Change to Reduce HIV/AIDS Infection in Predominantly Heterosexual Epidemics in Third World Countries* (Canberra, Australia: Health Transition Centre, 1999), 242.

50. Centers for Disease Control *Morbidity and Mortality Weekly,* June 5, 1981. The *MMWR* is a weekly report on diseases from around the world and methods of combating them.

51. Garrett, *The Coming Plague,* 301.

52. Ibid.

53. Ibid., 349.

54. Ibid., 318, 328.

55. Colin Norman, "Africa and the Origin of AIDS," *Science* 230, no. 4730 (December 6, 1985): 1141; Garrett, *The Coming Plague,* 226.

56. See, for example, "Tuberculosis and Acquired Immunodeficiency Syndrome—Florida," *Morbidity and Mortality Weekly Report,* September 19, 1986, 587–90; and J. R. Glynn et al., "The Impact of HIV on Morbidity and Mortality from Tuberculosis in Sub-Saharan Africa: A Study in Rural Malawi and Review of the Literature," *Health Transition Review* 7, supplement 2 (1997): 75–87.

57. Dennis C. Weeks, "The AIDS Pandemic in Africa," *Current History* 91, no. 565 (May 1992): 208; Sheldon J. Watts, *Epidemics and History: Disease, Power, and Imperialism* (New Haven, CT: Yale University Press, 1997), 277–78.

58. Lawrence K. Altman, "At AIDS Talks, Science Faces a Daunting Maze," *New York Times,* June 6, 1993, sec. 1, p. 20.

59. Michael Waldholz and Christopher J. Chipello, "AIDS Drug 3TC Significantly Prolongs AZT's Effectiveness, U.S. Tests Confirm," *Wall Street Journal,* February 2, 1995, B2.

60. R. Kroes and John H. Weisberger, "Nutrition and Cancer" and Melissa H. Olken and Joel D. Howell, "Nutrition and Heart-Related Diseases," both in Kiple and Ornelas, eds., *The Cambridge World History of Food.*

61. Kenneth F. Kiple, "The Ecology of Disease," in W. F. Bynum and Roy Porter, eds., *Companion Encyclopedia of the History of Medicine,* 2 vols. (New York: Routledge, 1993), 1:357–81.

62. Cliff, Haggett, and Smallman-Raynor, *Deciphering Global Epidemics,* 12.

63. Ackerknecht, *Short History of Medicine,* 160; Phillips and Sechzer, *Animal Research and Ethical Conflict,* 6.

64. Phillips and Sechzer, *Animal Research and Ethical Conflict,* 6–7.

65. Over forty years after the beginning of the controversy, in a lecture to the New York College of Physicians and Surgeons delivered on February 7, 1882, Dalton castigated Bell in a defense of the scientific method. See his "Nervous Degeneration and the Theory of Sir Charles Bell," reprinted in Dalton, *John Call Dalton on Experimental Method,* 72–108.

66. Jeri A. Sechzer, "Historical Issues Concerning Animal Experimentation in the United States," *Social Science and Medicine* 15, no. 1 (March 1981): 13–14.

67. Sechzer, "Historical Issues Concerning Animal Experimentation," 15; Steven J. Smith et al., "Use of Animals in Biomedical Research: Historical Role of the American Medical Association and the American Physician," *Archives of Internal Medicine* 148, no. 8 (August 1988): 1849.

68. Smith et al., "Use of Animals in Biomedical Research," 1849; Phillips and Sechzer, *Animal Research and Ethical Conflict,* 18.

69. Smith et al., "Use of Animals in Biomedical Research," 1850.

70. Ibid., 1149–51.

71. *Laboratory Animal Welfare Act of 1966,* Pub. L. No. 89–544, 80 Stat. 350 (1966) (codified as amended at 7 U.S.C. secs. 2131–56 (1982 and Supp. IV 1986)).

72. Smith et al., "Use of Animals in Biomedical Research," 1852; Rowan, *Of Mice, Models, and Men,* 56.

73. Peter Singer, *Animal Liberation: A New Ethics for Our Treatment of Animals* (New York: New York Review Books, 1975).

74. Tom Regan and Peter Singer, eds., *Animal Rights and Human Obligations* (Englewood Cliffs, NJ: Prentice-Hall, 1976).

75. Bernard E. Rollin, *Animal Rights and Human Morality* (Buffalo, NY: Prometheus, 1981).

76. An interesting fusion of feminism and the animal rights movement may be found in Birke and Hubbard, eds., *Reinventing Biology.*

77. Henry Salt, *Animals' Rights Considered in Relation to Social Progress* (1892; reprint, Clark's Summit, PA: Society for Animal Rights, 1980).

78. Peter Singer, *Animal Liberation,* rev. ed. (New York: Avon Books, 1990), 308 n. 22.

79. Tom Regan, *The Case for Animal Rights* (Berkeley: University of California Press, 1983).

80. Smith et al., "Use of Animals in Biomedical Research," 1852–53; Michael P. T. Leahy, *Against Liberation: Putting Animals in Perspective* (London: Routledge, 1991), 236–37; F. Barbara Orlans, *In the Name of Science: Issues in Responsible Animal Experimentation* (New York: Oxford University Press, 1993), 169–90.

81. Arnold Arluke and Boria Sax, "The Nazi Treatment of Animals and People," in Birke and Hubbard, eds., *Reinventing Biology,* 228–60.

82. Regan, *The Case for Animal Rights,* 14.
83. See Cohen and Loew, "Laboratory Animal Medicine," 1–16; James G. Fox, "Laboratory Animal Medicine: Changes and Challenges," *Cornell Veterinarian* 75, no. 1 (January 1985): 159–70; N. R. Brewer, "Personalities in the Early History of Laboratory Animal Science and Medicine," *Laboratory Animal Science* 30, no. 4 (August 1980): 741–58; and Henry L. Foster, "The History of the Commercial Production of Laboratory Rodents," *Laboratory Animal Science* 30, no. 4 (August 1980): 793–98.
84. Singleton, "Whither Goest Vivisection?" 55. For the rise of veterinary medicine, see Wilkinson, *Animals and Disease.*
85. Hugh LaFollette and Niall Shanks, *Brute Science: Dilemmas of Animal Experimentation* (London: Routledge, 1996), 260, 262.

Making Choices in the Laboratory

Adrian R. Morrison*

I. Introduction

This is a very personal, practical essay by one who has spent his working life trying to understand a bit of nature—a very small bit: the brain mechanisms of sleep and wakefulness. Because that effort has involved the use of animals in ways that harm them to varying degrees, my work and that of many fellow scientists has come under incredible scrutiny and worse. The reason, of course, is that apart from the majority of society, which is concerned about the welfare of laboratory animals but is supportive of their controlled use in experimentation, there are those firmly opposed to using them, even when human lives are at stake. At the heart of that opposition, in my opinion, lies evil.

Adherents of the animal rights movement—I do not speak here of the compassionate souls misled by animal rights propaganda into responding to fundraising appeals—are not necessarily evil themselves, of course. Indeed, many are simply individuals who, when they rail and demonstrate against biomedical research, do not appreciate the consequences of their support of the extreme aims of the animal rights movement or are naive in their understanding of the process of science. Their knowledge of biology is abysmal. Although they quite rightly do not like to be grouped with terrorists within the animal rights movement just because both groups share a very strong affinity for animals, I do not hesitate to

---

*I wish to dedicate this essay to the memory of Dr. Michael Goldberger, who in his way initiated this project. I am grateful to those who have provided funds that have partially supported my public education efforts. Others have been helpful in different ways. Drs. Charles Nicoll and Sharon Russell alerted me to the writings of Brandon Reines; I appreciate that and other assistance. I also want to thank Mary Brennan of the Foundation for Biomedical Research and Jacquie Calnan of Americans for Medical Progress for bibliographic assistance. Finally, with great gratitude, I thank my colleagues and students in my laboratory. They have been very supportive as I have pursued my mission to protect the integrity of biomedical research.

say that even the movement's nonviolent adherents work against the best interests of humanity (and of the animals that benefit from biological research). Most importantly, though, a morality that does not treat people as worthy of special consideration underlies the movement's thinking and many of its actions. This morality leads inevitably to evil: hate messages and other acts designed to intimidate researchers and their families, as well as the destruction of laboratories. These actions impede life-saving research.

The following statements by leaders of the animal rights movement exemplify this suspect morality: "The belief that all life is equal because all our planetary relations (both human and non-human) are sacred leads to the inevitable conclusion that it is unethical to value any one life over any other. Thus the life of an ant and the life of my child should be granted equal consideration."[1] "Animal liberationists do not separate out the human animal, so there is no rational basis for saying that a human being has special rights. A rat is a pig is a dog is a boy. They're all mammals."[2] Considering people to be precious individuals is certainly one of the hallmarks of the Western tradition; the discounting of this belief underlay the terrors of both Nazi Germany and Soviet Russia, in which millions of human beings lost their lives. Yet, those very deaths have been used by the animal liberationists to call attention to the plight of chickens on their way to slaughter: "Six million Jews died in concentration camps, but six billion broiler chickens will die this year in slaughterhouses."[3] The same individual offering that comparison, Ingrid Newkirk, the cofounder of People for the Ethical Treatment of Animals (PETA), was confronted in a radio interview with a question about abortion: "So a rat is worthy of more protection than a human fetus, is that correct?" Her response? "That's correct."[4] Not only do such statements trivialize humanity, they impede progress toward reaching consensus on how animals should be treated.

Section II of this essay presents my own responses to those philosophers who have argued for and against the propriety of using animals in biomedical research. In Section III, I discuss how I think about my work in the laboratory; that is, I consider practical decisions that I have made through the years. Sections IV and V consider objections to animal research and the misrepresentations of its value to medical progress that these objections embrace. I have included these discussions because I have considered it to be one of my roles as a scientist to educate and protect the public from the animal-rightists' misinformation campaign. Finally, in Section VI, I briefly describe the particular path that my career took; this will allow me to discuss the role that animals play in solving a fundamental problem faced by neuroscience: the failure of the central nervous system to repair itself after injury.

I would like to note, here, that rational commentary and recommendations on how one should use animals in research almost always comes from those "outside the arena," so this essay may well be unique. It is time to hear from scientists who must make the difficult decisions in the laboratory, in the service of science, and, I firmly believe, in the service of humanity.

II. General Thoughts

Several beliefs or principles have governed my life as a scientist who uses animals to solve the questions that he addresses. Foremost, I believe that human beings stand apart in a moral sense from all other species, though I also believe humans to be a product of the same physical, evolutionary forces that operate on all life. Furthermore, I am certain that animals have been and will continue for many years to be indispensable agents in advancing medical knowledge. Thus, my position is that using animals in biomedical research is necessary scientifically, justified morally, and required ethically.

Clearly, all scientists who use animals in ways that harm them must have similar views; otherwise, many would have to be sadists. We can immediately dismiss that as a preposterous proposition. Interestingly, belief among biomedical researchers in the appropriateness of animal use in research does not appear to depend on particular religious beliefs. I feel certain that among scientists who value fellow human beings above other species—even above the genetically similar chimpanzee—one would find a wide variety of religious views, from the formally devout to avowed atheists (although I know of no formal survey that has plumbed this question). While God may ultimately be behind every research scientist's having a belief in the sanctity of human life (whether the scientist recognizes it or not), He rarely enters directly into modern ethical conversations on the question of the rights of animals. When reference to God does appear in discussion, it is usually in animal-rightists' pejorative reference to the idea in Genesis that man was given dominion over the natural world.

But without God's blessing, how can one defend, for example, the use of perfectly healthy animals for research in preference to severely brain-damaged infants? This, in so many words, is a challenge frequently raised by the animal rights movement. What is my response to this particular concern? Having stood on the grounds of Auschwitz, I am ever mindful that one man's Jew, gypsy, or homosexual can be another man's guinea pig. If for no other reason, then, I can ground a response in self-preservation. I speak, really, of self-preservation in the larger sense, of protecting the weak and helpless from those who consider themselves competent to decide the fate of others in accordance with their own view of what is "best." I abhor the idea that "we cannot justifiably give more protection to the life of a human being than we give to a nonhuman animal, if the human being clearly ranks lower on any possible scale of relevant characteristics."[5]

This disturbing point of view, stated in Peter Singer's book, *Rethinking Life and Death: The Collapse of Our Traditional Ethics* (1994), stems from his proposal that we should abandon the "old-fashioned" belief in the sanctity of human life and move beyond excluding animals from our moral community. As is well known, he is committed to end "speciesism." Singer's thinking inspired the bizarre statements by animal rights leaders that I quoted in Section I. In the view of George Weigel, former president of the Ethics and Public Policy Center:

> Singer's proposed solution to "the collapse of our traditional ethics" would mean nothing less than the end of humanism, in either its Judeo-Christian or Enlightenment-secular form. . . . Far from pointing a way out of today's moral dilemmas, Singer's book is a roadmap for driving down the darkest of moral blind alleys, at the end of which, however spiffed-up and genteel, is Dr. Mengele: the embodiment of the triumph of power over principle, in the manipulation of life and death by the "fit" at the expense of the "unworthy."[6]

Lawyers David Schmahmann and Lori Polacheck commented on these ideas as they appeared in Singer's *Animal Liberation* (originally published in 1975 and reissued in a second edition in 1990).[7] In that work, Singer argued that "[to] introduce ideas of dignity and worth as a substitute for other reasons for distinguishing humans and animals is not good enough. Fine phrases are the last resource of those who have run out of arguments."[8] But consider the sources of these "fine phrases," urge Schmahmann and Polacheck in their reply:

> Singer is right, of course, that once one dismisses [as Singer does in *Animal Liberation*] Hebrew thought; the teachings of Jesus; the views of St. Thomas Aquinas, St. Francis, Renaissance writers, and Darwin; and an entire "ideology whose history we have traced back to the Bible and the ancient Greeks"—in short, once one dismisses innate human characteristics, the ability to express reason, to recognize moral principles, to make subtle distinctions, and to intellectualize—there is no way to support the view that humans possess rights but animals do not.[9]

As a utilitarian, Singer does not actually subscribe to the idea of rights; he does, however, support the aims of the animal rights movement.[10] He and the rest of the movement see speciesism as analogous to racism.[11]

To all but a few people—those captured by the extremes of the animal rights movement—the equation of speciesism with racism seems to trivialize bigotry. Most people sense a duty to their fellow man that supersedes obligations to other species. Among these duties is the relief of human suffering, an obvious objective of biomedical research employing animals; this research is clearly acceptable to most people. Remarkably, however, it is not acceptable to everyone; if it were, there would be no need for this volume.

Why do most of the rest of us set humans apart? Michael A. Fox, a Canadian philosopher,[12] put forth what I consider to be clear and sensible reasons, although he would quickly come to reject his own arguments on the urging of a radical feminist friend.[13] Humans are unique, Fox originally argued, in many obvious ways. Humans' brain complexity leads to the sophisticated use of language: consider Shakespeare's plays versus the simple sign language that humans laboriously teach apes. Furthermore, humans use intricately fashioned tools, even making tools to make other objects. I would add that those who try to draw other species (the great apes in particular) into our fold by emphasizing their intellectual abilities demean those animals. Their abilities are but shadows of our own; they cannot come close to us intellectually. We should appreciate those creatures in their own right—as wonderful creations of nature, not as defective humans.

A recent editorial in the *New Scientist* approached this question from another direction:

> Unfortunately, it has become fashionable to stress that chimpanzees and humans must have staggeringly similar psychologies because they share 98.4 per cent of their DNA. But this misses the point: genomes are not cake recipes. A few tiny changes in a handful of genes controlling the development of the [cerebral] cortex could easily have a disproportionate impact. A creature that shares 98.4 per cent of its DNA with humans is not 98.4 per cent human, any more than a fish that shares, say, 40 per cent of its DNA with us is 40 per cent human.[14]

Furthermore, we have a concept of ourselves that goes well beyond a chimp's ability to ape itself in a mirror. We can see ourselves "as independent individuals with our own integrity, sense of purpose, and worth. We have a concept of our own lives—their origin, duration, self-guided direction, and terminus in death—of world history, and of the limitless reaches of time and space beyond the self. . . . Humans are the beings who because of their acute sense of self experience anxiety, guilt, despair, shame, remorse, internal conflict, pride, hope, triumph, and so many other emotion-laden states."[15]

Only with such capacities can a being be called "cruel" or "humane" in its actions. My cat, playing with a dying mouse, cannot be judged cruel. But were I to torture the mouse to death, I would be considered cruel. Human beings may permissibly kill only when we do so respectfully, for a defined purpose, and— most importantly—as painlessly as possible. Anything else is cruel. (The duck hunter who follows the rules of his craft merits my respect; he who shoots at a passing crow for fun is a cad.) Of course, definitions of "defined purpose" and "painlessly" may well differ among reasonable people. However, I cannot include in this group those who would deny uses that are beneficial to suffering human beings.

Once we have an animal, a group of animals, a species, or even an entire ecosystem within our control, then, of course, we have a great obligation to it. During my early years as a researcher, when we lacked a centralized animal-care facility with veterinarians and a full-time staff, I hired veterinary students to provide food and water to the animals and clean their cages. Nevertheless, I never left for home without personally visiting my animal colony to make sure that each cat had sufficient water and food, and that none was in distress.

That simple responsibility had been fixed in my mind much earlier in life. As a horse-crazy fourteen-year-old boy, I read every book on horses that I could lay my hands on; among them was *My Friend Flicka* by Mary O'Hara. For some reason, I never forgot the following passage from that book, in which Rob McLaughlin talks to his elder son, Howard, about responsibility to animals. A wild mare, Rocket, was carrying the noose of a lariat around her neck because she had broken away and was impossible to catch. Rob worried that the end of the noose might get caught, which would cause the noose to tighten, choking Rocket:

> "What if it did choke her?" asked Howard. "You always say she's no use to you." "There's a responsibility we have toward animals," said his father. "We use them. We shut them up, keep their natural food and water from them, that means we have to feed and water them. Take their freedom away, rope them, harness them, that means we have to supply a different sort of safety for them. Once I've put a rope on a horse, or taken away its ability to take care of itself, then I've got to take care of it. Do you see that? That noose around her neck is a danger to her, and I put it there, so I have to get it off."[16]

One might say that Rocket had a right to that concern, and there are philosophers who argue that animals can have rights in this limited sense.[17] Indeed, lawyer and philosopher Jerrold Tannenbaum has cogently argued for this point of view from a legal standpoint: anticruelty laws clearly use rights language. We can be prosecuted for denying an animal food when in our care: this is because it has a "right" to be fed. He argues that the animal rights movement has stolen the concept of animal rights from those of us who use "rights" in this loose sense while really being concerned for their welfare in the traditional sense. Tannenbaum believes that we should take the term back by admitting that we believe that animals do have certain rights. Tannenbaum cautions that we risk losing public support for biomedical research by conceding this, yet thinks animals have rights in the limited sense that I have just described.[18] I am more comfortable emphasizing my strong *obligation* to animals in my power, but have no problem expressing that obligation by saying they have a right to good care when in my hands. However, I believe that such an admission in writing, at least if not carefully circumscribed as Tannenbaum and philosopher Joel Feinberg do in their scholarly writings, runs the risk of showing up as an out-of-context quotation in a fundraising letter for an animal rights group.

Not surprisingly, animal rights activists are zealous in pressing any perceived advantage from articles in respectable scientific journals into service for their fundraising efforts. For example, in February 1997, the once dependable *Scientific American* foolishly published an article by two animal-rightists (with medical credentials) who argued against the value of animals in biomedical research. One month later, a reprint of that article appeared in a fundraising letter from the deceptively named, animal-rights-promoting Medical Research Modernization Committee (MRMC). In pleading with *Scientific American* to think more carefully about their plan to publish that article, I predicted its triumphant use by the animal rights movement. In this episode, *Scientific American* harmed science.[19]

It should be obvious by now that I believe I have a very strong obligation to treat as humanely as possible those animals that I am privileged to use in research. In my experience the overwhelming majority of biomedical researchers feel this same obligation. At the same time, we are not eager to be regulated, certainly not overregulated, which definitely occurs at times. Two laws administered by the Public Health Service (PHS) of the Department of Health and Human Services (HHS) and the U.S. Department of Agriculture (USDA) govern the use of animals in biomedical research. Both require local oversight committees, generally called Institutional Animal Care and Use Committees (IACUCs), which must include in their membership a veterinarian, a nonscientist, and someone who is not affiliated with the institution. These committees are charged with reviewing and ultimately approving (or disapproving) all proposals for animal use. USDA inspectors regularly inspect facilities and review the actions of the IACUC. PHS requires that the IACUC review all facilities of PHS grantees (i.e., the vast majority of those doing biomedical research) semiannually. A third nongovernmental organization, the Association for the Assessment and Accreditation of Laboratory Animal Care International (AAALAC), responds to institutional requests by veterinarians and scientists seeking examination of their programs and facilities, hoping to receive the AAALAC's greatly desired seal of approval. Steering a research project through the hurdles posed by this morass of oversight groups can be enervating.

It is clear, though, that some confuse researchers' anger against animal-rightists and overly zealous regulators with an uncaring attitude. Thus, there are those who have labeled themselves the "troubled middle," interposed between scientists and animal rights extremists; this term suggests the unfortunate implication that only this "troubled middle" is truly concerned about the care of research animals.[20] In my opinion, this designation is presumptuous and the implication erroneous. While individuals can honestly differ about what constitutes an appropriate or a necessary (ignoring bureaucratic demands) level of care, or even about what constitutes important research, only a "muddled middle" can claim to stand between biomedical researchers and the animal rights movement. A tenable middle ground between "yes" and "no" cannot logically exist.

While I am keenly aware of my obligations as a member of the species that far surpasses any other in intellectual capacity, I still can think as a biologist about the issues. Given that the two leading philosophers of the animal rights movement, Singer and Tom Regan, have each demolished each others' philosophical positions,[21] a biological perspective seems just as worthy as a philosophical perspective in dealing with the question of the appropriateness of animal use by humans. (But let me hasten to add that because we are what we are, we cannot avoid thinking about what we do.) Animals use other animals (and other living organisms) in nature; this is what holds the animate world together. Why, then, should we be any different in our struggle to stay alive? To a biologist, the following oft-quoted proclamation by Regan makes no sense: "If [abandoning animal research] means that there are some things we cannot learn, then so be it. . . . We have then no right against nature [because nature is not a moral agent] not to be harmed by those natural diseases we are heir to."[22]

Beyond working for the survival of ourselves and our species, there is a second, related reason for engaging in biomedical research, stated amusingly yet accurately by H. L. Mencken:

> The value the world sets upon motives is often grossly unjust and inaccurate. Consider, for example, two of them: mere insatiable curiosity and the desire to do good. The latter is put high above the former, and yet it is the former that moves one of the most useful men the human race has yet produced: the scientific investigator. What actually urges him on is not some brummagem idea of Service, but a boundless, almost pathological thirst to penetrate the unknown, to uncover the secret, to find out what has not been found out before. His prototype is not the liberator releasing slaves, the Good Samaritan lifting up the fallen, but a dog sniffing tremendously at an infinite series of rat-holes.[23]

Mencken recognized that we are a very curious species and that scientists are the most curious of us all. I agree with him. Of course, with our exceptional brains we have made wonderful use of that curiosity, to the benefit of both man and animals. No other species has this capability. Why, then, can anyone argue that we should not continue? I think that to refrain from exploring nature in every way possible would be an arrogant rejection of evolutionary forces. Further, to abandon those who look to biomedical research to relieve their suffering would be irresponsible. I need only mention those who have or will suffer paralyzing spinal cord injury. Each year approximately ten thousand people will be condemned to spending their lives in wheelchairs (or worse) as a consequence of such injury.[24] Only continuing research—and great progress is being made, as I will discuss later—will tell us why the central nervous system is unable to regenerate; this will allow us to help those thousands of people.

The philosophical arguments that fuel the concerns, anger, and/or violence of the animal rights movement, the arguments of Regan and Singer chief among them, are completely removed from this terrible reality. Yet, to the best of my knowledge, neither of these gentlemen nor any of the movement's political leaders has publicly stated that he would reject the benefits of medical research. Worse, Singer's utilitarian calculus requires him to demonstrate that the benefits that humans receive from animal research are not sufficient to justify the harm done to animals. To his discredit, he resorted to unconscionable misrepresentations of such research in order to tip the balance against it.[25] Because Regan argues from a rights point of view, he does not have to attack the benefits of research, but only our failure to respect animals' rights. However, he really leaves no hope for those depending on research, stating that "[n]ot even a single rat is to be treated as if the animal's value were reducible to his *possible utility* relative to the interests of others, which is what we would be doing if we intentionally harmed the rat on the grounds that this *just might* 'prove something,' *just might* 'yield' a 'new insight,' *just might* produce 'benefits' for others."[26] This position would effectively eliminate biomedical research, for Regan would only allow the use of one rat at a time, and only when such use would definitely better the life of a person. Scientific advances do not happen one rat at a time.

Rather than focus on some of the features of humanity (such as those I listed earlier) that separate us from all other animals, Singer emphasizes the one thing that unites us with many animal groups: the capacity to suffer. Yet even this separates us from other animals, I believe. Consider the following example. A bright young teenager receives a severe blow to the head in a car crash; this transforms him from a boy with a boundless future into one that must be fed, clothed, and wheeled around by grieving parents for the rest of his or their lives. What animal can match such suffering?

It is a curious fact that the vast majority of animal rights attacks have been directed at laboratories studying various aspects of brain function. Singer's *Animal Liberation* itself devotes an inordinate number of pages to such research.[27] One reason may be that much of brain research has been conducted with monkeys and cats, species of particular concern to people. Yet dogs, another favored species, are used in studies of the cardiovascular and digestive systems, but laboratories doing such work are never in the news. One possible explanation for the choice of targets is that the leaders of the movement sense the qualms that the public has about "fooling around" with the brain; another factor might be a perception by the activists that the public has little sympathy for the beneficiaries of brain research, that is, the mentally ill or those with addictions. But could there also be a subconscious wish to destroy the research that benefits the one organ, the human brain, that most differentiates us from animals?

To sum up, Regan and Singer have spawned a movement that Charles Griswold, Jr., a philosopher at Boston University, characterized this way: "The animal rights movement illustrates the incoherent nature of a moral passion become immoral by virtue of its extremism. In the name of the laudable quality of humaneness, the use of animals for food, clothing and medical experimentation is prohibited. Research that could save your child's life, or save you from an excruciating disease, is declared unethical. The result is inhumanity toward man."[28] This is evil, by my definition.

III. In the Laboratory

Although heavily regulated, scientists, alone in their laboratories, are the ultimate arbiters of their animals' welfare. The scientist chooses which experiments to do and which species to use. These decisions are far from mechanical, and can be idiosyncratic. Let me illustrate this by drawing on my own experience of forty years in the laboratory. I begin with a statement I made elsewhere:

> [T]he invasiveness of vivisection is [not] something I prefer or participate in without reflection. Because I do experimental surgery, I go through a soul-searching every few months, asking myself whether I really want to continue working on cats (we've had up to four of them at a time as pets over the years) or other animals for that matter. The answer is always "yes" because from my knowledge of medical history I know that medicine cannot progress without animal experimentation and that such basic research leads ultimately to unforeseen benefits.[29]

I will add, however, that I am very happy that the scientific questions I am now trying to answer are best answered by studying laboratory rats rather than cats. I am now studying how chemicals placed in certain structures of the brain affect sleep and wakefulness.[30] These substances work by attaching to specific receptors on the surfaces of nerve cells. The anatomical study of the locations of various receptors has for the most part been done using rats rather than cats, so it makes more sense for me to use rats in my work. Please note, however, that my relief in being able to avoid using cats reflects a personal sensitivity: cats are among my family's favorite pets. I can easily imagine that some scientists have avoided a whole line of research because they could not bring themselves to work on a particular species most suited for those studies, avoiding heart research, for instance, in order to avoid working on dogs.

Given that I have decided that using animals in research that will harm them is both necessary and morally defensible, what ethical questions do I think I face? What about killing animals, which is necessary to complete many experiments? I see no ethical problem here, provided that the number of animals used and killed is appropriate to the results sought and that the killing is performed humanely. This killing carries an emotional cost, though, which can be considerable. Having to euthanize cats with which I have worked for weeks and even months while studying their sleep behavior has always saddened me. Scientists who must kill a large number of rodents at one time in order to obtain a sufficient sample of a particular organ for biochemical analysis have told me that the experience is distasteful and depressing.

The daunting ethical question that research presents is the morality of inflicting any degree of pain. By doing so, we enter a realm of activity that is peculiarly human: harming an animal in order to learn. In general, pain is secondary to the purpose of the experiment; for example, animals generally feel postoperative discomfort following the surgical implantation of various recording devices. But pain is also the subject of a small percentage of experiments that are aimed at understanding brain mechanisms in order to develop better, safer analgesics and anesthetics. Pain research, therefore, presents a particularly sensitive ethical problem. Recognizing this, pain researchers have devised procedures that permit an animal to escape pain when the animal finds it intolerable. Studies of chronic pain, in which animals are not given relief mechanisms, require even more thought and attention.

I noted above that I am more comfortable working on rats than on cats. There are, as well, other personal considerations that may dictate one's choice of experiments. For example, many years ago my research pointed in a direction that would have required partially damaging the spinal cord in the necks of cats. I never did those experiments because I knew from my veterinary training that displaced cervical discs, which are not rare in certain breeds of dogs, are very painful. At the time, I reasoned that the experimental surgery in the necks of cats would be similarly painful. The question was of real scientific importance to me twenty-five years ago, but now it is not because today there are other feasible approaches to the question in which I had originally been interested. For example, that question could now be studied by manipulating nerve cells in the brain pharmacologically rather than by using a surgical procedure. But as I look back on the development of my field, I do not think it would have been wrong had I done the surgical experiment. One does not have a crystal ball—otherwise, research would be much easier.

IV. Analyzing Objections

Aside from determining when it is appropriate to inflict pain on animals, a scientist in the current climate is also faced with another choice. He could choose to ignore the threats posed by the animal rights movement to biomedical research and, closer to home, to individual scientists; this would be done by staying safely in the laboratory and hoping to be overlooked. Alternatively, he could decide to engage the issue by entering the public debate. I chose the latter course, ultimately earning me a raid on my facilities by the so-called Animal Liberation Front (ALF).

During a weekend in January 1990, unknown individuals ransacked my office and stole a variety of things, including grant applications, data, and manuscripts; they also took correspondence and addresses that could lead them to other victims. On my walls, these individuals left their "signature"—"ALF." The raid occurred exactly one month after I had blown the whistle on an animal rights course being taught to children in a special program at my university by an associate of the American Anti-Vivisection Society. Adding to the extremists' anger, undoubtedly, was my defense a few months earlier of another scientist whose offices had been raided by the ALF and who had then been vilified by PETA; I had also revealed in a radio debate that PETA's legal machinations were preventing the humane euthanasia of an experimental animal, a revelation that angered my PETA opponent. A few weeks after the raid itself, an article about the raid—and about me as a scientist—appeared in *The Village Voice*. In that piece, Ingrid Newkirk was quoted as saying "PETA intends to use Morrison to persuade other vivisectors who were heartened by his strong stand on animal research that it doesn't pay off. Now the spotlight is on him, and what happens next will deter others who might want to follow in his footsteps."[31]

I was subsequently harassed in a variety of ways. Following a large demonstration at the University of Pennsylvania, PETA sent a letter to neighbors in my zip code outlining my alleged cruelties to animals (this backfired, for my neighbors spoke on my behalf). My family and I received many threatening phone calls and much hate mail. Colleagues abroad were also harassed. Finally, a series of articles—commissioned by the American Anti-Vivisection Society and written by a former employee of the Humane Society of the United States—attempted to destroy my scientific reputation.

Although I can make light of the events now, they were an emotional drain at the time. Clearly, though, I had to continue my public efforts. What is required to assume such a role? First of all, an individual must think more deeply about his own beliefs than he did in more halcyon days. He also needs to steep himself in medical history in order to appreciate more fully the complexity of the process of science; this will allow him to discuss this process with a non-scientific audience. Finally, he should recognize and appreciate the powerful attraction that animals have for people and communicate his own empathy for the animals under his control.

Dealing with the animal rights movement's challenge to biomedical research is not easy. A segment of society has objected to using animals in research ever since animal experimentation began, especially after experimental physiology started in earnest during the nineteenth century. Experiments in this field involved cutting into animals while they were living (*vivisection*) and, unfortunately, not anesthetized. (Of course, the same held for people undergoing surgery in that era.) Those opposing these practices grouped into the antivivisection movement. Although even then some individuals went beyond expressing a concern about cruelty and argued that humans were not special enough to warrant subjecting animals to the rigors of experimentation,[32] the ideas that would inspire the present social force known as the animal rights movement awaited the latter half of the twentieth century.

The publication of the first edition of Peter Singer's *Animal Liberation* in 1975 is generally regarded as the source of inspiration for the modern animal rights movement.[33] In my view, the major factor contributing to that book's extraordinary success in energizing the movement is the presence of a largely urban (perhaps more importantly, suburban) populace considerably removed from the realities of natural animal life. Consider that in 1880, one in two people derived a living from agriculture; in the early 1990s, one in fifty did.[34] This means that a very large segment of the population deals with animals primarily as pets and as part of the family, making these people more vulnerable to animal rights propaganda.

Frederick K. Goodwin, a psychiatrist and former director of the National Institute of Mental Health, has suggested that the general erosion of trust in our institutions, brought about by events such as Vietnam and Watergate, has undoubtedly contributed to the climate of moral confusion surrounding the use of animals in research.[35] In other words, why should scientists be trusted any more than government? We are also pummeled by the idea that there can be no absolutes, expressed by cultural relativism and its many admirers. Indeed, I think that the animal rights movement carries cultural relativism to a bizarre extreme: humans are to be considered no better than animals. Indeed, one of Singer's newly minted Five Commandments is the proscription of "speciesism."[36]

Of course, the powerful imagery of television, transmitting distorted pictures of laboratory practices, is of great assistance to the movement. A flagrant example of this was the transmission of a video, provided by PETA, which showed a tiny kitten in a research hospital at Boys Town; with a surgical wound on its head, the kitten stumbled around on a barren floor while pathetically crying for its mother. Viewers were not informed that the animals at the facility were very well cared for, that the video was set up by the undercover people filming it (who had taken the kitten from its mother), or that the Boys Town researchers who had been targeted by PETA were a highly respected, caring husband-and-wife team. They had been researching the causes of defective development of the hearing apparatus in the human fetus; the stage of development that was the subject of their research appears postnatally in kittens but in the third trimester in a human fetus, making the kitten a very important animal for such research.

Two additional problems face those of us who wish to persuade society at large that it is being misled—to its detriment—by animal rights propaganda. First, those born after 1955 are the healthiest generations in history and cannot fully appreciate their good fortune. They have no concept of the horror, for example, of a polio epidemic, since the last one occurred in the early 1950s. Sir William Paton makes this point in a graphic description of the contrast between the 1930s (when he was training to become a physician) and the 1990s:

> One no longer sees infants with ears streaming pus, school boys with facial impetigo, beards growing from heavily infected skin, faces pocked by smallpox or eroded by lupus, or heads and necks scarred from boils or suppurating glands. Drugs and a better diet have transformed haggard patients with peptic ulcers. The languid, characteristically brown-skinned case of Addison's disease of the adrenals; the pale, listless patients of chronic iron deficiency or pernicious anemia; and the cretin or, conversely, the young woman with "pop eyes" and overactive emotional behavior—due respectively to thyroid deficiency or excess—are all being treated. The soggy hulk of a patient in the edematous stage of chronic kidney disease is relieved by diuretics. As a result of polio vaccine and control of tuberculosis, we see few crippled children: as one walks behind a group of youngsters today, varied as ever in shape and size, the marvel is how straight their limbs and backs are. The chronic arthritics with their sticks are being replaced with septuagenarians swinging along on their plastic hips. The patients now are rare that once one saw dying from an infected mastoid, struggling for breath in the last stages of heart failure, or dying from appendicitis, leukaemia, pneumonia, or bacterial endocarditis.[37]

The second additional problem, referred to above, is the difficulty that even those sympathetic to the idea of using animals in research have in appreciating how convoluted the path to discovery really is. Let me first hint at it with a quotation from well-known psychopharmacologist Seymour S. Kety's forward to Judith Swazy's wonderful book, *Chlorpromazine in Psychiatry*. Chlorpromazine is a drug that revolutionized the treatment of schizophrenia; discussing its discovery, Kety says:

> One conclusion, immediately apparent and rather surprising, is that none of the crucial findings or pathways that led, over the course of a century,

to the ultimate discovery of chlorpromazine would at first have been called relevant to the treatment of mental illness by even the most sophisticated judge. If scientists had decided in the middle of the last century to target research toward the treatment of schizophrenia, if they had been able to organize such a program, and if they had engaged the greatest minds, which of those crucial discoveries and pathways would they have supported as relevant to their goal? Certainly not the synthesis of phenothiazine by a chemist interested in methylene blue; nor the study of anaphylaxis in guinea pigs (which is more clearly related to asthma [than to schizophrenia]) . . . nor the study of the role of histamine in allergy and anaphylaxis and the search for antihistaminic drugs . . . nor the studies on operant conditioning in animals; and not the search by an anesthesiologist for an antihistaminic-sympatholytic drug that might be useful in mitigating surgical shock.[38]

Consider now the tortuous path to the modern treatment of cardiopulmonary disease. In the late 1960s, physiologist Julius Comroe, Jr., and anesthesiologist Robert Dripps began a truly awe-inspiring study that deserves reconsideration in this era of attacks on biomedical research. Their purpose was not to defend biomedical research from attacks by the animal rights movement. Instead, by providing nonanecdotal support for the value of basic research to the advancement of medicine, they sought to assist the federal government in establishing sound policies for funding biomedical research. In the mid-1960s, the idea of funding targeted, clinically oriented research was much in vogue in governmental circles, and Comroe and Dripps tried to provide a counterweight to this trend. Ironically, Comroe and Dripps published a summary article of their study in *Science*[39] just months after the appearance of Singer's *Animal Liberation*. The latter purported to demonstrate that basic research using animals did not provide sufficient benefits to warrant harming them.

Comroe and Dripps had decided to determine the key steps leading to the top ten clinical advances in cardiovascular and pulmonary medicine since the early 1940s. (Note that among these advances was the first successful open-heart surgery with complete cardiopulmonary bypass apparatus; this procedure was first performed in the mid-1950s.) Did they alone decide what were the major clinical advances? No, although they were eminently qualified to do so. Instead, to avoid their own biases, they asked 40 physicians to list the advances that they considered the most important for their patients. They then divided the master list developed by the physicians into cardiovascular and pulmonary lists. These they sent to 40–50 specialists in each field, asking them to vote on the items in their respective lists (and to add others, if they wished). The ten advances with the most votes were cardiac surgery, vascular surgery, drug treatment of hypertension, medical treatment of cardiac insufficiency, cardiac resuscitation, oral diuretics, intensive care units, chemotherapy and antibiotics, new diagnostic methods, and the prevention of polio (in particular, respiratory paralysis).

Next, 140 consultants—clinicians, basic medical scientists, science writers, and others—assisted Comroe and Dripps in identifying the essential bodies of knowledge required for each of the advances to have reached their respective levels of achievement at the time of the study. For example, 25 different essential bodies of knowledge were identified for cardiac surgery, including electrocardiography, cardiac catheterization, blood groups and preservation, asepsis, anesthesia/analgesia, anticoagulants, the bubble oxygenator, and management of infection. They found that altogether, the top ten advances depended upon 137 essential bodies of knowledge.

Comroe and Dripps "limited" their further study to examining 4,000 articles, recognizing that centuries of work by thousands of people had contributed to the development of the major advances. They identified 2,500 articles that were particularly important for creating one or more of the bodies of knowledge, and arranged these articles into 137 chronological tables in preparation for their final analysis. For example, the list for electrocardiography contained 46 events, each with an associated publication. It extends from the "ancients" (who recognized various manifestations of electricity) through Benjamin Franklin in 1752 (for proving the identity of lightning and electricity) to those who, in 1967, recorded from the heart's electrical conducting system by using a catheter placed in a person's heart.

Comroe and Dripps then identified a group of "key articles" in each list. Key articles were those that "reported new data, new ways of looking at old data, a new concept or hypothesis, a new method, new drug, new apparatus, or a new technique that either was essential for full development of one or more of the clinical advances (or necessary bodies of knowledge) or greatly accelerated it." An article could also be regarded as key if "it described the final step in [a] clinical advance even though it was an inevitable step requiring no unusual imagination, creativity, or special competence (for example, [the] first person to report on a new drug in humans *even though basic work on animals had been done and results in humans were largely predictable*) [emphasis added]."[40]

Concerned about bias, Comroe and Dripps sent 42 of their tables, containing more than 50 percent of the key articles, to 42 reviewers (32 clinicians and 10 basic medical scientists) without telling them which articles on the tables had been selected as key. The reviewers were asked to choose which of the articles they thought were key; their selectors were compared to those of Comroe and Dripps. The result was almost complete agreement on the type of article chosen as key, if not on the same article. Comroe and Dripps then reread each of the 529 key articles they had identified in the 137 tables and found that 41 percent of the articles were not clinically oriented.

Thus, a high percentage of the articles deemed important for the major clinical advances in cardiopulmonary medicine and surgery (as identified by the initial groups of physicians and specialists) reported work that "sought knowledge for the sake of knowledge." Comroe and Dripps also identified a second group of "clinically oriented" studies that were liberally interpreted as such; studies were included in that category if the author mentioned "even briefly an interest in diagnosis, treatment, or prevention of a clinical disorder or in explaining the basic mechanisms of a sign or symptom of the disease itself." With this liberal definition of "clinically oriented," the category contained numerous studies "performed entirely on animals, tissues, cells, or subcellular particles."[41]

One can imagine from the preceding discussion that the medical advances that Paton noted in the brief passage I quoted earlier represent a monumental amount of work. An analysis of the history of any one of the cures that he mentions would reveal a path as tortuous as those that led to any of the ten advances in cardiopulmonary medicine studied by Comroe and Dripps. Furthermore, as one who has worked in basic research, I know that some experiments that lead nowhere may still inspire an idea that is productive.

This is clearly a cautionary tale, for in the current climate there is a distinct push to avoid experiments that seek "knowledge for knowledge's sake." Keep in mind that the "right" experiment to do given current knowledge and insights may not show up in a future Comroe-and-Dripps-style study. I believe we must be very wary, lest we reach a point where certain research cannot be done simply because a crystal ball is unavailable, that is, because the potential benefits of the research are not immediately foreseeable. Of course, experiments that have the potential to cause considerable pain require careful examination and defense, but if they can be shown to be careful, vital science, then they must be done. Those in the "troubled middle" who believe that they are wise enough to decide which experiments should or should not be done are quite mistaken.

V. Fudging the Data

The foregoing examples of the complexity of the progress of science illustrate why scientists find it so difficult to deal with a particularly troublesome subset of the animal rights movement. This subset is comprised of a small band of health professionals, including even physicians, who reinforce their ethical beliefs with damaging analyses of experimental work. These individuals have written a number of books and articles with the express aim of demonstrating that the study of biological and physiological processes in animals is of no use for understanding human diseases, and that animal studies have often stood in the way of medical progress. Laypersons, unfortunately, lack the knowledge to evaluate such claims, for these advocates typically do not accurately trace the twisting paths—such as those described by Kety, Comroe, and Dripps—that lead to discoveries.

Of course, scientists argue, often vehemently, over theories, hypotheses, and even the significance of the sets of data that lead to a hypothesis; during these arguments, they brand each other as wrong. However, I do not speak here of serious disagreement among men and women arguing solely about scientific data. Rather, I am concerned about those with medical credentials, conferred on them by society, who use their status to pursue a radical agenda. Medical or scientific training, or training as a scholar in a nonscientific field, confers a high level of believability to statements that one makes on intellectual matters. With that status, of course, comes the requirement to behave responsibly. Lamentably, many health professionals in the animal rights movement fall short of this standard. In their analyses, they fudge the data in order to strengthen their case in the service of a new worldview.

Underlying their work is either a dim understanding of the process of science or, worse, a seeming willingness to distort medical history. Frequently, practitioners of this art claim that because an observation from the clinic has led to insight into the causative agent of a particular disorder, the necessity of laboratory research is discounted. Those who advance such "proofs" do not consider the need for many, many controlled experiments with animals (and humans) in order to unravel the basic mechanisms that will lead to specific treatments. This could be chalked up to the ignorance of these authors, but I believe that a fanatical belief in the rightness of their cause clouds their thinking as well. The pronouncements of such "experts" then lead individuals untutored in science, philosophers among them, to feel that their ethical beliefs in opposition to animal experimentation have been vindicated by reputable scientists.

Some scientists and their supporters assume that, to counter such dangerous illusions, all that is needed is an accounting of the wonders of medical science. The public will then naturally gravitate to our side. I am not one of these people; I think it important to expose the charlatans, because the average person is not sufficiently tutored in science to weigh statements made by those with medical credentials who argue against animal experimentation. This is why *Scientific American* must be criticized for the recent incident in which they allowed two animal-rightists to sully their pages.

In reporting on efforts of science to conquer disease, animal-rightist "medicine men" (and women) typically describe the glass as half-empty rather than as half-full. By that I mean that they focus on the defects of various experimental approaches using animals—and, needless to say, no method is perfect—without ever providing a *practical, ethical* (as most of us understand this word) alternative.

Rather, as a total substitute for experiments involving animals, they offer the study of naturally occurring diseases in people as the proper way to conduct medical research, without recognizing that scientists must perform a myriad of experiments to unravel any biological phenomenon. This is not to say that study on humans is not an important part of research; after a drug is developed, for example, it must be tested on human volunteers as well as on animals before it reaches the market. This step, however, is well beyond the stage of invasive basic research.

Using epidemiological studies of disease patterns is also frequently mentioned as a method of avoiding animal research. (*Epidemiology* is the study of the patterns of disease occurrence: the ages, sexes, and races affected; the relative prevalence of a disease in geographical terms; and the distribution of cases over the course of a year.) Yet recognition of when a particular disease is more likely to occur—say, in certain individuals living in particular locales during the summer—will not define cellular mechanisms that have gone awry or develop vaccines or medicines to prevent, cure, or alleviate the disease. It contributes nothing toward alleviating the suffering of those who find themselves ill at that time, in that place. And what of the three-year-old discovered unconscious at the bottom of a flight of stairs with what turns out to be a serious brain injury rather than an illness? How will epidemiological studies of the incidence of various types of accidents in the home help that particular child?

Far worse than proposing inferior alternatives to animal research is the practice of using fragments from the writings of a responsible scientist to support a claim that is actually contrary to the scientist's stated beliefs. In 1632, Galileo revealed the same intellectual dishonesty among those who opposed his belief that the solar system was heliocentric. In this instance, his various opponents had been assembling arguments by picking and choosing from among the works of Aristotle to prove whatever they wished. In his *Dialogue on the Great World Systems,* Galileo used the literary device of a discussion among three individuals: one representing himself; another, Sagredo, representing a wise, dead friend; and Simplicio, a composite of all his opponents. At one point, Sagredo says this to the aptly named Simplicio:

> But, good Simplicio, this reaching the desired conclusion by connecting several small abstracts which you and other egregious philosophers easily find scattered throughout the texts of Aristotle I could do as well by the verses of Virgil or Ovid, composing patchworks of passages which explain all the affairs of men and secrets of Nature. But why do I talk of Virgil or any other poet? I have a little book much shorter than Aristotle or Ovid, in which are contained all the sciences, and with very little study one may gather out of it a most perfect system, and thus is the alphabet.[42]

Let us now consider some examples of modern Simplicios, who pluck words from a publication, if not simple letters from the alphabet, and arrange them to suit their purpose. Betsy Todd, a nurse with a master's degree in public health who serves with the MRMC, is one such individual. In 1991, she sought to align the American Public Health Association (APHA) with the animal rights agenda by presenting a resolution for adoption at the APHA's annual meeting; this resolution was a model of deception.[43] When read with no knowledge of what some of the authorities that she used to bolster her argument actually said, the resolution appears reasonable to a reader schooled in the rules of normal scientific debate. Its stated purpose was to encourage "public discussion and debate of the scientific issues pertinent to the use of animals in medical research, testing, and education."[44] The introduction to the proposal contained two seemingly authoritative claims supported by several references:

> . . . that there are documented problems with animal research methodologies, including the difficulties of species extrapolations, dose extrapolations, and animal "models" that only crudely mimic human diseases, and that these limitations directly affect the relevance of animal research to human health; and . . . that respected medical historians, sociologists and public health scholars have long disputed researchers' claims about the contribution of animal research to human health . . . .[45]

These statements certainly seem to raise legitimate concerns about the value of animal-based research.

Turning to some of her references, however, one finds that Todd grossly misrepresented respected scientists. A number of her sources provide no support for her contention that research with animals has been of dubious value in advancing human health; some of these sources, in fact, support the opposite position.

For example, just because there may be "scientific problems with animal research methodologies" (viewed from a glass-half-empty perspective) does not mean that important insights may not be gained from the use of animals. Indeed, Todd's very first reference, a paper by biochemists Bruce Ames and Lois Gold, states that "[e]pidemiologists are frequently discovering clues about the causes of human cancers, and their hypotheses are then refined by animal and metabolic studies."[46] They conclude that "the most important contribution that animal studies can offer is insight into carcinogenesis mechanisms and into the complex natural world in which we live."[47] These authors were really only urging good judgment in evaluating animal test results.

One of Todd's supposedly supporting references is from Sir Richard Doll, Regius Professor of Medicine at Oxford University, who emphasized the important role that epidemiology plays in determining causative factors in cancer (and who would disagree?).[48] Yet Doll hardly commented on animal research at all, and then only positively. Todd's next reference, a paper by Sir George Pickering, an earlier Regius Professor, discusses the difficulty—but importance—of physicians' engaging in scientific observations.[49] Only in a couple of sentences does Pickering comment on the obvious foolishness of trying to apply what is learned in the laboratory directly to a sick patient.

Grouped with these distinguished physicians' names in Todd's list of references are those of a number of oft-heard-from animal-rightists whose methods of misrepresentation equal Todd's.[50] For example, Brandon Reines, a veterinarian, argues that significant medical advances are primarily due to observations made on human patients. Without question, the keen observations of brilliant physicians have been invaluable to the advancement of medicine—who would disagree? But Reines goes overboard to support his claim. For example, he quotes Walton Lillihei, the developer of the pump-oxygenator used in heart-lung bypass, as saying that his research team had been "feeling our way along as far as flow was concerned. . . . Then we got more experience with our heart-lung machine and it worked for all sizes of people."[51] Reines then concludes that "[t]hus, Dr. Lillihei and his associates made the heart-lung machine safe and effective during the course of practice on actual patients—not from studies on healthy laboratory animals."[52]

But what is omitted by the ellipsis points? Read what they supplant: "For patients whom we thought were too big for those first of our bubble oxygenator heart-lung machines, we used dogs' lungs. About fifteen times in all."[53] A lengthy paragraph follows in which the procedures for cleaning the lungs are described; only after this description does one reach the words after the ellipsis points.

Another example of Reines's attempts to force a scientific advance into his scheme is his narrow view of William Harvey's seventeenth-century achievement: the seminal recognition that blood pumped from the heart makes a complete circuit, passing via arteries into capillaries and thence to veins that empty back into the heart. Reines would like all credit for this accomplishment to be given to an aspect of Harvey's work that had nothing to do with animal experimentation.

Harvey had performed many experiments on a wide variety of warm- and cold-blooded animals to determine anatomical relationships of the heart with the arteries and veins and how blood left and entered the heart via these vessels. His experiments, which involved interference with blood flow by tying off a variety of vessels, showed that the blood leaving the heart had to return via the veins. Furthermore, the blood had to circulate through a closed system because more blood passed through the heart in a short time than was found in the entire body. One series of experiments involved blocking, with ligatures, the return of blood through the veins where they can most easily be seen: the almost hairless human arm. Reines chooses to ignore all Harvey's work leading up to this brilliant choice of experimental subject by stating that work with humans was the key to Harvey's discovery that the circulation of blood occurs in a closed system.[54]

I close this saga of manipulation with yet one more example. In this case the issue is the discovery of insulin, which depended greatly on experimental surgeries in dogs. As historian Michael Bliss said in his magnificent book, *The Discovery of Insulin,* "[t]he discovery of insulin at the University of Toronto in 1921–22 was one of the most dramatic events in the history of the treatment of disease."[55] He added, with absolutely no exaggeration, that "[t]hose who watched the first starved, sometimes comatose, diabetics receive insulin and return to life saw one of the genuine miracles of modern medicine. They were present at the closest approach to the resurrection of the body that our secular society can achieve. . . ."[56]

The story of insulin's discovery is complex, though, with a mixture of uncertainties, egos, academic politics, and, by today's standards, horrific laboratory conditions; this makes the achievement just perfect for chicanery by presenters of the case against the contributions of animals to medical progress. Both Reines and the animal-rightist team of physicians Neal Barnard and Steven Kaufman (see note 19) have indulged themselves. Fortunately, medical researchers Charles S. Nicoll and Sharon M. Russell contacted Bliss directly. He had this to say about Reines's attempt to twist the facts: "Reines' interpretation of my work is thoroughly distorted, wrong-headed and silly. I informed him of this several years ago when I first read his mindless writings on the subject. . . . Insulin would not have been isolated, at Toronto or anywhere else, without the sacrifice of thousands of dogs. These dogs made it possible for millions of humans to live."[57]

VI. Tragedy and (Potential) Triumph

Finally, let me discuss one more important choice that a scientist makes. Indeed, it is his first choice: the research problem on which to spend his career. As noted earlier, my choice was to study sleep, but I could have just as easily chosen something else: for example, the problem of the central nervous system's refusal to regenerate when damaged. In my opinion, the worst that can happen to someone, short of death, is an accident that destroys that person as we know him due to brain trauma, or that confines an active teenager to a wheelchair or worse due to a severed spinal cord. I agree with the statement that "[r]egeneration of injured brains and spinal cords is the Holy Grail for many neurobiologists."[58]

In the early 1960s, though, the prospects for solving this problem seemed nearly hopeless. No less than Santiago Ramón y Cajal, the Spanish genius who had mapped the entire central nervous system, said in 1913 that "[i]n adult centres the nervous paths are something fixed, ended, immutable. Everything may die, nothing may be regenerated."[59] Given this, Cajal issued the following challenge:

It is for the science of the future to change, if possible, this harsh decree [lack of regeneration in the central nervous system]. Inspired with high ideals, it must work to impede or moderate the general decay of the neurones, to overcome the almost invincible rigidity of their connections, and to re-establish normal nerve paths, when disease has severed centres that were intimately associated.[60]

I turned away from this important field, even though it engaged some of my professors. During the 1960s, researchers could only demonstrate—in mammals at least—minimal new growth after damage to the central nervous system.[61] Processes of nerve cells (or *axons*) in the spinal cord were observed to "sprout" into areas in which other axons had degenerated (as a result of being severed from the cell bodies giving them life), though even this ability was disputed.[62] The difficulty in obtaining more extensive growth was that stimulus to growth seemed to be lacking while, at the same time, toxic substances and the physical barrier of scar tissue acted to impede extensive axonal regeneration.

However, the intervening years have witnessed exciting progress. Many researchers have entered the field, and significant advances in understanding have followed. In addition to gaining insights into the mechanisms of sprouting and its variability in various central neural systems, scientists have revealed a much greater potential for regeneration and restoration of function than was imagined even long after Cajal's pronouncement. With appropriate manipulations, some central neural pathways have been induced to regenerate sufficiently to permit some centrally directed movements, although these movements fall well short of being adequate for normal walking.[63] Now, a neurosurgeon and researcher in the field, Wise Young, has been emboldened to say that "the possibility of effective regenerative therapies for human spinal cord injury is no longer a speculation but a realistic goal."[64]

Furthermore, much has been learned about the cascade of chemical events initiated by trauma by replicating these events experimentally in animals.[65] Possessing such knowledge, scientists are learning when and how to intervene in clinical situations, and are developing drugs that can block or minimize pathological events. For example, if a stroke has already caused an individual irreversible damage, a method of rehabilitation developed in monkeys is proving to be beneficial.

Edward Taub and his colleagues have demonstrated that stroke victims can be trained to use an arm rendered "useless" by a stroke.[66] This is accomplished by restraining the normal limb and, hence, forcing the patient to employ the affected limb for various tasks. Taub came to this idea as a result of his studies of monkeys that were deprived of sensory input into their spinal cords. He had shown that these animals could be trained to use the affected arm without sensory feedback. However, these monkeys also gnawed and licked their denervated arms, which resulted in ugly-looking wounds. The unfortunate condition of these monkeys created a wonderful situation for animal rights extremists to exploit; they did so in 1981, and the resultant publicity gave a tremendous boost to the fledgling PETA.

Michael Goldberger, Taub's colleague and a former classmate of mine, asked me to defend Taub; he knew that I was fully aware that no treatment other than nursing was possible for these animals. I chose to come to Taub's aid. I believed that Taub had been unjustly accused of cruelty due to misdiagnoses by two zoo veterinarians and subsequent manipulation of the facts by animal-rightists. The National Institutes of Health (NIH), which funded Taub's work, was forced by a misled Congress to agree that no further research would be done on the monkeys until they reached a condition in which they had to be euthanized for humane reasons. Consequently, by the time the monkeys could finally be studied, several years had elapsed since the denervations.

Ironically, the delay proved to be extremely beneficial to science. While the monkeys were under anesthesia before death, recordings from single nerve cells in their brains revealed that adult nervous systems are capable of a much greater degree of reorganization than was previously thought possible.[67] Future stroke victims are fortunate that the scientists involved were skillful enough to obtain this information in the four hours that they were permitted to work on the monkeys (the limit set in an agreement between NIH and Congress) before having to administer the extra dose of anesthetic required to kill them. The findings stimulated a variety of new investigations.[68] These studies have given us hope that the mechanisms of adult brain reorganization being uncovered may be exploited in the future to ameliorate the effects of brain damage—hope unwittingly provided by animal rights extremists.

VII. Conclusion

I have tried to impart a sense of what it is like to work with animals in biomedical research. Although the story is personal, I am certain that other scientists share my views, but most prefer to remain silent, fearing retaliation from animal rights extremists. Regrettably, the animal rights movement tries to block the advancement of scientific knowledge. At its heart this movement is evil, for it diminishes humanity while it seeks to elevate animals to our level, all the while pretending that the central concern is animal welfare. Not only does the movement attack individual scientists and their laboratories, it does violence to the truth. It grossly misrepresents the history of scientific discovery; it twists the arguments of reputable researchers beyond recognition; and it elevates the views of misanthropic charlatans who would stifle the scientific advancement that promises healthier lives for our children and grandchildren.

NOTES

1. Michael W. Fox, *Inhumane Society: The American Way of Exploiting Animals* (New York: St. Martin's Press, 1990), 98.
2. Katie McCabe, "Who Will Live, Who Will Die?" *The Washingtonian,* August 1985, 115.
3. Ingrid Newkirk, quoted in Chip Brown, "She's a Portrait of Zealotry in Plastic Shoes," *Washington Post,* November 13, 1983, B1, 10. At the time of the article, People for the Ethical Treatment of Animals (PETA) was just becoming a household word, and biomedical research was only beginning to recognize that it had a real problem on its hands.
4. Ingrid Newkirk, "Dialogue and Debate with Ingrid Newkirk, National Director, People for the Ethical Treatment of Animals (PETA)," interview by Dennis Prager, *Prager Perspective* (July 1–15, 1997): 6. One does not know how the average activist would view such an extreme statement, although it is reasonable to assume many would be pro-choice on the abortion issue. The typical animal rights activist is white, female (more than 75 percent are women), and in her thirties. See Scott Plous, "Signs of Change Within the Animal-Rights Movement: Results From a Follow-up Survey of Activists," *Journal of Comparative Psychology* 112, no.1 (1998): 48–54.
5. Peter Singer, *Rethinking Life and Death: The Collapse of Our Traditional Ethics* (New York: St. Martin's Press, 1994), 205–6.
6. George Weigel, "Are Humans Special?" review of *Rethinking Life and Death: The Collapse of Traditional Ethics,* by Peter Singer, *The Washington Post Book World,* March 26, 1995, 1.
7. Peter Singer, *Animal Liberation,* 2d ed. (New York: Random House, 1990). The first edition of *Animal Liberation* appeared in 1975.
8. Ibid., 239.
9. David R. Schmahmann and Lori J. Polacheck, "The Case against Rights for Animals," *Boston College Environmental Affairs Law Review* 22, no. 4 (Spring 1995): 747–81.
10. Tom Regan and Peter Singer, "The Dog in the Lifeboat: An Exchange," *The New York Review of Books,* April 25, 1985, 56–57.
11. Singer, *Animal Liberation,* 6.
12. Michael Allen Fox, *The Case for Animal Experimentation: An Evolutionary and Ethical Perspective* (Berkeley: University of California Press, 1986).
13. Michael Allen Fox, "Animal Experimentation: A Philosopher's Changing Views," *Between the Species* 3, no. 2 (Spring 1987): 55–60, 75, 80, 82.
14. Editorial, "The Great Divide?" *New Scientist,* February 13, 1999, 3.
15. Fox, *The Case for Animal Experimentation,* 45.
16. Mary O'Hara, *My Friend Flicka* (Philadelphia: Lippincott, 1941), 43.
17. See Joel Feinberg, "Human Duties and Animal Rights," in Richard Knowles Morris and Michael W. Fox, eds., *On the Fifth Day: Animal Rights and Human Ethics* (Washington, DC: Acropolis Books, 1978), 45–69; and Jerrold Tannenbaum, *Veterinary Ethics: Animal Welfare, Client Relations, Competition, and Collegiality,* 2d ed. (St. Louis, MO: Mosby, 1995), 133–40.

74   Adrian R. Morrison

18. Jerrold Tannenbaum, comments in forum on "Rights, Welfare and Protection: What's in a Name?" at Scientists Center for Animal Welfare meeting, San Antonio, TX, December 1998.
19. Neal Barnard and Steven Kaufman, "Animal Research is Wasteful and Misleading," *Scientific American* 276, no. 2 (February 1997): 80–82. In that issue, Jack Botting and I published a piece opposing Barnard and Kaufman's views; the essays were published together in order to provide a debate on the merits of animal experimentation. Despite the pleadings of Botting and me, the editor of *Scientific American* decided that the authors would not be given space to print rebuttals following the articles. He did this in spite of the fact that we demonstrated to him that Barnard and Kaufman, on more than one occasion, had misrepresented medical history in clever, deceptive ways. This concerned Botting and me because the average reader exposed to the Barnard and Kaufman piece would have no way of knowing the accuracy of the statements they made. When Botting and I reviewed drafts of the essay by Barnard and Kaufman, we saw that if we were to respond to all of the misrepresentations in that piece, we would use up all of our allotted space. Given these limitations, we decided to use our space in *Scientific American* to promote our positive message. Jack Botting and Adrian Morrison, "Animal Research is Vital to Medicine," *Scientific American* 276, no. 2 (February 1997): 83–85. Our rebuttal of Barnard and Kaufman's claims about medical history had to wait for another forum; it ultimately appeared in an Internet magazine, *HMS Beagle,* at http://biomednet.com/hmsbeagle/25/people/op_ed.htm.

Incredibly, an introductory article to the "debate" in *Scientific American,* by Andrew Rowan of the Humane Society of the United States, stated that "[t]here is also much room to challenge the benefits of animal research and much room to defend such research." I have found no reason to believe the former. It ignores historical fact. Andrew Rowan, "The Benefits and Ethics of Animal Research," *Scientific American* 276, no. 2 (February 1997): 79.
20. Strachan Donnelley, "Speculative Philosophy, the Troubled Middle, and the Ethics of Animal Experimentation," *Hastings Center Report* 19, no. 2 (March/April 1989): 15–21.
21. Richard P. Vance, "An Introduction to the Philosophical Presuppositions of the Animal Liberation/Rights Movement," *Journal of the American Medical Association* 268, no. 13 (October 7, 1992): 1715–19. Vance adds, though, that "Regan and Singer have agreed that theoretical differences shouldn't prevent them from seeking a common practical goal: to attack the use of animals in research." See Regan and Singer, "The Dog in the Lifeboat," 57. See also the exchange of letters that followed Vance's article: Mark Bernstein et al., "Is Justification of Animal Research Necessary?" *Journal of the American Medical Association* 269, no. 9 (March 3, 1993): 1113–15.
22. Tom Regan, *The Case for Animal Rights* (Berkeley: University of California Press, 1983), 388.
23. H. L. Mencken, *A Mencken Chrestomathy* (1949; reprint, New York: Vintage Books, 1982), 12.
24. Robert J. White, "Superman's Plight and Animal Paladins," *Washington Times,* August 6, 1995, B4.

25. Sharon M. Russell and Charles S. Nicoll, "A Dissection of the Chapter 'Tools for Research' in Peter Singer's *Animal Liberation*," *Proceedings of the Society for Experimental Biology and Medicine* 211, no. 2 (February 1996): 109–38. The same issue includes a rebuttal by Singer (139–46) and a reply by Russell and Nicoll (147–54).

26. Regan, *The Case for Animal Rights,* 384.

27. See Russell and Nicoll, "'Tools for Research' in Singer's *Animal Liberation.*"

28. Charles Griswold, Jr., "The Immorality of 'Animal Rights,'" *Washington Post,* January 5, 1986, D7.

29. Adrian R. Morrison, "Thoughts of a Working Scientist," *Science and Animal Care* 9, no. 2 (Fall 1998): 1–2, 4.

30. Adrian R. Morrison, Larry D. Sanford, and Richard J. Ross, "Initiation of Rapid Eye Movement Sleep: Beyond the Brainstem," in Birenda N. Mallick and Shojirou Inoué, eds., *Rapid Eye Movement Sleep* (New York: Marcel Dekker, 1999), 51–68.

31. Ingrid Newkirk (national director of PETA), quoted in Jack Rosenberg, "Animal Rites," *Village Voice,* March 6, 1990, 33.

32. Andreas-Holger Maehle and Ulrich Tröhler, "Animal Experimentation from Antiquity to the End of the Eighteenth Century: Attitudes and Arguments," in Nicholaas A. Rupke, ed., *Vivisection in Historical Perspective* (London: Routledge, 1990), 14–47.

33. Peter Singer, *Animal Liberation* (New York: The New York Review, 1975).

34. Rod and Patti Strand, *The Hijacking of the Humane Movement* (Wilsonville, OR: Doral Publishing, 1993), 2.

35. Frederick K. Goodwin, "Animal Research, Animal Rights and Public Health," *Conquest* 181 (August 1992): 1–10.

36. Singer, *Rethinking Life and Death,* 201–6.

37. William Paton, *Man and Mouse: Animals in Medical Research,* 2d ed. (Oxford: Oxford University Press, 1993), 93.

38. Seymour S. Kety, forward to *Chlorpromazine in Psychiatry: A Study of Therapeutic Innovation,* by Judith Swayzy (Cambridge, MA: MIT Press, 1974), xii–xiii.

39. Julius Comroe and Robert Dripps, "Scientific Basis for the Support of Biomedical Research," *Science* 192 (April 9, 1976): 105–11.

40. Ibid., 108.

41. Ibid., 108, 111.

42. Galileo, *Dialogue on the Great World Systems* (Chicago: University of Chicago Press, 1953), quoted in Hal Hellman, *Great Feuds in Science: Ten of the Liveliest Disputes Ever* (New York: John Wiley, 1998), 13–14. Publication of the *Dialogue* in accessible Italian (rather than Latin) publicized Galileo's theory to an extent that the Church could not ignore. The *Dialogue* finally brought the full wrath of Pope Urban VIII down upon Galileo, for the pope read some of it as a direct insult to him. After Galileo recanted at his trial, saving himself from death, he suffered house arrest for the remainder of his days.

43. Betsy Todd, "Medical Research for APHA, 1991" (resolution for consideration at the annual meeting of the American Public Health Association in Atlanta, GA, November 1991), published in *The Nation's Health* 21, no. 9 (September 1991): 16. The resolution failed.

44. Ibid.
45. Ibid.
46. B. N. Ames and L. S. Gold, "Too Many Rodent Carcinogens: Mitogenesis Increases Mutagenesis," *Science* 249, no. 4972 (August 31, 1990): 970.
47. Ibid., 971.
48. Richard Doll, "The Epidemiology of Cancer," *Cancer* 45, no. 10 (May 15, 1980): 2475–85.
49. George Pickering, "Physician and Scientist," *British Medical Journal* (December 26, 1964): 1615–19.
50. Among these were Barnard and Kaufman (see note 19).
51. Walton Lillihei, quoted in Lael Wertenbaker, *To Mend the Heart* (New York: Viking Press, 1980), 155, quoted in Brandon Reines, *Heart Research on Animals: A Critique of Animal Models of Cardiovascular Disease* (Jenkintown, PA: The American Anti-Vivisection Society, 1985), 52.
52. Reines, *Heart Research on Animals,* 52.
53. Lillihei, quoted in Wertenbaker, *To Mend the Heart,* 155.
54. Reines, *Heart Research on Animals,* 44–45.
55. Michael Bliss, *The Discovery of Insulin* (Chicago: University of Chicago Press, 1982), 11.
56. Ibid.
57. Michael Bliss, quoted in Charles S. Nicoll and Sharon M. Russell, "Animal Rights Movement Evokes Concern," *American Biology Teacher* 56, no. 2 (February 1994): 70–71.
58. Wise Young, "Spinal Cord Regeneration," *Science* 273, no. 5274 (July 26, 1996): 451.
59. Santiago Ramón y Cajal, *Degeneration and Regeneration of the Nervous System,* ed. and trans. Raoul M. May (New York: Hafner, 1959), 2:750.
60. Ibid.
61. Chan N. Liu and William W. Chambers, "Intraspinal Sprouting of Dorsal Root Axons," *Archives of Neurology and Psychiatry* 79 (1958): 46–61.
62. Michael M. Goldberger, Marion Murray, and Alan Tessler, "Sprouting and Regeneration in the Spinal Cord: Their Roles in Recovery of Function after Spinal Injury," in Alfredo Gorio, ed., *Neuroregeneration* (New York: Raven Press, 1993), 241–64.
63. See Henrich Cheng, Yihai Cao, and Lars Olson, "Spinal Cord Repair in Adult Paraplegic Rats: Partial Restoration of Hind Limb Function," *Science* 273, no. 5274 (July 26, 1996): 510–13; and Martin F. Schwab, "Regenerative Nerve Fiber Growth in the Adult Central Nervous System," *News in Physiological Sciences* 13 (December 1998): 294–98.
64. Young, "Spinal Cord Regeneration," 451.
65. Tracy McIntosh, Marianne Juhler, and Tadeusz Wieloch, "Novel Pharmacologic Strategies in the Treatment of Experimental Traumatic Brain Injury: 1998," *Journal of Trauma* 15, no. 10 (October 1998): 731–69.
66. See Edward Taub, Jean E. Crago, and Gilendra Uswatte, "Constraint-Induced Movement Therapy: A New Approach to Treatment in Physical Rehabilitation," *Rehabilitation Psychology* 43, no. 2 (Summer 1998): 152–70; and Bruno Kopp

et al., "Plasticity in the Motor System Related to Therapy-Induced Improvement of Movement after Stroke," *NeuroReport* 10, no. 4 (March 17, 1999): 807–10.

67. Tim P. Pons et al., "Massive Cortical Reorganization after Sensory Deafferentation in Adult Macaques," *Science* 252, no. 5014 (June 28, 1991): 1857–60.

68. Michael Merzenich, "Neuroscience—Long-Term Change of Mind," *Science* 282, no. 5391 (November 6, 1998): 1062–63.

Basic Research, Applied Research, Animal Ethics, and an Animal Model of Human Amnesia

Stuart Zola

I. Introduction

In September 1947, the University of California, Berkeley issued a set of eleven rules regarding the use of animals on its campus. Rule No. 3 stated that "[a]ll animals must receive every consideration for their bodily comfort; they shall be kindly treated, properly fed, and their surroundings kept in a sanitary condition."[1] Many research institutions around the country voluntarily developed similar sets of rules in order to insure the welfare of animals used in research. In 1966, with the passage of the Animal Welfare Act (AWA), concern about animal welfare became nationalized.[2] Since then, federal, state, and local regulatory agencies have passed literally thousands of rules and regulations directed at systematizing and legally enforcing the spirit of Rule No. 3.

Other essays in this volume deal admirably with the wisdom (or lack of wisdom) of this enterprise and with various moral issues concerning the use of animals in research. As evidenced by the range of opinions presented in these essays, it is clear that questions about whether or not animals should be used in biomedical research continue to be the subject of vigorous debate. Since the eighteenth century, when the British utilitarian Jeremy Bentham drew his famous conclusion about animals—"The question is not, Can they reason? Nor Can they talk? But Can they suffer?"[3]—there has been an almost endless variety of views on the issue of the use of animals in biomedical research. Nearly two centuries of discussion have not resolved the issue, and it is unlikely that this essay will do so. It is hoped, however, that in setting out the facts about the aims and methods of biomedical research and explaining how these facts "map on" to moral questions about the use of animals, at least some aspects of the debate will be clarified.

In this essay, I will focus on one particular issue in the debate: the distinction between *basic research* and *applied research*. I will discuss how misunderstanding the relation between these two domains of research has led some animal rights activists to make an artificial distinction between kinds of animal research that are not justifiable and kinds of animal research that might be justifiable. In the process of clarifying this issue, I will discuss historical, philosophical, and contemporary lay perspectives on the basic/applied distinction. Additionally, I will describe the contributions that animal research has made to our current understanding of how memory function, a critical cognitive ability, is organized in the brain. I will conclude that the distinction between basic research and applied research is an arbitrary one, that it is often muddy, and that it has not helped resolve the debate over the use of animals in research.

II. Basic Research and Applied Research: Definitions

In order to embark on a discussion of basic research and applied research, it would be useful to first define the two terms. It turns out, however, that this is not an easy task. There have been few contemporary attempts to develop formal definitions of the two terms. Instead, discussions of the basic/applied distinction typically involve delineating the processes or ideas used in carrying out particular kinds of research thought to be associated with each of the terms. Perhaps the best and clearest definitions of the two terms come from Sir Francis Bacon, the lord chancellor of England during the early 1600s. Bacon was a leader of his day in both law and science, and he is considered by many to be the founder of modern scientific thinking. Although the terms "basic" and "applied" were not in use during his lifetime, he did divide research into two domains with definitions that were simple and informative. According to Bacon, "experiments shedding light" (*experimenta lucifera*) could be contrasted with "experiments yielding fruit" (*experimenta fructifera*).[4] These expressions capture the essence of current parlance, as there has been little improvement since the 1600s in distinguishing the activities of basic research from those of applied research. Although it could be argued that even Bacon's definitions are not entirely mutually exclusive, his view of the basic/applied distinction has held sway for almost four centuries. It is this view that serves as the framework for the sections that follow.

III. Basic Research and Applied Research: Several Perspectives

The distinction between basic research and applied research has been of particular use in two contexts. First, biomedical ethics committees and/or Institutional Animal Care and Use Committees (IACUCs), when they are considering whether or not to allow a particular research program using animals to move forward, often take this distinction into account. This may be done either explicitly (e.g., by asking what the potential benefits of the proposed research are) or implicitly. Second, animal rights groups use the distinction to dismiss out of hand a large portion of biomedical research using animals, on the ground that the research is entirely worthless (i.e., it has no immediate practical application).

The important question, however, is how distinguishable the two domains of research are in practice. If the distinction between basic research and applied research turns out not to be sharp and clear, but is instead often arbitrary or even misleading, then decisions based upon the view that the distinction is sharp and clear might turn out to be less valid than was supposed. The remainder of this section will focus on the attempts of three quite different scientific organizations to distinguish between the activities associated with basic research and those associated with applied research. As will be seen, these two types of activities overlap to such an extent that it is often difficult to determine to which domain a particular activity belongs.

In 1986, the Institute of Medical Ethics (IME) in the United Kingdom set up a working party to study the ethical issues involved with using animals in biomedical research. Its members included scientists, officers of animal-welfare organizations, physicians, veterinary surgeons, philosophers, theologians, and a lawyer. In the context of the working party's discussions, the IME report concluded that in basic research (also referred to as fundamental or pure research), the goal is simply and solely to increase knowledge: there is no practical application in mind. Examples of basic research include a zoologist studying the ecology of a species of bat, a biochemist engaging in the identification of receptor sites on the surface of mammalian cells, and a pharmacologist investigating the distribution of chemical transmitters in the brain. The IME defined applied research as work dedicated to the solution of practical problems. Under this definition, applied research includes the development of medical and veterinary pharmaceuticals, the development and testing of medical and surgical materials (e.g., sutures, artificial replacement parts), and the experimental study of disease and pathology (e.g., ways to improve healing in experimental burns, studies of tumor induction and control in animals).[5]

Having made this distinction, the IME then went on to make clear that, in practice, basic research and applied research often go hand in hand. Indeed, in the discussion of the definition of basic research, the point was made that "investigators carrying out fundamental research . . . may have in view a practical [applied] problem, the solution of which would require further fundamental biological knowledge."[6] Moreover, as observed by pharmacologist Sir William Paton, researchers often commingle basic questions and applied questions, and switch back and forth between them during the course of a research project.[7] That is, there is often interplay between the two domains: basic research often

leads to applied research, and fundamental knowledge is often derived from applied research. As the IME report pointed out: in pharmacology, for example,
basic research on receptor sites for neurotransmitters has resulted in findings
that have been critical to the development of effective drug therapies for a wide
range of debilitating neurologic and psychiatric illnesses, including depression
and schizophrenia. In work on organ transplantation, many practical, applied
aspects are in place (e.g., surgical techniques), but for this field to advance further, there still needs to develop a better basic understanding of immunology.
These examples suggest that basic research and applied research can be closely
intertwined. Thus, as the IME report concluded, it is sometimes difficult, in a
practical sense, to separate the two domains of research.

Administered by the Masons of New York State, the Masonic Medical Research Laboratory (MMRL) is a research facility with a multimillion-dollar annual budget. It conducts basic biomedical research, particularly on heart disease,
aimed at generating knowledge and information necessary for the development
of the medical cures and treatments of tomorrow. By their definition, basic
research in the biomedical sciences involves fundamental studies into life
processes, where the major goal is to obtain an understanding of the principles
of living organisms. In contrast, applied and/or clinical research involves investigations aimed at implementing or putting to use available information. Both
applied and clinical research depend on knowledge initially gained through basic research.[8]

The MMRL also makes the point that history has taught us that the major discoveries essential to the development of medical breakthroughs have emerged
from studies committed to answering basic questions. For example, open-heart
surgery would not be possible today without the thousands of discoveries provided through basic research into how blood clots, how the heart beats, or how
antibiotics combat infection. Thus, the MMRL takes perhaps a more linear
view of the process of research than did the IME's working party. Whereas the
IME views the research process as consisting of two modes of research that mutually provide each other with ideas and insights, the MMRL's conception of
research seems to stress the role of basic research in laying the groundwork for
applied research. Nevertheless, the MMRL still considers basic research and
applied research to be closely interconnected. Moreover, at least by one example provided by the MMRL, basic and applied research activities are difficult
to untangle; for example, immunologists at MMRL are investigating interventions that alter the function of the immune system as a means to reducing blood
pressure. Indeed, in its opening discussion of the laboratory and its programs,
the MMRL provides a more general definition of research, describing it as the
conduct of investigations aimed at obtaining new knowledge and information.
This definition clearly embraces activities found in both the basic and applied
domains of research.

A website at the University of Wisconsin, Whitewater (UWW) has also grappled with the problem of defining basic research and applied research. Basic research can be thought of as being driven by a scientist's curiosity or interest in a scientific question.[9] The main motivation of such research is to expand knowledge, not to create or invent something or to develop a treatment, cure, or intervention. The website also notes a facet of basic research that is not mentioned by the IME or the MMRL: the discoveries that result from such research have no obvious commercial value. Basic research focuses on topics such as the origins of the universe, the process by which slime molds reproduce, and the specific genetic code of the fruit fly. Applied research, according to the site, is designed to solve practical problems rather than to acquire knowledge for knowledge's sake.[10] The goal of the applied scientist is to improve the human condition, by learning how to treat or cure a specific disease, for example.

The definitions on the UWW website, like those of the MMRL, tend toward the linear view that in all branches of science, basic, fundamental understanding of a field is needed in order for progress to take place. Basic research lays down the foundation for the applied science that follows. If basic work is done, then applied spin-offs often result from the research. Nevertheless, the UWW website describes how the discovery of superconductivity involved the continued back-and-forth interaction between the two research domains.[11] Thus, as in the previous examples, we see that during the course of science the borders between basic research and applied research can become blurred so that the distinction is no longer clear or even useful.

Indeed, if science has taught us anything, it is that the process of scientific discovery cannot be arbitrarily legislated or defined. For example, consider a major medical treatment like cardiac bypass surgery, which is carried out thousands of times each year in hospitals around the country. A review of all the research studies that were necessary for the development of bypass surgery revealed that about 40 percent of the studies, when initially carried out, had nothing to do with any clinical applications.[12] They were purely basic research studies, yet the information derived from them was critical to the successful development of bypass surgery. Thus, even though these studies were not applied research, they did contribute to a discovery that saves thousands of lives per year. The point here is that science has taught us an important lesson. Arbitrary distinctions, like separating research into the categories of "basic" and "applied," might serve important bookkeeping purposes, but these kinds of distinctions should not be used to form policies about the use of animals in research (such as deciding whether or not a particular project using animals should be allowed to go forward). Unfortunately, the basic/applied distinction is often used in making such decisions. In particular, as discussed in the next section, the question of whether a particular research proposal falls within the domain of basic research or applied research is often where the moral question of the use of animals in research is played out.

IV. The Moral Issue Regarding Animals

One could argue that the modern debate about basic research and applied research began in the seventeenth century, when Descartes "set out to rethink philosophy by doubting everything that could not be established by reason alone."[13] The essence of this idea culminated in his view that the bodies of animals and humans were nothing but machines. Descartes maintained within his newly developing view that only humans had souls, and that accordingly, animals lacked reason, as well as consciousness and any capacity to suffer pain. "Descartes' denial that animals (despite all appearances to the contrary) were able to suffer, appears to have been widely used as a justification for experimenting on live animals, at a time when the practice was becoming more common."[14]

By the late eighteenth century, philosophical debate about the morality of using animals for human purposes (including biomedical research) began to be framed in terms that we would recognize today, partially as a result of Bentham's aforementioned question regarding the capacity of animals to suffer. The response to this debate was the establishment in the nineteenth century of legislative and other developments to insure animal welfare and prevent animal cruelty. In the United States enormous amounts of animal-welfare regulation (such as the University of California's rules) have continued to cumulate in the twentieth century. Yet debate about the use of animals in biomedical research persists.

For some individuals, animal research is simply not a debatable topic. From their perspective, animals should not be used in biomedical research under any circumstances. There is presumably no argument or discussion that could alter this viewpoint, and this viewpoint will not be considered further here. Other people, however, have a point of view that is less extreme, one that on its surface, at least, appears more reasoned. This view allows for the possibility that under some circumstances it might be justifiable to use animals in biomedical research. Individuals holding this view claim that for a research program to be justifiable, it must be possible to predict some benefit from the research that will assist in the diagnosis, treatment, or prevention of disease or ill health, either in humans or in animals. I will call this claim the *justification rule*. This does not seem too unreasonable a requirement. However, it turns out that the justification rule is unreasonable in many cases. In particular, when the justification rule intersects with the presumption that there is a clear-cut distinction between basic research and applied research, the progress of scientific investigation can be harmed considerably.

This possibility for harm arises, in part, because it is not always possible to predict any specific benefits to humans or animals that might result from a research project that uses animals. Therefore, it is not always reasonable to use this criterion as the one by which to determine whether or not a study will be allowed. Uncertainty about future benefits often characterizes studies that fall within the domain of basic research. Indeed, as noted in Section III, one could argue that these kinds of studies are rarely if ever designed with applied or clinical goals in mind. If this argument were accepted in conjunction with the justification rule, one logical implication would be that basic research studies with animals could never be justified; only studies that involve applied research would be acceptable. An entire domain of research would thus be disenfranchised. But it is also true that one might not be able to predict the future benefits of projects that are clearly applied research. For example, an experimental heart valve being tested in dogs, may turn out not to work effectively, causing the entire program to be abandoned; or an experimental cancer drug being tested in rats might not impede the growth of tumors, leading to that project's termination as well. In point of fact, the aim of the research in each of these cases is to discover whether the respective treatments will be effective; if it were already known that they would be effective, there would have been no reason to do the studies.

The lack of a clear basic/applied distinction creates further complications for those who determine the permissibility of research projects. As noted above, some projects do not obviously belong to either category; other projects involve interdependent studies that represent both types of research. Thus, when one advocates the justification rule and believes in a sharp line dividing basic research from applied research, one's consequent decisions will prevent a substantial body of research from taking place. This is likely to be harmful in the long run.

One way to avoid this outcome would be to soften the justification rule. For example, one might require that research using animals need only *possibly* provide benefits to humans or animals. If the justification rule were interpreted loosely, some, but not all, basic research studies would then qualify as acceptable. But by this view, potentially very good science could still be precluded from being done simply because (1) it is basic research, and (2) its *possible* benefits are not clear or immediately obvious. That is, the notion that there is an easy way to demarcate basic and applied research in making the decision is still problematic. Why? Because it superimposes a decision based on a category of work, without regard to the quality of the work.

Another way to preserve research possibilities is to reconsider what is meant by "benefits." For example, one could hold the moral position that while possible benefits to humans and animals are important, the advancement of scientific knowledge is itself a benefit as well. On the surface, this position appears to run the risk of justifying almost any research project.[15] In reality, however, this is countered by the underlying assumption that a permissible project must be based on good science, that is, science that has been peer-reviewed and found to be of acceptable quality. With that caveat in mind, treating scientific knowledge itself as a benefit would seem to be reasonable from a variety of perspectives. First, it would not artificially disenfranchise one domain of research. Decisions about whether a research project using animals was morally justified would not be based on an arbitrary categorical determination, but instead on a more general principle, namely, quality of science. Second, this position recognizes that the discovery of fundamental knowledge is valuable in its own right. Third, it underscores one of the valuable lessons of science alluded to in Section III: when a discovery is made, it is sometimes difficult or even impossible to know how important it will turn out to be. Therefore, it might not be reasonable to preclude the possibility of carrying out a study simply because it has no obvious immediate relevance, either potential or real.

V. An Animal Model of Human Amnesia

Laboratory animals can play an important role as biological models for the study of physiological functions and cognitive functions in humans, and as disease models for understanding the mechanisms of human diseases and medical conditions. Animal models can help clarify many aspects of a disease or medical condition by providing a means of systematically studying the circumstances necessary to produce impairments observed in humans, and by providing the possibility for assessing the effectiveness of potential interventions, treatments, and cures.

This section will present findings that have resulted from research involving an animal model of human amnesia. Considerable research on memory has been carried out in nonhuman primates. This work can be characterized as involving "basic" research (e.g., neuroanatomical studies involving the connectivity of brain structures) as well as "applied" research (e.g., attempts to clarify what parts of the brain are important for memory and how damage to these regions impairs memory). (For the remainder of this essay, the terms "basic" and "applied" appear in quotes to underscore the lack of a clear distinction between them.) The sections that follow briefly describe the discovery of a system of interconnected structures, located in the medial portion of the temporal lobe of the brain, that support *declarative memory,* a particular type of memory function that deals with the conscious recollection of facts and events from one's life.[16] (This is also known as *explicit memory*.) The description of this work underscores two points made in the preceding sections. First, research programs often lack a sharp division between "basic" research and "applied" research. Second, it can be very important to grant approval to work that, at the time it is proposed, can only be described with respect to *possible* benefits.

Development of an Animal Model of Human Amnesia

In 1978, an important study by Mortimer Mishkin, a neuroscientist interested in the process of memory, signaled the development of an animal model of human amnesia in nonhuman primates.[17] In human amnesia, individuals can have problems remembering facts and events from their lives as a result of a wide range of medical conditions in which brain damage occurs (e.g., Alzheimer's disease, stroke). The animal model of amnesia has allowed us to identify with certainty regions within the medial temporal lobe that are important for normal memory function, such as the hippocampal region (see below). It has also let us begin to determine systematically how individual structures within the medial temporal lobe contribute to memory function ("applied" or clinical research). At the same time that behavioral work was being carried out with monkeys to accomplish these goals, important information about the neuroanatomy of the monkey brain was being discovered. No particular clinical issue motivated the anatomical work. Instead, the motivation was simply to understand and describe the interconnectivity of several adjacent brain regions in the temporal lobe ("basic" or fundamental research).[18]

In the behavioral work with monkeys, researchers made bilateral lesions (i.e., lesions on both sides of the brain) to the medial temporal lobe. These were intended to reproduce the surgical lesions sustained by a well-studied amnesic patient, H. M.[19] To relieve intractable seizures, this patient had undergone bilateral surgical removal of large portions of his temporal lobes. The lesions in monkeys reproduced many of the features of memory impairment exhibited by H. M. and other amnesic patients.[20] As in human amnesia, damage to the medial temporal lobe in monkeys impaired memory in both visual and tactual modalities. For example, in one kind of memory test, a monkey is shown a single object referred to as the sample object (e.g., a small toy). Then, after a variable delay that could range from eight seconds to forty minutes, the sample object and a novel object (another toy, different in color, shape, and size) are presented together. To obtain a food reward, the monkey must remember which object it had seen initially and must choose the novel object. This task is called the *delayed nonmatching task,* and the work with monkeys has depended upon several tasks, like this one, with which human amnesic patients are known to have difficulties.[21] Monkeys with damage to the hippocampal region of the medial temporal lobe have impaired memory ability: they do not remember as well as normal monkeys which of the two objects they had previously seen. Distracting the animals during the retention interval exacerbates the deficit in monkeys with hippocampal damage, as it does in human amnesic patients. In contrast to their memory problems, the monkeys with bilateral lesions of the medial temporal lobe have normal perceptual and sensory abilities, as do human amnesic patients.

Identification of a Memory System in the Medial Temporal Lobe

This behavioral research in monkeys, together with the aforementioned neuroanatomical research, has resulted in the identification of a system of anatomically related structures that is important for memory; this system is located in the medial temporal lobe. The anatomical research has revealed that this *medial temporal lobe system* is comprised of the hippocampal region and adjacent cortical areas. The cortex adjacent to the hippocampal region includes the entorhinal, perirhinal, and parahippocampal cortices. All of these cortical areas are, as we now know, anatomically related to the hippocampal region. In particular, the perirhinal cortex and the parahippocampal cortex provide nearly two-thirds of the cortical input to the entorhinal cortex. The entorhinal cortex, in turn, is the major source of cortical projections to the hippocampus.

The medial temporal lobe system is necessary for establishing declarative memory, i.e., the capacity for conscious recollection of facts and events. This kind of memory is often thought of as "everyday" memory; examples of it include remembering what you had for breakfast this morning, or remembering the details of a telephone conversation you had a few days ago. When components of the medial temporal lobe system are damaged, memory is impaired. For example, as described earlier, bilateral damage to the hippocampal region in monkeys impairs their performance on the delayed nonmatching task. The monkeys have difficulty identifying which object they initially saw, even after only a few minutes. Memory problems also result when a human's hippocampus is damaged (e.g., the patient will have difficulty recalling a conversation from earlier in the day). Thus, normal memory requires the integrity of this system of interconnected structures.

Memory Impairment and Severity of Damage to the Medial Temporal Lobe System

Work with monkeys and humans has led to the understanding that the severity of memory impairment increases as more components of the medial temporal lobe system are damaged.[22] This idea has been supported by a large number of individual studies in monkeys. In these studies, groups of monkeys with varying damage to the medial temporal lobe performed memory tasks, and the results were compared. The main finding from this work was that the severity of memory impairment depended on the locus and extent of damage within the medial temporal lobe system. Damage limited to the hippocampal region (H) caused significant memory impairment. More severe memory impairment occurred following H damage that extended to the adjacent entorhinal and parahippocampal cortices. The severity of impairment was greater still following H damage that also included all the adjacent cortical regions (i.e., the perirhinal, entorhinal, and parahippocampal cortices). The finding that monkeys with damage affecting both the hippocampal region and adjacent cortical regions exhibited more severe impairment than monkeys with damage limited to the hippocampal region parallels findings from human amnesia. For example, patient H. M., who had extensive bilateral damage to his medial temporal lobe region, is more severely amnesic than other patients with less extensive medial temporal lobe damage.[23]

VI. Overview and Relevance of the Animal Model Research to the Issue of Animal Ethics

The above findings based on work with monkeys also share numerous points of correspondence with findings in humans. In particular, the findings show that circumscribed bilateral lesions limited to the hippocampal region are sufficient to produce amnesia. Additional findings indicate that the cortical regions adjacent to and anatomically linked to the hippocampal region — the perirhinal, entorhinal, and parahippocampal cortices — are also important for memory function. Moreover, the findings from these studies of monkeys also relate to several additional human disorders that involve memory. For example, memory impairment is typically the earliest symptom of Alzheimer's disease. There is considerable evidence that the medial temporal lobe regions, the site of the most prominent pathological alterations caused by Alzheimer's disease, are precisely the regions that have been identified as important for memory in monkeys. Human memory impairment associated with pathology in the medial temporal lobe region is also prominent after strokes, viral infections (e.g., encephalitis), head traumas, and even chronic stress, as researchers have found a link between chronically elevated stress hormones and potential damage to the hippocampus. Memory problems are also an important issue generally for the increasingly aged normal population. As efforts continue to develop treatments for human memory disorders and to prevent memory deterioration, it will be important to understand the neurological organization of memory as completely as possible.

VII. Conclusion

The research on monkeys that I have just described illustrates my main argument — that the distinction between "basic" research and "applied" research is arbitrary, often vague, and not helpful in determining beforehand what kinds of research with animals are justifiable. The findings from research with monkeys have had important theoretical implications and have illuminated important points about the organization of memory in the medial temporal lobe in humans and animals. One could reasonably argue that this project involved both "basic" research and "applied" research. The work with monkeys involved gathering both clinical information about memory impairment and fundamental information about the neuroanatomy of the brain. Moreover, the "basic"/"applied" distinction has not been helpful in any obvious way with respect to the progress of this research. For example, this framework cannot easily characterize the work with monkeys described above. In fact, the distinction, when applied in conjunction with the aforementioned justification rule, has the potential for impeding the progress of this kind of research, because at least some aspects of it, such as the neuroanatomic components of the study, did not have direct or obvious benefits to humans.

It is useful to make one final point. Even for biomedical research projects on animals that seem to be the most abstruse—devoted simply to increasing knowledge—the potential findings may benefit humans or animals, often in entirely unanticipated ways. It behooves scientists to educate the public and remind IACUCs about precisely this point: the serendipitous nature of science. Both "applied" and "basic" research have their place in the advancement of science, and as we have seen, the distinction between them is neither a clear nor a desirable one. Animal rights advocates, by insisting on this artificial distinction, do much to jeopardize *both* the advancement of knowledge and the remediation of human and animal diseases.

NOTES

1. Memo from the Office of the President, University of California, Berkeley, September 1947.
2. The House version of the Animal Welfare Act was passed in May 1966; the Senate passed the bill in an 85–0 roll call vote in June of that year. Later that summer, the act was signed into law by President Lyndon B. Johnson. *Animal Welfare Act*, Pub. L. No. 89-544, 80 Stat. 350 (1966) (codified as amended at 7 U.S.C secs. 2131 et seq. [1994]). The AWA is this nation's primary federal law regarding animal care, and it sets standards for the treatment of animals by breeders, exhibitors, transporters, and those research facilities that use animals in research. The act has been modified through subsequent amendments, and the issue of whether or not it sufficiently protects animals continues to generate philosophical, economic, and regulatory discussion among government regulators, commercial and academic institutes, and humane-treatment advocates.
3. Jeremy Bentham, *An Introduction to the Principles of Morals and Legislation*, ed. J. H. Burns and H. L. A. Hart (1970; reprint, London: Clarendon Press, 1996), 282–83 n. b. First published in 1789, the *Introduction* contains Bentham's most famous analy-

sis of the principle of utility, in which he distinguishes between utility's role in explaining why agents act as they do and its role in pointing out the way that they ought to act.

4. Jane A. Smith and Kenneth M. Boyd, eds., *Lives in the Balance: The Ethics of Using Animals in Biomedical Research—The Report of a Working Party of the Institute of Medical Ethics* (New York: Oxford University Press, 1991), 8.

5. Ibid., 8–10.

6. Ibid., 9.

7. William Paton, *Man and Mouse: Animals in Medical Research,* 2d ed. (Oxford: Oxford University Press, 1993), 28.

8. "The Importance of Basic Research," at http://www.mmrl.edu/Imprtnc.htm, accessed May 10, 2000.

9. "What Is Basic Research?" at http://facstaff.uww.edu/lscore/STS/mirrored_docs/basic2.htm, accessed May 10, 2000.

10. "What Is Applied Research?" at http://facstaff.uww.edu/lscore/STS/mirrored_docs/basic4.htm, accessed May 10, 2000.

11. The Gray Zone," at http://facstaff.uww.edu/lscore/STS/mirrored_docs/basic5.htm, accessed May 10, 2000.

12. Julius Comroe, *Retrospectroscope: Insights into Medical Discovery* (Menlo Park, CA: Von Gehr Press, 1977), 12. This volume is a collection of Comroe's essays showing that scientists depend on the work of other scientists and that important discoveries crucial to later medical breakthroughs were often made by those not directly concerned with diagnosing, curing, or preventing disease. Indeed, as Comroe points out in the preface of *Retrospectroscope,* many of these important earlier discoveries were initially judged to be impractical or irrelevant.

13. Smith and Boyd, *Lives in the Balance,* 299–300.

14. Ibid.

15. Ibid., 31–32.

16. Stuart Zola, "Amnesia: Neuroanatomical and Clinical Aspects," in Todd E. Feinberg and Martha J. Farah, eds., *Behavioral Neurology and Neuropsychology* (New York: McGraw-Hill, 1997), 447–61. See also Larry Squire, "Memory, Human Neuropsychology," in Robert Wilson and Frank C. Keil, eds., *The MIT Encyclopedia of the Cognitive Sciences* (Cambridge, MA: MIT Press, 1999), 520–22.

17. Mortimer Mishkin, "Memory in Monkeys Severely Impaired by Combined but Not Separate Removal of the Amygdala and Hippocampus," *Nature* 273, no. 5660 (May 25, 1978): 297–98.

18. For two good examples of the neuroanatomical work, see Gary Van Hoesen, "The Parahippocampal Gyrus: New Observations Regarding Its Cortical Connections in the Monkey," *Trends in Neuroscience* 5 (1982): 345–50; and Ricardo Insausti, David Amaral, and Maxwell Cowan, "The Entorhinal Cortex of the Monkey: II. Cortical Afferents," *Journal of Comparative Neurology* 264, no. 3 (October 15, 1987): 356–95.

19. A very good historical perspective that underscores the contributions that the study of patient H. M. has made to memory research can be found in Brenda Milner, Larry Squire, and Eric Kandel, "Cognitive Neuroscience and the Study of Memory," *Neuron* 20, no. 3 (March 1998): 445–68.

20. Nancy Rempel-Clower, Stuart M. Zola, and Larry R. Squire, "Three Cases of Enduring Memory Impairment Following Bilateral Damage Limited to the Hippocampal Formation," *Journal of Neuroscience* 16, no. 16 (August 15, 1996): 5233–55; S. Zola-Morgan and L. R. Squire, "Medial Temporal Lesions in Monkeys Impair Memory on Tasks Sensitive to Human Amnesia," *Behavioral Neuroscience* 99, no. 1 (1985): 22–34.
21. Stuart M. Zola et al., "Impaired Recognition Memory in Monkeys after Damage Limited to the Hippocampal Region," *Journal of Neuroscience* 20, no. 1 (January 1, 2000): 451–63.
22. Stuart Zola-Morgan, Larry R. Squire, and Setu J. Ramus, "Severity of Memory Impairment in Monkeys as a Function of Locus and Extent of Damage within the Medial Temporal Lobe Memory System," *Hippocampus* 4, no. 4 (August 1994): 483–95.
23. Rempel-Clower, Zola, and Squire, "Three Cases of Enduring Memory Impairment."

The Paradigm Shift toward Animal Happiness: What It Is, Why It Is Happening, and What It Portends for Medical Research

Jerrold Tannenbaum

I. Introduction

This essay discusses what I believe to be the most dangerous contemporary threat to the use of animals in medical research. This threat is not, as many supporters of animal research assume, the growth of the contemporary animal rights movement and the aim of this movement to terminate all use of animals in experimentation and testing. Calls for the end of animal use tend to come from people who dispute, on empirical grounds, the relevance of using animals in developing medical treatments, or from those who openly reject fundamental ethical values that are reflected in animal research. Among these values is the view that animals are not as valuable as human beings and that it is therefore sometimes appropriate to use them in research that benefits humans. Such criticisms of animal research are easy to recognize, and they tend to elicit vigorous responses from the medical community.

Far more dangerous is a relatively new approach to animals that is espoused, with increasing frequency and fervor, within the research community itself. This view asserts that animals used in research are entitled not just to freedom from unnecessary or unjustifiable pain or distress, but to well-being, pleasure, and even happy lives. This approach is dangerous precisely because its endorsement by people who are committed to using animals obscures the fact that it threatens animal research.

II. The Traditional Approach to Animal Welfare

For at least the past century, the great majority of people in Western societies have adhered (at least in principle) to a general ethical position regarding the

93

treatment of animals that we humans use or with which we interact. This general view, which I shall call the *traditional approach* to animal welfare, focuses on unpleasant mental states in animals, such as pain, suffering, stress, distress, and discomfort. (Because the term "pain" is often used in the animal-ethics literature to refer to any or all of these mental states, I shall use that term here, but within single quotation marks to indicate this broad sense.) The traditional approach asserts that many animals that humans use or interact with are capable of experiencing 'pain', and that the experience of 'pain' is a harm or evil to animals just as the experiencing of these states is a harm or evil to humans. According to the traditional approach, because it is always desirable not to cause an evil that one need not cause, the ideal, when we use animals for our own purposes, is to avoid causing them 'pain'. However, the traditional approach also asserts that many uses of animals are ethically acceptable, and that some of these uses may sometimes cause animals 'pain'. Thus, an important tenet of the traditional approach is that although we should always try to avoid inflicting 'pain' on animals, when we use them in legitimate ways that may cause them 'pain', we are obligated not to cause them *unnecessary* or *unjustifiable* 'pain'.[1]

In prohibiting the infliction of "unnecessary" animal 'pain', the traditional approach employs a weak (and some have suggested an inappropriate[2]) sense of "necessity." Strictly speaking, it is rarely if ever necessary to cause animals 'pain': in most cases, we could stop using them in ways that cause 'pain'. In regarding certain animal 'pain' as necessary, the traditional position regards certain uses of animals as ethically *appropriate,* but insists that no more 'pain' should be inflicted on the animals than is required for these uses. For example, if raising and slaughtering cows to produce beef (which most adherents of the traditional view believe is ethically acceptable) does cause cows some 'pain', such 'pain' is not, strictly speaking, necessary. We could stop raising cows for beef, however much difficulty, discomfort, or displeasure this may cause for people who want to eat beef. Nevertheless, most adherents of the traditional approach countenance as necessary some animal 'pain' that occurs when we use cows to produce beef. They do so because they believe that using the animals for this purpose is ethically acceptable and that some 'pain' may be inevitable in the context of this use. Likewise, research that causes animal 'pain' is not, strictly speaking, necessary, because we *could* cease using animals in research, even if terminating animal research would cause widespread human suffering. The traditional approach accepts some animal 'pain' as necessary in research because it accepts the appropriateness of some research that causes some animal 'pain'.

Although the traditional approach focuses on animal 'pain' and seeks to avoid or minimize it, the approach is not utilitarian. Utilitarian ethical theories claim that the rightness of actions derives solely from their *utility,* that is, their contributions toward intrinsically good states of affairs such as pleasure, happiness, or the satisfaction of preferences. A utilitarian justification of an animal experiment (or of animal experimentation generally) would argue that any animal 'pain' it causes is outweighed by its benefits to humans or to other animals. A utilitarian will claim that an animal use that causes 'pain' to animals is acceptable only if that use, when compared to alternative uses of animals, minimizes the total amount of 'pain' felt by all beings capable of feeling such sensations. For example, from a utilitarian perspective, a proposed animal experiment would be wrong if there were another approach to the relevant research—an alternative experiment, or a procedure avoiding animal use—that would cause less total 'pain' than would the proposed experiment.

In contrast to a utilitarian approach, the traditional approach does not make the appropriateness of animal uses turn on whether, on balance, the total 'pain' experienced by all beings affected is minimized. Instead, the traditional approach holds that a number of animal uses are legitimate, and may employ as a justification for this legitimacy a range of different ethical or religious principles. For example, adherents of the traditional approach need not justify the use of animals for meat on the ground that people who eat meat experience, on balance, total satisfactions that outweigh all the 'pain' caused to the animals used in meat production. An adherent of the traditional approach might justify raising cows for meat on any of various grounds: that eating meat is natural for the human species, that it brings great pleasure to humans, that God decreed that certain animals may be eaten by people, or that there is simply nothing wrong with raising and killing certain animals for food.

Although the traditional approach is not utilitarian, it generally engages in a balancing or weighing of what is done to animals, on the one hand, against the purported results of these uses, on the other. In the United States, the federal Animal Welfare Act (AWA)[3] and the Health Research Extension Act of 1985 (HREA)[4] require that institutions create Institutional Animal Care and Use Committees (IACUCs), which must approve all of the experimentation and testing on animals covered under these laws. (The laws of other countries require similar committees.) IACUCs typically ask whether an animal experiment that will cause animals pain or distress is justified by the aims and likely results of the experiment. This balancing or weighing is sometimes phrased in terms of comparing the "costs" to the animals against the "benefits" to people or animals. The traditional approach does not preclude employing a strict utilitarian argument to justify some uses of animals. Nevertheless, the traditional approach is not in and of itself utilitarian, because what counts as justified animal 'pain' under the traditional approach often does not turn on calculations of utility.

Another important feature of the traditional approach is that its adherents do not believe that it is in and of itself wrong to kill an animal, or that animals have a moral right not to be killed by humans. This follows from the fundamental tenet of the approach, that our overriding ethical obligation to animals is to avoid causing them unjustifiable 'pain'. However, the traditional approach does not treat all animal killings that do not cause 'pain' as perforce acceptable. Adherents of the traditional approach presumably would not approve of an "experiment" in which animals are killed without 'pain' and then thrown against a brick wall to determine the decibel level of sound caused when various sizes and species of animals hit the wall. Such an activity would doubtless be regarded as unjustified, because even though the experiment causes no animal 'pain', it lacks any redeeming value.

British cancer researcher Harold Hewitt provides a succinct expression of the traditional approach. "My concern," he states,

> is really not with the number of animals [used in an experiment], in the sense that I should be more upset by my having caused one animal to suffer by my neglect or ineptitude than I should be by administering euthanasia to fifty at the termination of an experiment in which none had been caused suffering. The question the prospective animal experimenter has to ask himself is whether he considers that the painless taking of animal life is itself an immoral act. For me it is not.[5]

Hewitt does not speak explicitly of the "interests" animals have in not experiencing pain. However, clearly embedded in his view is the idea that even if we should say animals have an "interest" in living or not being killed by researchers, this interest is not sufficiently strong to render ethically wrong their painless killing in scientifically justified experiments. However, Hewitt would say that we have an obligation not to subject research animals to unnecessary pain. Indeed, he would say that this obligation is so strong that it may never be overridden.

Although Hewitt does not speak of animal "welfare" in the passage above, his view of the permissibility of the painless killing of animals appears to reflect the position that the painless killing of an animal is not in and of itself a *harm* to that animal. (Hewitt appears to believe—as do adherents of the traditional approach—that there is *no* ethical import in killing an animal per se. Presumably, he would not come to this conclusion if he believed that painlessly killing an animal harms it. If one acknowledges that painlessly killing an animal harms it, this implies that there can be at least some ethical issue regarding whether it should be harmed, even if one resolves this issue in favor of harming it.) The view that the painless killing of animals does not harm them—and therefore does not diminish their welfare—is stated explicitly by A. F. Fraser and D. M. Broom, two prominent animal-welfare scientists and proponents of the traditional approach. According to Fraser and Broom,

> [i]f an animal is suddenly shot, with no previous warning that this might happen, and it dies instantaneously, then there is a moral question about whether such killing should occur but there is no welfare problem. If an animal dies slowly with much pain, or is wounded by a shot which

results in pain and difficulties in normal living, then its welfare is poor. . . . If animals are kept in order that they will eventually be eaten, their welfare could be good throughout their lives even up to the point of slaughter.[6]

In sum, the traditional approach asserts the following principles:

1. The only significant interest animals have is in not experiencing 'pain'.
2. Our primary ethical obligation when we use animals (in research or agriculture, for example) is to avoid causing them 'pain' or more 'pain' than is necessary or justifiable.
3. Death is not a harm to animals if death comes without 'pain'.
4. Therefore, killing animals without causing them 'pain' does not have an effect upon, and does not constitute a diminution of, their welfare.
5. We are obligated to protect and assure the welfare of animals that we use in research and for other purposes.
6. Therefore, insofar as we kill research animals without causing them 'pain', we satisfy our ethical obligation to assure their welfare.

III. The Traditional Approach in Current Laws and Regulations

Although the traditional approach is under assault, it is still reflected in the great bulk of laws and regulations in the United States that apply to a wide range of animal uses. State cruelty-to-animals laws, for example, prohibit the infliction of unnecessary or unjustifiable pain, suffering, or distress upon animals.[7] These laws do not prohibit simply killing an animal, nor can one be prosecuted for animal cruelty for failing to provide one's own animal with love, affection, or positive pleasures. The gist of the offense of animal cruelty is the infliction of unnecessary or unjustified 'pain'.[8] Humane-slaughter laws likewise prohibit subjecting animals that are killed for meat to unnecessary or unjustified pain or distress.

With one major exception that will be discussed below, the fundamental motivation of current U.S. laws and regulations relating to animal research reflects the traditional approach. The federal Animal Welfare Act regulates research on dogs, cats, primates, guinea pigs, hamsters, rabbits, and other warm-blooded species that the U.S. Department of Agriculture (USDA) determines shall be included under the law, with the exception of animals used in agricultural research.[9] (At the time of this writing, the USDA has not yet included rats, mice, and birds under the AWA.) As amended in 1985, the AWA requires that regulations be effected assuring that

- "animal pain and distress are minimized, including adequate veterinary care with the appropriate use of anesthetic, analgesic, tranquilizing drugs, or euthanasia";

ꭓ • "the principal investigator considers alternatives to any procedure likely to produce pain to or distress in an experimental animal";
  • "in any practice which could cause pain to animals" a veterinarian will be consulted in the planning of such procedures, and these procedures will provide for "the use of tranquilizers, analgesics, and anesthetics"; and
  • "the withholding of tranquilizers, anesthesia, analgesia, or euthanasia when scientifically necessary shall continue for only the necessary period of time."[10]

These provisions, all of which reflect the traditional approach, are elaborated in regulations that reiterate or apply the approach more concretely. The following provisions of the AWA and regulations are illustrative:

  • "[P]rocedures involving animals will avoid or minimize discomfort, distress, and pain to the animals[.]"[11]
  • Investigators must provide the IACUC a written narrative showing that they have considered "alternatives to procedures that may cause more than momentary or slight pain to the animals[.]"[12]
  • Animal research proposals must contain a "description of the procedures designed to assure that discomfort and pain to the animals will be limited to that which is unavoidable for the conduct of scientifically valuable research, including provision for the use of analgesic, anesthetic, and tranquilizing drugs where indicated and appropriate to minimize discomfort and pain to the animals."[13]
  • Paralytics may not be used on animals without using anesthesia.[14]
  • Animals "that would otherwise experience severe or chronic pain or distress that cannot be relieved" must be "painlessly euthanized at the end of the procedure, or, if appropriate, during the procedure[.]"[15]
  • Activities that involve surgery must include "appropriate provision for preoperative and post-operative care of the animals in accordance with established veterinary medical and nursing practices."[16]
  • The methods of euthanasia used by researchers are not to involve any pain or distress to the animal.[17]

Furthermore, the AWA requires that each institution's IACUC inspect, at least twice per year, all areas in which animals are used or housed. The law describes the purpose of these inspections in terms of minimizing pain. Although the statute requires that an inspection uncover all deficiencies, the only matters specifically mentioned are inspection of "practices involving pain to animals" and "the condition of animals." The goal of the inspections is "to ensure compliance with the provisions of this [act that attempt] to minimize pain and distress to animals."[18]

The primary purpose of the AWA and its regulations is to minimize animal pain, distress, and discomfort, and this is underscored by the requirement that all institutions file an annual report. This report must contain not only an assurance that the facility has adhered to all standards and regulations under the act, but must state that there has been "appropriate use of anesthetic, analgesic, and tranquilizing drugs, prior to, during, and following actual research"[19] and that "each principal investigator has considered alternatives to painful procedures."[20] The main feature of the report is the specification of the number of animals that have been subjected to pain. This requirement is in harmony with the traditional approach, which permits the infliction of pain if it is unavoidable and justifiable. Thus, the report includes a category for animals that experience "pain or distress . . . for which the use of appropriate anesthetic, analgesic, or tranquilizing drugs would have adversely affected the procedures, results, or interpretations" of research projects. Reports must explain why such drugs were not used.[21]

Public Health Service (PHS) policies relating to animal use, which are promulgated pursuant to the Health Research Extension Act, apply to all vertebrates at institutions receiving PHS funds for animal research. (These policies thus regulate species not yet covered under the AWA, such as rats, mice, and birds. Institutions receiving PHS funds must comply with both the AWA and PHS policies.) The PHS policies incorporate the requirements of the AWA regulations relating to 'pain' minimization and state that:

- "[p]rocedures with animals will avoid or minimize discomfort, distress, and pain to the animals, consistent with sound research design";
- "[p]rocedures that may cause more than momentary or slight pain or distress to the animals will be performed with appropriate sedation, analgesia, or anesthesia, unless the procedure is justified for scientific reasons in writing by the investigator"; and
- "[a]nimals that would otherwise experience chronic pain or distress that cannot be relieved will be painlessly killed at the end of the procedure or, if appropriate, during the procedure."[22]

The U.S. Government Principles for the Utilization and Care of Vertebrate Animals Used in Testing, Research, and Training (hereafter referred to as the "Principles") were originally promulgated by the PHS for animal research in federal government facilities, and are now incorporated into the PHS policies relating to animal research. The Principles declare the following:

- "[P]roper use of animals, including the avoidance or minimization of discomfort, distress, and pain when consistent with sound scientific practices, is imperative. Unless the contrary is established, investigators should consider that procedures that cause pain or distress in human beings may cause pain or distress in other animals."

- "[P]rocedures with animals that may cause more than momentary or slight pain or distress should be performed with appropriate sedation, analgesia, or anesthesia. Surgical or other painful procedures should not be performed on unanesthetized animals paralyzed by chemical agents."
- "[A]nimals that would otherwise suffer severe or chronic pain or distress that cannot be relieved should be painlessly killed at the end of the procedure or, if appropriate, during the procedure."[23]

The traditional approach also underlies a key statement of the *Guide for the Care and Use of Laboratory Animals,* a comprehensive handbook of recommendations for IACUCs, veterinarians, and scientists that was developed by the National Research Council[24] and the Institute for Laboratory Animal Resources. Often called the "Bible of animal research," the *Guide* has been incorporated into the PHS policies involving such research. Under these policies, all research institutions that receive federal funds for animal research must consult the *Guide.* The *Guide* emphasizes that "an integral part of veterinary medical care [for laboratory animals] is prevention or alleviation of pain. . . . The proper use of anesthetics and analgesics is an ethical and scientific imperative."[25]

Pain and Death in the Current Regulatory Scheme

The primacy in the current regulatory approach of avoiding unnecessary research-animal 'pain' is strikingly illustrated by how the killing of animals is treated. Nothing in the AWA or in the PHS policies states or suggests that there is a problem or issue raised by the killing of animals. AWA regulations require that each institution's IACUC is assured by all investigators that their uses of animals "do not unnecessarily duplicate previous experiments."[26] The Principles state that the "animals selected for a procedure should be . . . the minimum number required to obtain valid results. Methods such as mathematical models, computer simulation, and *in vitro* biological systems should be considered."[27] However, neither of these provisions suggests that using too many animals is wrong because too many will be killed. Indeed, the provision from the AWA appears among several provisions requiring the avoidance or minimization of pain or distress, which suggests that the discouraging of unnecessary duplication is intended to reduce animal 'pain'.

Altogether, AWA regulations and PHS policies explicitly mention the killing of animals only twice, both times in the context of reducing 'pain'. AWA regulations require that killing be accomplished without causing the animals pain unless the investigator can demonstrate that there are scientific reasons for doing otherwise.[28] Both the AWA regulations and the PHS policies state that "animals that would otherwise suffer severe or chronic pain or distress that cannot be relieved should be painlessly killed at the end of the procedure or, if appropriate, during the procedure."[29] Killing is thus viewed as a method of pain control. The focus of current laws and regulations, then, is on avoiding or minimizing research-animal pain, suffering, distress, and discomfort—not on preserving the lives of research animals or making those animals happy when they are alive.

IV. The Traditional Approach: Issues and Theoretical Underpinning

The traditional approach is not without conceptual, ethical, and practical problems. Nevertheless, this approach is generally supported by its adherents with a relatively clear—and, I would argue, extremely persuasive—set of ethical principles.

There is disagreement among and between animal scientists, veterinarians, and philosophers about how the terms "pain," "suffering," "distress," and "discomfort" should be defined when applied to animals. There is also disagreement about what kinds of animals are capable of experiencing these mental states, when and to what extent animals experience such states, and how what I have generically termed 'pain' can be prevented, terminated, or lessened. Finally, opinions also differ over whether and to what extent certain animal species experience more complex negative mental states, such as fear, depression, anxiety, and boredom. Some of these issues are not just empirical, but conceptual: A number of thinkers adopt definitions of certain mental terminology ("anxiety" is a good example) that make it relatively easy to conclude that some animals experience complex negative mental states. Applying these definitions, however, may lead to the relevant terms being used differently from how they are ordinarily employed when applied to humans. This may result in overestimation of the ethical costs of animal experiments and calls for stronger justification for such experiments than would otherwise be required.[30]

In addition to suffering from these conceptual problems, the traditional approach is sometimes difficult to apply. It can be extremely difficult, for conceptual and empirical reasons, to estimate the 'pain' that animals are likely to experience as a result of an experiment, and it is often difficult to predict the results of an experiment that involves animal 'pain'. Thus, the task of weighing likely research benefits against 'pain' in order to determine whether an experiment is justified often depends on estimation and intuition. Some of the lack of rigor in articulating and applying the traditional approach is avoidable and should be addressed. In determining whether an experiment or research protocol is justified, IACUCs tend to consider and balance the animal 'pain' that an experiment is likely to cause and the importance or value of the experiment.

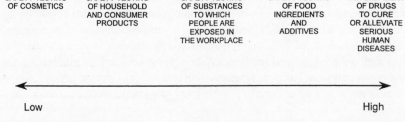

| SAFETY TESTING OF COSMETICS | SAFETY TESTING OF HOUSEHOLD AND CONSUMER PRODUCTS | SAFETY TESTING OF SUBSTANCES TO WHICH PEOPLE ARE EXPOSED IN THE WORKPLACE | SAFETY TESTING OF FOOD INGREDIENTS AND ADDITIVES | DEVELOPMENT OF DRUGS TO CURE OR ALLEVIATE SERIOUS HUMAN DISEASES |

Low   High

Figure 1. Possible Perceived Value of Selected Animal Uses, under the Traditional Approach

The more 'pain' an experiment is likely to cause, the greater the justification that must be shown. The more important the work, the higher its justification. Thus, the more 'pain' an experiment causes, the less willing an IACUC is likely to be to approve it and the more importance the IACUC is likely to demand for sufficient justification. Conversely, the less animal 'pain' an experiment causes, the more likely an IACUC will be to approve the experiment and the less importance the IACUC is likely to require.

Problems can arise in determining the level of importance of animal research. Figure 1 above summarizes a way of ranking selected general categories of animal use in terms of importance; I believe that this method of ranking is accepted by a large number of IACUCs in the United States. (It is not clear why many IACUCs tend to rank kinds of animal use in this way; no empirical studies have been done to confirm the pervasiveness of this ranking or to explain why it occurs. My impression in speaking with IACUC members is that the rankings in Figure 1 correspond to a hierarchy of values that members believe they share with laymen and scientists.) Some individuals and IACUCs may disagree with this ranking. There is sometimes disagreement within categories about which animal uses are more or less important. In my recent *Veterinary Ethics* text, I offered several criteria for determining the relative importance of animal experiments, and several tests relating to the justification of animal 'pain'.[31] For example, the more people who suffer from a disease the understanding of which requires animal research, the more important such experimentation is likely to appear. Alternatively, if this disease can already be treated successfully, the value of an experiment that inflicts 'pain' (and certainly of one that inflicts great 'pain') on animals to obtain another cure will seem lessened. An animal experiment aimed at alleviating a disease that very few people suffer from can still be of great value, if, for example, the disease causes death or significant suffering and successful treatments are unavailable. One important issue that some IACUCs face, and about which there is considerable disagreement,[32] is determining the value (and thus the justifiable level of associated animal 'pain') of *basic research.* (This is research that is not intended to prevent or cure disease, but is aimed at obtaining knowledge about humans or animals that might or might not be medically beneficial in the future.[33]) There have been very few published discussions by ethicists or scientists about how we should evaluate the importance or value of such animal experiments relative to the 'pain' they might cause, and more work on this issue is clearly needed.

The traditional approach can also present thorny practical issues for investigators and IACUCs. Although more research on understanding and alleviating 'pain' in animals is being conducted at present than ever before, a great deal remains to be discovered.[34] Researchers and laboratory-animal veterinarians are still learning what kinds of anesthesia, sedatives, and analgesia can prevent or minimize research-animal pain. Even less is known about how to prevent or alleviate unpleasant sensations that do not, strictly speaking, constitute pain—sensations such as distress, discomfort, fear, boredom, and depression—in species to which it is appropriate to attribute such states. The use of drugs and other techniques that prevent or minimize research-animal 'pain' also raises practical issues. IACUCs and investigators must ask how much these techniques cost, who shall pay for them, and whether and how they can be integrated into experimental procedures as well as normal housing and husbandry conditions.

Although these issues may not always be capable of easy resolution, they do not strike most of us as problematic in principle. These issues seem unavoidable because underlying the traditional approach is a series of ethical principles that strike most of us as persuasive. As I have noted above and discussed in detail elsewhere,[35] the traditional approach rests on the principle that because 'pain' is an evil, the intentional infliction of it must have a good justification. The more 'pain' or more severe 'pain' that is to be caused, the stronger must be the justification for inflicting it. In the realm of research, this principle is usually stated in terms of the value of an experiment that will cause animal 'pain': IACUCs, investigators, and regulators assert regularly that the more 'pain' an experiment causes, the greater its value must be for it to be justified. The general principle that infliction of pain (in the strict sense of the term) requires a corresponding justification also applies to the causing of unpleasant mental states such as distress or discomfort. Because such states are usually (but not always) less unpleasant than pain, the intentional infliction of them on research animals generally requires a lower level of justification than does the infliction of pain. Because pain and other unpleasant mental states that I have included under the rubric of 'pain' are all subject to the same requirement of justification relative to their amount or severity, most people agree that the infliction of 'pain' on animals in research must be justified. They also agree that the more animal 'pain' a given experiment or research project is likely to cause, the greater its justification or value must be.

V. The Decline of the Traditional Approach

For well over a decade, I have presented the following case to groups of medical researchers, veterinarians, veterinary students, and IACUC administrators and members.

> A researcher uses radioactive tracer chemicals to study the anatomical structure of the brains of rhesus monkeys. After the chemicals are injected intravenously, the animals are killed painlessly. The brain tissue is then removed for study. At no time do the monkeys experience any pain, distress, or discomfort other than the minimal amount associated with the injections.
>
> Does this experiment have a negative impact on the monkeys' welfare? (For the purposes of this discussion, do not consider how the animals have been housed, cared for, or treated prior to being killed.) Would your response to this question be different if the animals in the experiments were mice?[36]

When I began presenting this case, the overwhelming majority of people in my audiences responded to it in a manner reflecting the traditional approach. They agreed that whether the monkeys ought to be used in such a study is a legitimate question, but most felt that because the animals do not experience 'pain' in the process of being killed, their being killed does not raise a question of animal welfare.

When I present this case today, the first question evokes—in all the kinds of audiences to which I present it—immediate and substantial laughter. When I ask why people are laughing, I am told that it is *obvious* that the monkeys' welfare is affected—negatively—because they are *killed*. Moreover, the majority of respondents want to know precisely what kinds of direct medical benefits the study will generate, or at least what kinds of knowledge it might generate that could eventually be of clear practical benefit. When I ask whether they would require the same level of justification if this study were done on rats and mice, the vast majority say they would not, but almost all of these people insist that even the killing of mice or rats affects these animals' welfare—again, because they are killed. When I ask whether anyone adheres to the view that the monkeys' welfare is not affected because they are killed painlessly, a few people timidly raise their hands. When I read the quotations in Section II in which Hewitt and Fraser and Broom express aspects of the traditional approach, a few more audience members will sometimes admit their adherence to this approach. When I read the quotations in Section III that are taken from the AWA and the PHS policies and are representative of the traditional approach, the general reaction from audiences is that while it is important to spare animals avoidable or unjustifiable 'pain', laws and regulations should be amended to reflect the idea that painless killing of some species is problematic, and always constitutes a negation of welfare.

Yet this is not the end of the matter. Virtually everyone who responds to my case by saying that the painless killing of the monkeys would negatively affect the monkeys' welfare goes on to say that the reason death affects welfare is that death precludes additional experiences that living enables. If one asks why precluding future experiences affects welfare, one invariably hears that killing an animal prevents it from having positive experiences. Very few people say that keeping an animal alive is important because it perpetuates the animal's ability to be free from avoidable or unjustified pain, distress, or discomfort. In other words, behind the notion that animal welfare is negated by death is the view that animal welfare includes *enjoyable* experiences.

VI. The Emerging Approach: Beyond Freedom from 'Pain' to Positive Pleasures and Satisfactions

Even a cursory look at the animal research literature indicates that my contemporary respondents are by no means unique. One finds the following positions expressed repeatedly which collectively I shall call *the emerging approach to animal welfare:*

1. Although we are obligated to avoid causing animals used in research and for other purposes no more 'pain' than is necessary or justifiable, this is not our only obligation.
2. Many animals have a significant interest in positive and enjoyable experiences, such as feelings of satisfaction in activities including eating, socializing with members of the same species (where this is characteristic of a species's behavior), and sexual behavior.
3. Certain positive experiences that animals can undergo constitute part of their welfare.
4. Therefore, killing animals, even painlessly, harms these animals because it prevents them from having these experiences.
5. Therefore, killing animals harms their welfare.
6. We are obligated to protect and assure the welfare of animals that we use in research and for other purposes.
7. Therefore, we are obligated to provide animals that we use in research not just freedom from avoidable or unjustifiable pain; we must also provide them with pleasurable and satisfying experiences.

This set of views is voiced increasingly by IACUC members, investigators, and laboratory-animal veterinarians. For example, the introduction to a recent bibliography of resources for IACUCs that was published by the USDA's Animal Welfare Information Center states:

> Various terms are used to describe the welfare requirements of animals in captivity—"psychological well-being," "ethological" or "behavioral needs," and "environmental enrichment." Whatever the term used, they are essential requirements, not luxuries. Legislation and guidelines in the European Union (EU) and the United States recognize this. The Council Directive of the EU concerning all laboratory animals stipulates that facilities " . . . should permit the satisfaction of certain ethological needs. . . . " In the United States, the Animal Welfare Act requires facilities to provide exercise for dogs and programs to promote the psychological well-being of nonhuman primates, while the U.S. Public Health Service Guide to the Care and Use of Laboratory Animals encourages "enriching the environment as appropriate to the species."[37]

The above paragraph begins with the principle that all who keep animals in "captivity" (including research institutions) are ethically and legally required to assure their welfare. The statement also portrays animal welfare as more than freedom from 'pain'. The term "psychological well-being" certainly connotes positive, enjoyable experiences; so too does the concept of environmental "enrichment," which, as we shall see, is now often used interchangeably with "well-being." The meeting of various ethological "needs" is phrased in terms of "satisfaction"; moreover, this bibliography indicates that the satisfaction of needs that its compilers have in mind includes the enjoyment and pleasure that animals supposedly receive from "enriched" environments.

A striking and important expression of the emerging approach is found in the *Guide for the Care and Use of Laboratory Animals*; as noted above, research institutions that receive federal funds for animal research must consult the *Guide*. The first paragraph of the *Guide* states that:

> This edition of the *Guide for the Care and Use of Laboratory Animals* (the *Guide*) strongly affirms the conviction that all who care for animals in research, teaching, or testing must assume responsibility for their well-being. . . . Decisions associated with the need to use animals are not within the purview of the *Guide,* but responsibility for animal well-being begins for the investigator with that decision. . . . The goal of this *Guide* is to promote the humane care of animals used in biomedical and behavioral research, teaching, and testing; the basic objective is to provide information that will enhance animal well-being, the quality of biomedical research, and the advancement of biologic knowledge that is relevant to humans or animals.[38]

The term "welfare" does not appear in this statement. Indeed, the term does not appear in the *Guide*. The term "well-being," which implies positive satisfactions and enjoyments, has replaced "welfare," which was not interpreted as including such things when the traditional approach to animal welfare held sway.

Saying that we must afford research animals "well-being" appears to imply that we must afford them some—perhaps a great deal of—satisfactions, enjoyments, and pleasures. According to philosopher Bernard Rollin, current demands for environmental enrichment and well-being are just preliminary steps to societal attitudes and laws requiring that all animals kept and used for human purposes shall be provided happiness and, as Rollin puts it, "*happy lives*":

> In the 1985 Amendments [to the Animal Welfare Act] society mandated exercise for dogs and environments for nonhuman primates which "enhance their psychological well-being." These demands presage, I believe, moral requirements which society will very shortly extend to all animals kept in confinement for human benefit, be they animals used in agriculture, zoos, or research facilities. The research community must anticipate these demands and begin to seek animal-friendly housing, care, and husbandry systems that allow the animals to live happy lives while being employed for human benefit.[39]

Calls by scientists and IACUCs for "happy lives" for research animals are not yet commonplace. However, it is important to appreciate how quickly the view that research-animal welfare includes some positive satisfactions and enjoyments is spreading through the biomedical research community. Currently, federal law specifically requires "psychological well-being" only for nonhuman primates used in research.[40] (Among the species included in the taxonomic order "primates" are lemurs, marmosets, monkeys, gibbons, baboons, orangutans, chimpanzees, bonobos, and gorillas.) However, many IACUCs routinely expect (in accordance with the suggestions of the *Guide*) that investigators will provide enriched environments and well-being for other species as well. There has emerged a large and growing literature relating to well-being for many species used in research, including cats, farm animals, ferrets, rabbits, hamsters, gerbils, guinea pigs, rats, mice, and birds.[41]

VII. Problems and Theoretical Underpinnings of the Emerging Approach

The rapidity with which the emerging approach to research-animal welfare is being accepted is matched only by the enormity of the ethical, conceptual, and practical problems it raises.

Ethical Issues Raised by the Emerging Approach

Perhaps the most remarkable feature of the emerging approach is that there has been very little discussion of *why* it is supposedly correct. Most discussions of the moral obligation to assure animal enjoyments or well-being appear to begin with a reminder that in 1985 Congress amended the AWA to require that researchers afford primates "a physical environment adequate to promote their psychological well-being."[42] It is then supposed to be obvious that (1) if providing for the psychological well-being of nonhuman primates used in research is legally required, it must be ethically obligatory as well, and (2) if providing for the psychological well-being of nonhuman primates used in research is ethically required, then researchers have an ethical obligation to provide psychological well-being for all species of research animals capable of experiencing such well-being. Neither (1) nor (2) is self-evidently correct.

"Welfare" and enjoyments

One argument for the emerging approach might claim that welfare must include positive experiences, simply in virtue of what we mean by "welfare." Researchers, then, would be ethically obligated to assure the welfare (*of research animals.*) From this proposition it follows that research animals should be provided positive experiences. However, there are two significant problems with this argument. First, as noted above, for many years scientists and veterinarians spoke of animal welfare in a way that did not imply that "welfare" includes positive experiences; some experts still speak this way. Proponents of the emerging approach might respond that the traditional way of speaking does not employ a proper sense of "welfare," and that if we want to assure research-animal welfare, properly speaking, we must afford positive experiences. To this, adherents of the traditional approach can reply that if animal welfare implies positive experiences for animals, it is not self-evident that we have an ethical obligation to provide such welfare to research animals. Proponents of the emerging approach still need to give an argument explaining why animals *should* be afforded "welfare" in this sense. Second, adherents to the traditional approach can also maintain, as I have argued elsewhere, that what we include in either human or animal "welfare" embodies what we believe a human or animal ought to be provided or ought to have as part of a better rather than worse life.[43] Therefore, one cannot determine whether research-animal welfare includes positive experiences without determining whether research animals ought to be assured such experiences, an issue that is begged when one asserts that animals should be assured "welfare" in the sense in which welfare includes positive experiences.

Enjoyments "in return" for animal use

Adherents of the emerging approach might argue that we owe research animals positive experiences "in return" for our using them in certain ways. There are different possible variants of such an argument, none of which seems especially convincing. One could argue that the mere use—any use—of animals for any research purpose entitles these animals to some positive experiences. But although it seems clear that we should not cause research animals unnecessary or unjustifiable pain, I suggest that it is not self-evident that we must give positive experiences to any animal that we confine or use for any purpose. Perhaps this would often be a nice thing to do, but why is it obligatory if the animals do not suffer or feel 'pain'?

Perhaps advocates of the emerging approach believe that there must be a balancing between the harms inflicted on animals and the positive experiences that they must be given: as a matter of fairness, or perhaps as a matter of maximizing utility, the worse one treats an animal, the more one owes it in positive experiences. There are problems with such a position. First, one needs to get clear about what one means by the kinds of "bad" treatment that presumably require positive experiences. If, as some proponents of the emerging approach may think, the mere keeping of research animals "in captivity" (to use the popular phrase) or the mere killing of research animals entitles these animals to positive experiences, it is again not self-evident why. Perhaps we are supposed to give animals that we cause 'pain' enough positive experiences to "balance out" their 'pain' as a kind of compensation or making-whole. Even if this view has some cogency, however, it does not apply to the large number of animals in research that are not caused 'pain.' Thus, we find a second problem with the argument: it cannot show that assuring the welfare of research animals always requires positive experiences.

Enjoyments preventing or negating 'pain'

A number of scientists and animal behaviorists advocate providing research animals with enriched environments and enjoyable experiences on the ground that enjoyments are necessary to prevent or overcome 'pain' that animals experience in experiments or as a result of their housing conditions. Primatologist Viktor Reinhardt, for example, asserts that the 1985 amendment to the AWA that requires psychological well-being for nonhuman primates does so "in order to ameliorate the adverse effects attendant upon chronic understimulation."[44] Animal scientist Françoise Wemelsfelder states that "millions of laboratory animals are presently housed in small, extremely barren cages, in which opportunities for species-specific interaction with the environment are largely absent"; that in such environments, animals develop abnormal and distressful behavior; and that enriched environments and positive experiences can prevent abnormal behavior and distress.[45] The claim that enrichment or enjoyment should be provided to animals because they prevent or negate 'pain' may sometimes be correct. But this claim does not deviate from the traditional approach because this approach still aims at minimizing animal 'pain' and does not assert, as the emerging approach does, that research animals are entitled to positive experiences in their own right.

Happiness and an animal's "nature"

Bernard Rollin offers what is supposed to be an argument for the emerging approach. He maintains that all animals have a nature, "essence," or *telos*. For Rollin, these are not just biologically built-in attributes, but characteristics or interests the satisfaction of which constitutes the very definition of the kinds of animals we are considering. He asserts that "we protect those interests of the individual that we consider essential to being human, to human nature, from being submerged, even by the common good. Those moral/legal fences that so protect the individual human are called *rights* and are based on plausible assumptions regarding what is essential to being human."[46] Rollin believes that a "new social ethic" is beginning to apply this principle to animals, although this ethic does not attempt to give animals human rights.

> Since animals do not have the same natures and interests flowing from these natures as humans do, human rights do not fit animals. Animals do not have basic natures that demand speech, religion, or property: thus according them these rights would be absurd. On the other hand, animals have natures of their own (what I have, following Aristotle, called their *telos*) and interests that flow from these natures, and the thwarting of these interests matters to animals as much as the thwarting of speech matters to humans. The agenda is not, for mainstream society, making animals "equal" to people. It is, rather, preserving the common-sense insight that "fish gotta swim and birds gotta fly," and suffer if they don't.[47]

> [T]he spider . . . has an intrinsic nature connected with being a spider, one that requires it to be alive. When it ceases to be alive, it is like the rock, and there is little difference between a crushed dead spider and a dried-up dead spider. . . . But when the spider is alive, it has what Aristotle called a *telos,* a nature, a function, a set of activities intrinsic to it, evolutionarily determined and genetically imprinted, that constitute its "living spiderness." Furthermore, its life consists precisely in a struggle to per-

form these functions, to actualize this nature, to fulfill these needs, to maintain this life, what Hobbes and Spinoza referred to as the *conatus* or drive to preserve its integrity and unity.[48]

Rollin maintains that because of the importance to an animal of any inhibition or obliteration of its *telos,* we are ethically obligated to afford this *telos* great respect. We may sometimes be justified in thwarting or negating an animal's *telos,* but we may do so only for the most significant reasons. For example, according to Rollin, attempting to stay alive is part of an animal's *telos,* so that when we kill an animal, we violate its *telos.* The eating of animals, in Rollin's opinion, does not provide us with a sufficiently strong justification for violating their *telos.*[49]

In approving of this "new social ethic," which will require that all animals kept in captivity be afforded happy lives, Rollin appears to argue that it is part of the *telos* of research animals that they be happy and, indeed, that they live happy lives. He also appears to maintain that unless any animal in captivity lives a happy life, it will suffer, not just in the sense of not being happy (which would be an unusual and, I would argue, inappropriate sense of the term "suffering"), but in the sense of feeling unhappy and miserable. This claim—that unless animals in captivity are happy, they will be miserable—seems patently false, even if we assume that all research animals have a *telos* in some sense and that we have a clear idea of what it means for research animals of various species and in various circumstances to have happy lives. Some research animals may suffer by being deprived of certain experiences that seem natural to their species, and this may provide a strong reason not to deprive them of such experiences. But it is quite another thing to claim that such animals, or all research animals, will suffer if they do not have happy lives. (For example, many species of birds that would naturally fly but are artificially rendered incapable of flight appear to do just fine in zoos and in homes, Rollin's assertions to the contrary not withstanding. Some of these birds might be happier if they were allowed to fly, but it does not follow from this that they ought to be allowed to fly or that they will suffer if they cannot fly.) Some animals may feel some distress at not being able to experience a certain desired satisfaction (for example, by being deprived of food when they are hungry). But it is quite another thing to claim that such animals therefore suffer, and suffer to the extent (presumably a significant extent) that they must be accorded at least a *right* to such satisfactions. In fact many, perhaps the great majority of animals used in research, experience little if any 'pain' during their lives, and certainly do not suffer. Furthermore, even if Rollin can offer a persuasive reason for respecting an animal's *telos* other than that inhibiting its *telos* causes it to suffer, it is highly implausible to suppose that having a happy life or even not suffering is part of the *telos* of all research animals. Most animals in the wild spend most of their waking hours engaged in the difficult tasks of obtaining food or avoiding predators. It does not seem even remotely plausible to postulate that most animals in the wild or animals bred for use in research laboratories have a need or drive to be happy or to lead a generally happy life in the same way in which they have physiological needs to eat, drink, or eliminate. Indeed, some animal scientists argue that stressful and often *unpleasant* sensations such as hunger and stress are an essential part of many animals' experiences (part of what Rollin might call their *telos*) because such sensations help in obtaining food and avoiding predators.[50]

In sum, if there is a convincing reason why people who use animals in research have an obligation to assure these animals happy lives, Rollin does not provide it. He may be correct in predicting that society will soon demand happy lives for research animals. However, it does not follow from this that the emerging approach, or the demands for animal happiness that it includes, are ethically defensible.[51]

Conceptual Issues Raised by the Emerging Approach

Insufficient discussion of definitions

Just as there has been virtually no sustained argument in support of the emerging approach, neither has sufficient attention been paid to terms that are frequently used to express the approach, such as "enrichment," "well-being," "psychological well-being," and "happiness." It is beyond the scope of this paper to attempt a detailed analysis of such terms or to document the many different senses in which each has been used in the animal research literature. The following discussion is intended to point out that although advocates of the emerging approach confidently demand that research animals must be afforded positive experiences, these advocates do not clearly define what these experiences are supposed to be. Worse, the use of unclear or ambiguous terms that many people apparently find compelling appears to substitute for *arguments* in support of the emerging approach.

"Well-being," "psychological well-being," and "enrichment"

"Well-being" and "psychological well-being." A committee appointed by the National Research Council issued a lengthy report in 1998 intended to guide institutions using nonhuman primates about how to provide these animals the "psychological well-being" required by the AWA. This report announces that the term "psychological well-being" refers "to [the animal's] mental state. It cannot be defined in terms of the [the animal's] environment, although environments certainly influence individual well-being."[52] Having indicated that well-being is an experience or set of experiences, the report claims that "psychological well-being is an abstraction that is inferred by measuring behavioral

and physiological variables in the affected primates to determine whether a manipulation had the desired effect."[53] This suggests that psychological well-being is not an experience, but a concept that includes a number of different factors, some of which are not feelings or experiences. The report then states:

> An emerging consensus suggests that in addition to physical health the following criteria are important in assessing psychological well-being:
> - The animal's ability to cope effectively with day-to-day changes in its social and physical environment (with reference to meeting its own needs).
> - The animal's ability to engage in species-typical activities.
> - The absence of maladaptive or pathological behavior that results in self-injury or other undesirable consequences.
> - The presence of a balanced temperament (appropriate balance of aggression and passivity) and absence of chronic signs of distress as indexed by the presence of affiliative versus distress vocalizations, facial expressions, postures, and physiological responses (e.g., labored breathing, excessive cardiac response, and abnormal hormonal concentrations).[54]

Most of these criteria do not logically imply the presence of any positive mental states, and in many circumstances may not in fact involve them. Some animals may be able to cope with environmental challenges, engage in species-specific behavior, and avoid maladaptive or pathological behavior without living happy, pleasant lives, or without having many enjoyable experiences. Only the final suggested criterion speaks explicitly about mental states. The second part of this criterion appears to identify well-being with the absence of distress, hardly an adequate characterization of well-being. The first part of the criterion calls for a "balanced temperament," which could be part of well-being or happiness if by these states one means something like equanimity or peace of mind. However, by a "balanced temperament" the report means a balance between passivity and aggression. Not only is it unclear what this means, but it does not seem to require a great deal of enjoyments or satisfactions or, on balance, an enjoyable or happy existence. The report makes even more obscure what concept of psychological well-being it employs when it summarizes the above criteria for psychological well-being by calling them criteria for "a primate's psychological health."[55] No definition or characterization is offered of this latter concept.

As primatologists Stephen Suomi and Melinda Novak observe,

> [a]t this point it is safe to say that there is no universally accepted way of defining psychological well-being for nonhuman primates among researchers, let alone among veterinarians, regulators, animal rights activists,

or members of the general public. Instead, a wide range of specific definitions permeates the scientific literature, in many cases representing quite
different points of view or even general frames of reference. For example,
some definitions rely primarily on behavioral characteristics or the product
of behavioral events such as successful reproduction or care of offspring.
. . . Others focus more on physiological processes, on preestablished levels
of certain hormones, or on changes in the immune system. . . . Still others
eschew any specific definitions of what constitutes psychological well-being and focus instead on what it is not.[56]

"Enrichment." The term "enrichment" is also often used ambiguously and
uncritically. When the term was first proposed, it meant adding features to the
environment that would present animals additional and varied stimuli, usually
of the sort experienced by their species in the wild. For example, some studies
show that chickens housed in environments enriched in this sense exhibit less
fear of novel places as well as reduced aggressiveness, cannibalism, and mortality.[57] Other studies, however, have found that enriched environments cause
an increase in presumably unpleasant mental states such as aggression. (In one
such study male mice were found to be quicker to show signs of aggression
when in large wooden cages or in standard plastic cages to which additional objects and extra sources of water had been added.[58]) However, the assumption
that enrichment *must* make for happier animals has become so ingrained that
the term is now commonly used synonymously with "well-being" or "psychological well-being,"[59] or to refer to environmental manipulations that improve
the apparent functioning of animals.[60] Identification of enrichment with well-
being conflates mental states that animals might experience with manipulated
environments that supposedly produce these states. This often makes it unclear
whether one is supposed to produce a mental state in an animal or merely provide the animal with an objectively observable and manipulable environment.

Animal "enjoyment," "satisfaction," "comfort," and "happiness"

It is not self-evident what we should mean when ascribing to animals mental states such as enjoyment, satisfaction, comfort, and happiness. Images of
cats purring or dogs wagging their tails suggest pleasure and satisfaction. Even
if such descriptions of satisfied animals are sometimes accurate, in a wide range
of cases it is not clear that we can say research animals are enjoying themselves
or feeling satisfied or comfortable. One might *say,* for example, that a laboratory mouse eating mouse chow or drinking water feels the same feelings of
satisfaction that we do when we eat a meal or take a drink, but this is an assumption and no more. What are we to make of a mouse sitting quietly in its

bedding without overt signs of distress (such as shuddering or vocalizations)? Can we conclude that the animal is "satisfied" or "comfortable"? If this is supposed to mean that the mouse is experiencing feelings of satisfaction or equanimity, what evidence do we have for such an assertion? Many scientists are aware of problems in attributing positive mental states to animals, and typically respond not by relinquishing their claim that animals have these experiences, but by defining the experiences in ways that eliminate experiential elements essential to the use of mentalistic terms when applied to humans. For example, in its 1992 report, *Recognition and Alleviation of Pain and Distress in Laboratory Animals,* the Committee on Pain and Distress in Laboratory Animals convened by the National Research Council defined "comfort" as "a state of physiologic, psychologic, and behavioral equilibrium in which an animal is accustomed to its environment and engages in normal activities such as feeding, drinking, grooming, social interaction, sleeping-waking cycles, and reproduction. The behavior of such an animal remains relatively stable without noteworthy fluctuation."[61] This definition of "comfort" assures that virtually all laboratory animals, including those with the most rudimentary mental capacities (such as fish), experience comfort, because almost all animals are capable of meeting the purely behavioral conditions (the specified "normal activities") enumerated in the definition. But it hardly follows that all these animals are capable of feeling "comfort" in the ordinary sense, which implies subjective *experiences* of satisfaction or contentment. Employing the strictly behavioral definition might lead one to think that some laboratory animals are much more mentally sophisticated than they really are. Furthermore, regarding animals that may be capable of experiencing "comfort" in the ordinary sense, the strictly behavioral definition may, paradoxically, deprive them of positive experiences. This could occur if researchers assess whether animals are experiencing comfort simply by referring to the presence of behavioral conditions specified in the definition, rather than by referring to evidence of positive mental states in the animals themselves.

It is even more problematic to apply to animals the notions of "happiness" and "happy life." Presumably, happiness is more than a fleeting enjoyment, satisfaction, or comfortable moment. How many and what kinds of positive sensations or experiences are needed for a research animal to feel happiness or have a happy life? Do happiness or a happy life require not just positive experiences, but also an appreciation that one is having these experiences? If so, it is not clear that we can attribute happiness to all (or even most) species of laboratory animals, because it is not clear that they have a sense of *themselves* having positive experiences. In describing people who have had happy lives, we often mean that those individuals have had long lives with many pleasures and fulfillments. Is this a requirement that must be fulfilled for a research animal to have a "happy life"?

Practical Issues Raised by the Emerging Approach

Will animal enjoyments and satisfactions affect the science?

One question that has received very little attention in the animal research literature, but is becoming a concern to some scientists, is how providing enjoyments and satisfactions to research animals might affect the scientific results of important experiments. Primatologist John Capitanio has found that the survival of monkeys infected with simian immunodeficiency virus[62] is significantly decreased when they are exposed to social change (for example, by being moved into paired housing with other monkeys) either after infection or in a ninety-day period preceding infection.[63] It seems, therefore, that "enrichment" may significantly affect immune function, and not always for the better. If an investigator working on immune function in monkeys keeps his animals in pairs (as most advocates of "enrichment" or "psychological well-being" now insist), the animals might be substantially different, physiologically or immunologically, from monkeys not kept in pairs. As a consequence, the immune function of paired monkeys may not be a good model for monkey—or human—immune function generally. The desire to make such monkeys happier by keeping them in pairs may therefore make the data obtained from them questionable. Studies of animal enrichment and studies of animal models of human diseases are almost always completely divorced from each other, so there is no way to tell if attempts to provide animal enrichment are influencing the models. Yet many scientists assume that a happier animal makes for a better scientific model—usually without any evidence that this is the case.[64]

How much will animal enjoyments and satisfactions cost?

Other questions that must also be seriously considered by those who expect institutions to give positive satisfactions to research animals include how much this will cost and who will pay. A number of facilities have incurred expenses in the tens or hundreds of thousands of dollars by providing enlarged enclosures and social housing for nonhuman primates. General acceptance of the emerging approach would necessitate enriched environments and enjoyable experiences for *all* research species, and would thus require large expenditures. Until it is clear what constitutes such environments and experiences, and how much satisfaction is supposed to be furnished to various kinds of research animals under various circumstances, it is impossible to venture a guess about what such "enrichment" will cost. Nor is it clear who will pay. Many researchers already pay their institutions significant amounts for housing their animals; these payments usually come out of the grants that pay for the researchers' work. Furthermore, substantial competition exists for available grant money, and IACUCs typically have no budgets of their own or have only enough funds to run their administrative functions. Many research projects may be precluded altogether: investigators and their institutions could lack sufficient funds to do research in a manner that prevents and alleviates any attendant animal 'pain', much less in a way that provides the levels of animal enjoyment or happiness that may become mandatory. Perhaps grants for research will come to include funding for animal enrichment, but if this happens, the likely result is that fewer experiments will be funded.

How strongly must animal enjoyments and satisfactions count?

The most serious practical issue that the emerging approach will pose for IACUCs—if this approach replaces the traditional approach in committee evaluations of animal experiments—pertains to the deliberations the approach will demand when a committee is determining whether various experiments and housing conditions are acceptable. As noted in section IV, IACUCs now engage in a rough balancing of likely gains (practical and theoretical) from proposed research against the 'pain' that the relevant experiments, living environments, and husbandry conditions cause to the animals. This deliberation can be difficult enough, but at least it is restricted to balancing 'pain' against purported experimental results. Current laws allow investigators to subject animals to 'pain' when it is unavoidable given justified experimental aims and designs. Presumably, the emerging approach will also allow IACUCs to consider the importance and value of experiments in determining whether certain animals must be afforded positive experiences, what kinds of positive experiences they must have, and how many of these positive experiences they must have. However, it is not clear from current expressions of the emerging approach how strong the requirement is for positive experiences. Should committees begin with the presumption that research animals must be given lives filled with great pleasures and enjoyments? If so, what kind of research would be able to counter such a presumption and allow researchers to provide less? How much less? If IACUCs should not begin with an assumed strong obligation to provide animals great and long-lasting enjoyments, it is not immediately obvious how much enjoyment and satisfaction committees should ordinarily require. Will, for example, a few daily pleasures do? If not, why not? And again, how much will it take in terms of the value of an experiment to override such a requirement?

The traditional approach assumes that 'pains' are bad for animals, just as they are for humans, and does not make less of mouse 'pain', for example, than it does of 'pain' in cats, dogs, or primates. It is not clear whether advocates of the emerging approach believe we must (1) afford all research animals the same amount or degree of pleasure, (2) afford each animal the maximum amount of the kinds of pleasures it can experience, or (3) afford each animal an equal proportion of the amount of the kinds of pleasures it can experience. Do some animals deserve more pleasures, or more extensive kinds of pleasures, than others? If so, why, and how many and what kinds of pleasures?

Even primatologists—scientists who study primate behavior and psychology—cannot agree about how to define and measure "psychological well-being" in primates, the kind of animal in which well-being has been investigated the most. Given the inability of these specialists to clarify this concept with respect to *one* group of animals, how are *IACUCs* to know how to define "well-being" for *all* species used in research? Because we also lack clear ethical principles or even rough intuitions about how to factor animal enjoyments— assuming we can agree on how to define them—into deliberations about the appropriateness of experiments, the process of applying the emerging approach will be a nightmare for IACUCs and investigators. Many will simply not know how to proceed. Perhaps government regulations would help, but it is difficult to know where these will come from, because animal-use regulations are rarely adopted until there is already something approaching a consensus regarding the practice (or practices) in question. The experience of the USDA in attempting to regulate the psychological well-being of nonhuman primates indicates that government assistance in applying the emerging approach to all research species is quite unlikely. After Congress required in 1985 that primates be provided with psychological well-being, it soon became clear that scientists and veterinarians had little understanding of what they were required to promote. Although the USDA proposed specific rules to promote the psychological well-being of primates, there were so many objections and questions raised about whether these rules had any scientific basis that the department rescinded them, and then eventually issued "performance" standards rather than "engineering" standards. This distinction is an important one: *performance standards* set final goals that regulated entities must meet, but allow these entities to decide how to reach these goals; *engineering standards* impose specific steps that regulated entities must follow to reach specified goals. (For example, a requirement that research laboratories house their mice in cages that are sufficient to allow the mice to exhibit normal behavior would be a performance standard. A requirement that mice be kept in cages of a specified length, width, and height would be an engineering standard.) The USDA's current performance standards regarding primate psychological well-being require institutions to rely on whatever scientists and veterinarians believe about achieving primate psychological well-being. The government has been unable to provide clear guidance to IACUCs and investigators about the psychological well-being of primates; therefore, it seems highly unlikely it will be able to do so for other research animals.

Without clear or intuitively convincing ethical standards with which to apply the emerging approach, many IACUCs are likely to engage in protracted and rancorous deliberations. Some investigators may come to believe (correctly) that their research is not being judged by the same standards as the work of other investigators in their institution. IACUCs at different institutions will likely adopt different ethical standards and policies, leading to complaints by investigators that they are not being held to the same standards as researchers elsewhere. Inconsistency and disagreement among IACUCs at different institutions will create controversy and complaints in the research community and by the public, who may be influenced by opponents of research into believing that greater government control is needed. For all its flaws, the traditional approach has prevented many of these problems, because it has allowed IACUCs and investigators across the country (and indeed, throughout the world) to operate with a shared and strongly held set of ethical beliefs about appropriate animal care and use.

VIII. From Research Tools to Friends

The emerging approach will do more than create difficulties for IACUCs. It will fundamentally transform how research animals are viewed.

Application of the Emerging Approach to All Research Animals

As the reactions to my hypothetical monkey experiment indicate, once people believe that the welfare of one species consists of its not just avoiding 'pain' but enjoying positive experiences, it will be difficult for them not to extend this view to other species. It may be that the "welfare," so conceived, of a mouse would be composed of fewer and more primitive kinds of satisfactions than would the welfare of a rhesus monkey. However, if one believes that positive experiences for an animal are part of its welfare, it is not clear how one could restrict this belief to primates or a limited number of favored species.

From Enjoyments and Satisfactions to a Happy Life

Moreover, as Rollin argues, if society believes that all animals kept in confinement for human purposes are entitled to some positive enjoyments, it will be extremely difficult for society not to advocate providing such animals with happy lives. If pleasure or enjoyable experiences are goods for animals as they are for humans, it would appear that more pleasure is better than less. Therefore, an animal's welfare is better served the more pleasures and enjoyments it experiences. It would appear, moreover, that the *best* state of welfare for an animal would be a happy life, because happiness (by definition, the critical part of a "happy life") seems to be the ultimate positive good that a sentient being can experience.

Balancing Happiness Against Research

If we have an obligation to provide research animals with happiness and happy lives, we are saying that the animals' happiness is an end in itself, a fundamental requirement, that must (together with the likelihood of research-animal 'pain') be balanced against the potential benefits of experiments to determine the experiments' appropriateness. Thus, even if the supposed obligation to assure research-animal happiness does not always preclude animal experiments, any method of experimentation or housing that does not assure such happiness would provide another, new factor that would count, to some extent at least, against doing such experiments. However, happiness is not a minor condition; it is a major benefit. Therefore, if we have even a moral obligation to assure research-animal happiness, this must surely be a *strong* obligation, one with great weight. If this were so, we would be able to justify animal experiments that did not assure animal happiness only when such experiments were of great value, just as we already believe that very painful experiments can be justified only if they are of great value. It seems clear that many experiments and kinds of research that are now regarded as acceptable would no longer be so because one would not be able to demonstrate that they are of *great* value. For example, few if any IACUCs now object to using mice for the harvesting of tissues (such as those of the liver and kidney) to study the effects of various chemicals on such tissues. These animals are routinely euthanized soon after their arrival at a research facility, and doing this to animals is usually justified on the ground that they will experience no 'pain.' However, if investigators have a strong obligation to give these animals *happiness* or *happy lives* before they are killed, a demonstration of the research's great value would have to be made, something that often will not be possible. Moreover, fulfilling an obligation to provide research animals with happiness or happy lives would appear to require allowing such animals to enjoy themselves for at least some time before they are killed. This, in turn, might require that before a researcher may euthanize an animal, he must know the animal's prior history in order to gauge how many happy experiences it has had in the past. All these things would involve time and money that many investigators do not have.

Another inevitable consequence of viewing research animals as entitled to happy lives will be that some species—perhaps most—will be exempt from research altogether. I have spoken with a number of scientists who believe that it is never acceptable to do medical research using chimpanzees because of these animals' substantial intelligence and their capacity for sophisticated pleasures. (In fact, research on chimpanzees is uncommon.) I have spoken with members of many IACUCs who indicate that their committees would be extremely reluctant to approve experiments not only on chimpanzees, but on other primates as well, such as baboons and macaque monkeys. These IACUC members suggest that such experiments would only be approved if there were a showing of great benefit from the proposed research. As more species of primates and non-primates come to be viewed as capable of, and then entitled to, enjoyments and, indeed, happy lives, the same protection will be extended to them.

Caring about Beings Entitled to Happy Lives

Ultimately, the most important effect of the emerging approach will be that many—perhaps most—research animals will be viewed in much the same way as we view pets. We will come to care about them and their lives so much that experimenting on them will be unthinkable.

One does not care about or seek to assure an *animal's* happiness in a vacuum. We must distinguish between two different positions. On the one hand, one may want to respect an animal's natural tendencies and behaviors and to seek to give them opportunities for expression. On the other hand, one may want to make that animal *happy*. The former attitude is defensible on a number of grounds, including the fact that certain kinds of treatment that restrict natural behavior do sometimes appear to cause animals to suffer. However, animal happiness is not a common state in the wild. To want animals to live happy lives is to want animals to have something they do not ordinarily have, something that can require special manipulations of their environments and lives. Some of these manipulations, such as the provision of good veterinary care, can be very costly. Once one believes that research animals are entitled to happiness—as benevolent, humane, and obviously correct as this belief seems to be to many people—one has *already* committed oneself to viewing research animals in ways that prevent their use in research. The belief should not be embraced without an understanding of this implication.

There are animals about which we know enough to be able to say that they can have enjoyments and live happy lives (although we may sometimes exaggerate the nature and depth of their sensibilities). Society has gained this knowledge through generations of observation, and individuals have gained it through continuous, lengthy interaction that is sometimes quite close. These animals are pets: dogs, cats, birds, and other animal species typically regarded as friends, and often as members of the family. (Note that it may not be possible to attribute mental states such as happiness to all animals kept as pets—reptiles, for example—but there can be no doubt about the more sophisticated species.) Many people want to make such animals happy, and sometimes accept significant economic and personal sacrifices to do so. We do these things for our pets because we *care* about them. As I argue in *Veterinary Ethics,* it is not irrational or ethically indefensible to care about these animals while accepting the use of others, even members of the same species, in research.[65] We are generally justified in heeding the needs and desires of members of our families more closely than we do those of strangers, and we have ethical duties to family members that sometimes require ignoring or even slighting others. Likewise, it is both sensible and sometimes ethically *obligatory* for us to care about and seek the health, welfare, and happiness of pets. We are not obligated to befriend them and take them into our homes and lives, but once we get to know individual pets, we do things that make it psychologically impossible and sometimes morally impermissible not to seek good things for them. (I had a wonderful dog, a friend for eighteen years. In his younger days, there was never a moment in which he did not entertain or accompany me when I needed or wanted his attentions. I cannot confidently say that he consciously sought to please me, and I certainly cannot say that he did these things "in return" for my entertaining and caring about him. Nevertheless, when old age brought about the decline of his health and the loss of his eyesight, I spared neither time nor expense in keeping his life comfortable and pleasant. Many people can tell similar stories.) We make our pets dependent on us, not just for food and shelter but also for emotional satisfactions they clearly enjoy. Many of us become dependent on them for companionship and the happiness they can bring us. Once taken into our lives, pets can become an important part of them, and the complex patterns of dependency, interaction, and friendship or love that we have with our pets make it impossible not to care—and sometimes care deeply— about them.

It may be possible for some people who do not want to view research animals as friends or companions to attempt nevertheless to give them happy lives. However, I submit that over time, people who attempt to give animals happy lives in a research setting will come to view them as pets or friends. For once one does attend to a research animal's happiness, one comes to view the animal as an individual, the needs and interests of which are important. If it is not happy, one wants to make it so; if it is happy, one wants to make it happier. One attends to it often, seeking to know how it is doing. One develops a bond with any animal that one cares enough about to want it to have a happy life (assuming it is a kind of animal to which it is sensible to attribute happiness). Once this bond is established with an animal, it becomes extremely difficult to do anything that causes the animal 'pain', to use it in a scientific study, or to kill it. In short, it becomes extremely difficult to use the animal in research. This is precisely what sociologist Arnold Arluke has found in studies of laboratory-animal technicians. Animals to which the technicians became attached, about whose happiness they cared, came to be viewed as pets, which led to their being spared from research when the technicians could accomplish this.

> Workers still found ways to treat animals as pets and express their affection for them. Technicians and caretakers would single out an animal for a laboratory pet. Often a mouse, rat, or guinea pig, these animals were not experimented upon or at least not sacrificed. In addition to being named, caged singly, fed special foods, and given much attention, they would also sometimes be taught tricks and allowed occasionally to run free in the laboratory. They were safe animals with whom workers could become attached without fear of loss. Affection for animals also resulted in 'rescues' where they were taken home by workers who were strongly attached to them. For instance, in all seven dog laboratories studied, in the previous year staff members had quietly taken home at least one animal.[66]

In the short term, if the emerging approach gains ground and is applied to a wider range of research animals in a wider range of research settings, animal research will become more expensive, and more troublesome and difficult for IACUCs to approve. These factors will lead to reduced amounts of research. Eventually, if research animals come to be viewed as our friends—and as worthy of happiness and happy lives as we are—animal research will stop. This is precisely what animal activists who promote the emerging approach want.

IX. A Paradigm Shift: Why It Is Happening and Why It Matters

The contributions of animal research to the health, safety, and well-being of both humans and animals have been enormous. Without animal research, very few of the medical advances we expect today for ourselves and our loved ones would be possible.[67] Vaccines for rabies were developed using dogs and rabbits. Smallpox, which killed more than two million people, can now be prevented because of research on cows. Diphtheria was conquered with research on guinea pigs and horses. Polio, the scourge of the 1950s, would have been impossible to prevent without the use of monkeys. Because of animal research, we now have vaccines for measles, rubella, chicken pox, hepatitis B, and Lyme disease. The insulin that allows millions of people with diabetes to continue to live was developed using dogs. The effectiveness of penicillin and other antibiotics that have saved tens (perhaps hundreds) of millions of lives was established through research on mice and other rodents. So many procedures and medications that prevent death, spare pain, and make life productive and enjoyable have been developed through animal research that it would take a discussion many times the length of this paper to document them all. Cardiac bypass surgery, cardiac pacemaker implants, angioplasty to unblock clogged cardiac arteries, artificial hip replacements for victims of arthritis, fixation devices to mend broken bones, cataract surgery, kidney dialysis, antibiotics, medications for high blood pressure, anticoagulants to prevent clots and stroke, chemotherapy and radiation therapy for cancers, rehabilitation techniques for victims of stroke and spinal cord injuries, laparoscopic surgery—these are just a few of the medical advances that have been developed or tested on animals.

Animals, too, benefit immeasurably from animal research. Vaccines for distemper, parvovirus, rabies, and feline leukemia; antibiotics for infections; surgical treatments for injuries and infirmities; nutritional foods—all these and much more have been developed using research animals.[68] Indeed, many procedures and treatments (such as chemotherapy, antibiotics, hip replacement and other orthopedic surgical techniques, and medications to control glaucoma and blindness) were initially developed or tested on animals for use on humans, and are now used to treat animals as well.[69]

Today, researchers are using animals in attempts to understand (and hopefully cure) AIDS, breast cancer, diabetes, leukemia, Alzheimer's disease, amyotrophic lateral sclerosis (Lou Gehrig's disease), chronic pain, cystic fibrosis, and a myriad of diseases, injuries, and infirmities that continue to plague humans and animals alike. To stop or seriously curtail animal research would thus cause serious harm to many. The vast majority of physicians, veterinarians, and biomedical researchers know this. They refute the claims of activists that animal research has not done any good and is unnecessary for future medical progress with overwhelming evidence and compelling arguments. Yet many of these same scientists, physicians, and veterinarians are joining the increasing chorus of calls for animal happiness that threatens animal research. Why is this happening?

Although the notion of a "paradigm shift" may be overused, it is appropriate in the case of the movement, in society and the research community, from the traditional approach that seeks to minimize animal 'pain' to the emerging approach that calls for animal happiness. As noted in Section VII, one usually finds virtually no argument for the emerging approach or for claims that it is superior to the traditional view. The *Guide,* for example, does not explain *why* all who use animals in research are obligated to assure animal well-being instead of welfare.[70] This is supposedly a truism about which there neither is nor can be any disagreement. Many respondents to my hypothetical monkey case, as well as many laboratory-animal veterinarians and IACUC members, find it patently obvious—not even worth discussion—that environments should be enriched to promote research-animal well-being and psychological well-being. They may admit that this cannot be accomplished now in light of financial constraints and lack of knowledge about enrichment, but there appears to be little disagreement about its desirability. An apparently increasing number of IACUC members, veterinarians, and scientists are so certain that enrichment and animal happiness are good that they do not ask how they might affect scientific results. Futhermore, many of these same people admit that they cannot define or carefully characterize animal "well-being," but insist that it be promoted anyway. The term "enrichment," which need not imply animal happiness, has nevertheless become synonymous with "happiness" for many in the research community; this is because they simply assume that making housing environments more "normal" or "natural" will produce the happiness we supposedly must seek for research animals. With very little empirical evidence about what kinds of pleasures animals of various species are capable of experiencing, it is assumed that the vast majority of animals used in research are capable of the most varied and exquisite pleasures.

In short, a new way of viewing research animals appears to be taking hold, a way that is neither motivated by nor susceptible to factual verification. It is beyond the scope of this essay or my own expertise to speculate about why this is happening. Franklin Loew, former dean of the veterinary schools at Tufts University and Cornell University, has suggested in another context that most people are coming to view all animals through an urban and suburban prism.[71] Most people now live in cities or suburbs, and the only live animals with which they come into contact are pets. These people, Loew believes, begin with a paradigm of animals as pets and believe that all animals have the same capacities and are entitled to the same benefits as their beloved cats and dogs. Loew's hypothesis is interesting, but it does not explain why scientists and veterinarians, who presumably know more about research animals, would accept such a view. The passage of the amendments to the AWA in 1985 marked the first time that the provision of psychological well-being was required for certain research animals; this was a critical event in encouraging the view that some research animals should be given positive enjoyments. However, this too cannot explain why so many in the research community now find it obvious that all research animals deserve happiness. Note that most scientists and veterinarians who initially opposed the amendments' requirement did so on the ground that we simply do not know what psychological well-being is in primates, much less how to achieve it.

Unless we can understand why the emerging approach is gaining ground in society and the research community, there will be no way to combat it. The task of critical examination will become more difficult—and will require even more courage on the part of critics—the more the emerging approach insinuates itself into society's view of research animals. We will need more careful conceptual analysis of general terminology such as "enrichment," "welfare," "well-being," and "psychological well-being," as well as analysis of terms that

ᵉ positive mental states that animals (or at least some animals) may be
ᵗ to experience. We need more careful empirical study of what happens
to aɴimals in so-called "enriched" environments, and of the extent to which
these environments skew or invalidate experimental data. Most importantly,
however, we must understand that demands for animal happiness posed by the
emerging approach to animal welfare are dangerous to the research enterprise.

NOTES

1. Jerrold Tannenbaum, "Ethics and Pain Research in Animals," *ILAR Journal* 40, no. 3 (1999): 97–110.
2. Gary L. Francione, *Animals, Property, and the Law* (Philadelphia: Temple University Press, 1995), 17–32.
3. *Animal Welfare Act,* 7 U.S.C. sec. 2131 et seq. (1994).
4. *Health Research Extension Act of 1985,* 42 U.S.C. sec. 289(d) (1994).
5. H. B. Hewitt, "The Use of Animals in Experimental Cancer Research," in David Sperlinger, ed., *Animals in Research: New Perspectives on Animal Experimentation* (Chichester, UK: John Wiley and Sons, 1981), 170.
6. A. F. Fraser and D. M. Broom, *Farm Animal Behaviour and Welfare,* 3rd ed. (London: Baillière Tindall, 1990), 257.
7. Jerrold Tannenbaum, "Animals and the Law: Property, Cruelty, Rights," *Social Research* 62, no. 3 (Fall 1995): 567–77.
8. Hewitt, "The Use of Animals in Experimental Cancer Research," 170.
9. 7 U.S.C. sec. 2132(g) (1994).
10. These requirements may all be found at 7 U.S.C. sec. 2143(a) et seq. (1994).
11. 9 C.F.R. sec. 2.31(d)(1)(i) (2000).
12. 9 C.F.R. sec. 2.31(d)(1)(ii) (2000).
13. 9 C.F.R. sec. 2.31(d)(1)(x) (2000).
14. 7 U.S.C. sec. 2143(a)(3)(C)(iv) (1994); 9 C.F.R. sec. 2.31(d)(1)(iv)(C) (2000).
15. 9 C.F.R. sec. 2.31(d)(1)(v) (2000).
16. 9 C.F.R. sec. 2.31(d)(1)(ix) (2000).
17. 9 C.F.R. sec. 2.31(d)(1)(xi) (2000); 9 C.F.R. sec. 1.1."Euthanasia" (2000).
18. 7 U.S.C. sec. 2143(a)(7)(A) (1994).
19. 9 C.F.R. sec. 2.36(b)(1) (2000).
20. 9 C.F.R. sec. 2.36(b)(2) (2000).
21. 9 C.F.R. sec. 2.36(b)(7) (2000).
22. National Institutes of Health—Office for Protection from Research Risks (NIH-OPRR), *Public Health Service Policy on Humane Care and Use of Laboratory Animals* (Washington, DC: U.S. Department of Health and Human Services, 1996), 9.
23. "U.S. Government Principles for the Utilization and Care of Vertebrate Animals Used in Testing, Research, and Training," in NIH-OPRR, *Policy on Humane Care and Use of Laboratory Animals,* i.
24. The National Research Council (NRC) was organized by the U.S. National Academy of Sciences (NAS) in 1916 to undertake studies and produce reports for agen-

cies of the federal government on issues relevant to science. Currently administered by the NAS, the National Academy of Engineering (NAE), and the Institute of Medicine, the NRC is the principal operating agency of the NAS and the NAE in providing scientific studies and policy recommendations for the government, the public, scientists, and engineers.

25. National Research Council and Institute for Laboratory Animal Resources, *Guide for the Care and Use of Laboratory Animals,* 7th ed. (Washington, DC: National Academy Press, 1996), 64.
26. 9 C.F.R. sec. 2.31(d)(1)(iii) (2000).
27. Principle 3 of the "U.S. Government Principles," in NIH-OPRR, *Policy on the Humane Care and Use of Laboratory Animals,* i.
28. 9 C.F.R. sec. 2.31(d)(1)(iv)(c) (2000).
29. 9 C.F.R. sec. 2.31(d)(1)(v) (2000); principle 6 of the "U.S. Government Principles," in NIH-OPRR, *Policy on Humane Care and Use of Laboratory Animals,* i.
30. For example, in 1987 the American Veterinary Medical Association (AVMA) convened a Colloquium on Recognition and Alleviation of Animal Pain and Distress; the AVMA asked the group to promulgate definitions of important mentalistic terminology for use by veterinarians and animal researchers. The Colloquium Panel Report defined "anxiety," for example, as "an emotional state involving increased arousal and alertness prompted by an unknown danger that may be present in the immediate environment." "Panel Report of the Colloquium on Recognition and Alleviation of Animal Pain and Distress," *Journal of the American Veterinary Medical Association* 191, no. 10 (1987): 1187. This definition does not accord with how "anxiety" is used in common discourse. Aside from the fact that one can be anxious about a known danger and one that is not present in the immediate environment, anxiety requires a sense of self. Anxiety typically involves feelings of uncertainty, fear, or dread about oneself. To say that one is anxious about a pending event, for example, is to say that you see yourself—your plans, your happiness, your state of mind—threatened by that event. Experiences of anxiety typically involve a highly developed sense of the future because being anxious typically involves an appreciation that one does not know what the future will bring. It is questionable whether most animal species used in research have the kind of self-consciousness that is a prerequisite for, and a component of, anxiety. Anxiety as we commonly speak of it is a very unpleasant and distressing emotion, precisely because it typically involves feelings of threat to the self. If, as the report asserted, most animals used in research (even mice and rats) routinely experience anxiety, that would seem to be a serious matter, and scientists would have to meet a very high burden to justify such research. Unfortunately, if most research animals experience anxiety, they do so by virtue of an idiosyncratic definition that makes anxiety a relatively mild emotion—one not worthy of the same level of moral concern. For a discussion of the role of definitions of mentalistic terminology in exaggerating ethical problems in animal research, see Jerrold Tannenbaum, *Veterinary Ethics,* 2d ed. (St. Louis, MO: Mosby, 1995), 417–18.
31. Tannenbaum, *Veterinary Ethics,* 485–86. I also consider numerous issues related to the concept of 'pain' in my "Ethics and Pain Research in Animals."
32. See Mary Midgley, "Why Knowledge Matters," in Sperlinger, ed., *Animals in Research,* 319–36.

33. For excellent discussions of such so-called "basic" research, see Adrian R. Morrison, "Making Choices in the Laboratory," in this volume, 49–77; and Stuart Zola, "Basic Research, Applied Research, Animal Ethics, and an Animal Model of Human Amnesia," in this volume, 79–92.

34. See Charles E. Short and Alan Van Poznak, eds., *Animal Pain* (New York: Churchill Livingstone, 1992).

35. Tannenbaum, "Ethics and Pain Research in Animals."

36. This case describes a standard procedure in neuroanatomical studies. I started using the case shortly before the U.S. Congress enacted the 1985 amendments to the AWA that required the provision of "psychological well-being" for nonhuman primates used in research. I explain the hostility many scientists expressed toward these amendments at the time in part by those scientists' acceptance of the traditional approach.

37. Animal Welfare Information Center, *Environmental Enrichment Information Resources for Laboratory Animals: 1965–1995* (Washington, DC: U.S. Department of Agriculture, 1995), 1.

38. National Research Council and Institute for Laboratory Animal Resources, *Guide for the Care and Use of Laboratory Animals,* 1.

39. Bernard E. Rollin, "Preface," in Bernard E. Rollin and M. Lynne Kesel, eds., *The Experimental Animal in Biomedical Research,* vol. 2, *Care, Husbandry, and Well-Being: An Overview by Species* (Boca Raton, FL: CRC Press, 1995), unpaginated.

40. 7 U.S.C. sec. 2143(a)(2)(B) (1994).

41. See Animal Welfare Information Center, *Environmental Enrichment Information Resources.*

42. 7 U.S.C. sec. 2143(a)(2)(B) (1994).

43. Jerrold Tannenbaum, "Ethics and Animal Welfare: The Inextricable Connection," *Journal of the American Veterinary Medical Association* 198, no. 8 (1991): 1360–76; Tannenbaum, *Veterinary Ethics,* chap. 13. In these sources, I discuss several definitions of animal "welfare" that have been proposed by prominent scientists, and demonstrate that each of these definitions reflects an ethical position about what is owed to animals under certain circumstances. For example, many scientists define research- or farm-animal welfare as the absence of suffering. They do so because they believe that animals used by people in research or farming ought not to be caused any suffering if at all possible; indeed, they assert that the primary obligation humans have to animals that we use for our own benefit is to cause them no suffering if possible, and as little suffering as we can if some is necessary. In contrast, scientists who define animal welfare as well-being, or as a state of complete mental and physical health in which the animal is in complete harmony with its environment, adopt such definitions because they believe that animals are owed certain positive goods in addition to freedom from suffering.

44. Viktor Reinhardt, "Foraging Enrichment for Caged Macaques: A Review," *Laboratory Primate Newsletter* 32, no. 4 (October 1993): 1.

45. Françoise Wemelsfelder, "Animal Boredom—A Model of Chronic Suffering in Captive Animals and Its Consequences for Environmental Enrichment," *Humane Innovations and Alternatives* 8 (1994): 587.

46. Bernard E. Rollin, *Farm Animal Welfare: Social, Bioethical, and Research Issues* (Ames: Iowa State University Press, 1995), 17.

47. Ibid.

48. Bernard E. Rollin, *Animal Rights and Human Morality,* 2d ed. (Buffalo, NY: Prometheus Books, 1992), 75.

49. Ibid., 88–91.

50. Françoise Wemelsfelder and Lynda Birke, "Environmental Challenge," in Michael C. Appleby and Barry O. Hughes, eds., *Animal Welfare* (New York: CAB International, 1997), 35–47.

51. Rollin's views regarding animal *telos* are subject to other objections, which do not need to be discussed in detail here. It is not obvious, for example, that all animals have inborn needs or behaviors that we would regard as part of their "nature" or "essence" in the sense that if these needs were not met or behaviors were not present, we would say that the affected animals are thus different kinds of animals. One can argue that it is wrong to prevent birds that ordinarily fly from flying. However, it is not correct to say that these birds are not really birds, or that they are not really birds of their respective species. One could still insist that their essential "birdness" has been removed, but this would merely be a way of restating that they *ought* not be prevented from flying. For this claim, one needs an argument.

52. National Research Council, *The Psychological Well-Being of Nonhuman Primates* (Washington, DC: National Academy Press, 1998), 1.

53. Ibid., 10.

54. Ibid., 11.

55. Ibid.

56. Stephen Suomi and Melinda Novak, "The Role of Individual Differences in Promoting Psychological Well-Being in Rhesus Monkeys," in Melinda Novak and Andrew Petto, eds., *Through the Looking Glass: Issues of Psychological Well-Being in Captive Nonhuman Primates* (Washington, DC: American Psychological Association, 1991), 52.

57. R. Bryan Jones and David Waddington, "Modification of Fear in Domestic Chicks, *Gallus gallus domesticus,* via Regular Handling and Early Environmental Enrichment," *Animal Behaviour* 43, no. 6 (1992): 1021–33; R. Bryan Jones, Christopher Larkins, and Barry O. Hughes, "Approach/Avoidance Responses of Domestic Chicks to Familiar and Unfamiliar Images of Biologically Neutral Stimuli," *Applied Animal Behaviour Science* 48, nos. 1 and 2 (June 1996): 81–98.

58. Peter K. McGregor and Samantha J. Ayling, "Varied Cages Result in More Aggression in Male CFLP Mice," *Applied Animal Behaviour Science* 26, no. 3 (May 1990): 277–81.

59. See, for example, Animal Welfare Information Center, *Environmental Enrichment Information Resources,* v.

60. See, for example, Ruth C. Newberry, "Environmental Enrichment: Increasing the Biological Relevance of Captive Environments," *Applied Animal Behaviour Science* 44, nos. 2–4 (September 1995): 230.

61. National Research Council, *Recognition and Alleviation of Pain and Distress in Laboratory Animals* (Washington, DC: National Academy Press, 1992), 3.

62. Simian immunodeficiency virus, or SIV, is similar in structure to HIV, the human immunodeficiency virus. The virus has been endemic to monkeys for many years. Some monkey species carry the virus without symptoms, but others succumb to diseases similar to those suffered by human AIDS patients. Some researchers hope that understanding SIV will assist them in understanding and combating HIV.

63. John Capitanio, "Social Experience and Immune System Measures in Laboratory-housed Macaques: Implications for Management and Research," *ILAR Journal* 39, no. 1 (1998): 12–20.

64. Joy Mench, personal communication with author, 1999.

65. Tannenbaum, *Veterinary Ethics,* 125–26, 184–91, 333–407.

66. Arnold Arluke, "Trapped in a Guilt Cage," *New Scientist* 134, no. 1815 (April 4, 1992): 34. See also Arnold Arluke, "Moral Elevation in Medical Research," *Advances in Medical Sociology* 1 (1990): 189–204; and Arnold Arluke, "Uneasiness Among Laboratory Technicians," *Lab Animal* 19, no. 4 (May/June 1990): 21–39.

67. See Committee on the Use of Animals in Research, *Science, Medicine, and Animals* (Washington, DC: National Academy Press, 1991); William I. Gay, ed. *Health Benefits of Animal Research* (Washington, DC: Foundation for Biomedical Research, undated); and Kenneth F. Kiple and Kriemhild Coneè Ornelas, "Experimental Animals in Medical Research: A History," in this volume, 23–48.

68. See Norval B. King, "Contributions and Needs of Animal Health and Disease Research," *American Journal of Veterinary Research* 42, no. 7 (July 1981): 1093–108; and Bruce H. Ewald and Douglas A. Gregg, "Animal Research for Animals," in Jeri A. Sechzer, ed., *The Role of Animals in Biomedical Research* (New York: New York Academy of Sciences, 1983), 48–58.

69. Franklin M. Loew, "Animals as Beneficiaries of Biomedical Research Originally Intended for Humans," *ILAR News* 30, no. 4 (Fall 1988): 13–15.

70. Joy Mench reports that a number of British scientists use the term "animal well-being" rather than "animal welfare" because they know the term "welfare" is used in the United States to refer to government subsidies for the poor. These scientists do not want the negative associations that some make with such programs to be associated with efforts to improve the conditions of laboratory, farm, and zoo animals (Mench, personal communication). This is a terrible reason to adopt terminology that appears to require research-animal happiness.

71. Franklin M. Loew, "Animals and the Urban Prism," *Journal of the American Veterinary Medical Association* 202, no. 10 (1993): 1658–61.

Defending Animal Research: An International Perspective

Baruch A. Brody

I. Introduction

In a recent article, "The Ethics of Animal Research," philosopher David De-Grazia asks the very important question of whether or not there is room for at least some agreement between "biomedicine" and "animal advocates" on the issue of animal research.[1] This is an important question, but one on which we are unlikely to make any progress until the contents of both positions are clearly understood. This essay is devoted to better articulating the position which supports animal research, the position that DeGrazia labels the "biomedicine" position; I leave the analysis of the animal-advocacy position for other occasions.

My reason for adopting this strategy is as follows: There has been in recent years an extensive philosophical discussion of various versions of the animal-advocacy position, and the variations on this position have been analyzed by several authors.[2] Much less attention has been paid to development of the pro-research position. DeGrazia himself describes the articulation of that position in negative terms:

> It seems fair to say that biomedicine has a "party line" on the ethics of animal research, conformity to which may feel like a political litmus test for full acceptability within the professional community. According to this party line, animal research is clearly justified because it is necessary for medical progress and therefore human health. . . . [M]any or most animal researchers and their supporters do not engage in sustained, critical thinking about the moral status of animals and the basic justification (or lack thereof) for animal research.[3]

Whether or not this is fully accurate, this perception of the status of the pro-research position seems to be widespread. It therefore seems important to attempt a better articulation and defense of a reasonable version of that position.

What do I mean by a reasonable pro-research position on animal research, the type of position that I wish to defend? I understand such a position to be committed to at least the following propositions:

1. Animals have interests (at least the interest in not suffering, and perhaps others as well), which may be adversely affected either by research performed on them or by the conditions under which they live before, during, and after the research.
2. The adverse effect on animals' interests is morally relevant, and must be taken into account when deciding whether or not a particular program of animal research is justified or must be modified or abandoned.
3. The justification for conducting a research program on animals that would adversely affect them is the benefits that human beings would receive from the research in question.
4. In deciding whether or not the research in question is justified, human interests should be given greater significance than animal interests.

Some preliminary observations about these propositions are in order. Propositions (1) and (2) commit the reasonable pro-research position to a belief that animal interests are morally relevant, and that the adverse impact of animal research on these interests should not be disregarded. This distinguishes the position I am trying to articulate from positions (such as the classical Cartesian position) that maintain that animals have no interests or that those interests do not count morally.[4] In light of their ability to experience pleasures and pains, it is implausible to deny animals interests or to give those interests no moral significance at all. Propositions (3) and (4) distinguish the pro-research position from the animal-advocacy position by insisting that it is permissible for animals to be adversely affected by legitimate research—they do not have a trumping right not to be used adversely for human benefit.[5] Toward this end, proposition (4) asserts that human benefits have greater significance than harms to animals in determining the legitimacy of the research, as animals have less moral significance than humans.[6]

What is the nature of humans' greater significance? It seems to me that this is the crucial question that must be faced by any reasonable pro-research position, for it is the answer to this question that will determine when animal research that has an adverse impact on animal subjects is justified. Many pro-research positions are possible; these positions differ over the research they accept as justified precisely because they differ over the nature of the priority of human interests over animal interests. It seems to me, moreover, that this crucial question must be answered before one even begins any discussion of possible justifications for an actual pro-research position, since the justification of any specific pro-research position will have to involve justifying a specific view of the priority of human interests.

Another way of putting this point is as follows: The reasonable pro-research position is actually a family of positions that differ both theoretically (on their conceptions of the nature of the priority of human interests) and practically (on the resulting types of justified research). What is needed first is a full examination of this family of positions, an examination that explores the plausibility of different views on the priority of human interests. Once we can identify the more plausible of these views, we can begin the attempt to justify one of them.

It is this observation that structures this essay. In Section II, I will present two very different understandings of the priority of human interests. The first understanding is involved in official U.S. policies governing animal research; the second underlies some official European policies. In Section III, I will argue that the U.S. understanding is less plausible than the European one, and that defenders of the pro-research position should focus on trying to articulate and justify some version of the European position. In Section IV, I will show that there is an important structural analogy between the European position and certain familiar positions on the prerogative, and on the obligation, to give priority to the interests of some humans over the interests of others. This will suggest that the pro-research position is part of a larger family of positions that deny the thesis that all interests count equally; it will also suggest that the justification of the pro-research position is to be found in the arguments that are used to justify that larger family of positions. In the final section of this essay, I will raise a fundamental concern about this whole family of positions, designed not to challenge their validity but rather to open a new type of investigation into such positions.

II. The U.S. and European Positions

The best statement of the U.S. policy on animal research is found in a 1986 document from the Public Health Service entitled "U.S. Government Principles for the Utilization and Care of Vertebrate Animals Used in Testing, Research, and Training."[7] This document plays the same role for animal research that the Belmont Report[8] does for research on human subjects, by identifying the principles that lie behind and justify the specific regulations governing the research. I want to highlight what is and is not present in the U.S. principles; they call upon researchers to:

- Use the "minimum number [of animals] required to obtain valid results"
- Consider alternatives such as "mathematical models, computer simulation, and in vitro biological systems"

- Practice the "avoidance or minimization of discomfort, distress or pain when consistent with sound scientific practices"
- Use "appropriate sedation, analgesia, or anesthesia"
- Kill animals painlessly after experiments when the animals "would otherwise suffer severe or chronic pain or distress that cannot be relieved"
- Provide living conditions that are "appropriate for their species and contribute to their health and comfort"[9]

All of these principles are compatible with the familiar program, developed by W. M. S. Russell and R. L. Burch in 1959, which has come to be called the 3R program.[10] This program calls for the *replacement* of animal experimentation with other research methods where possible; this is why the U.S. principles request the consideration of alternative research techniques. The program also calls for the *reduction* of the number of animals used; hence, the U.S. principles state a commitment to minimizing the number of animals used as much as is consistent with obtaining scientifically valid results. Finally, the 3R program calls for *refining* both the conduct of the research and the environment in which the research animals live; the aim is to minimize the animals' pain and suffering. This is why the U.S. principles talk about pain relief, euthanasia when necessary, and species-appropriate living conditions.

These U.S. principles are not the only place in which this 3R approach (without being officially designated by that name) is adopted as official U.S. policy. The 1993 National Institutes of Health (NIH) Revitalization Act calls upon the NIH to support research on using alternative models to animals, on reducing the number of animals used in research, on producing less pain and distress for these animals, and on using nonmammalian marine life as a research substitute for the use of more advanced animals. This research is to help establish "the validity and reliability" of these methods; for those "methods that have been found to be valid and reliable," the research is aimed at encouraging acceptance of those methods and at training scientists to use them.[11]

All of this is very much in the spirit of propositions (1) and (2) of my account of the responsible pro-research position on animal research. It is because animals have interests that may be adversely affected by the research—interests that count morally—that we are called upon to replace, reduce, and refine the use of animals in research. Proposition (3) is also explicitly part of the U.S. principles, which assert that "procedures involving animals should be designed and performed with due consideration of their relevance to human or animal health, the advancement of knowledge, or the good of society."[12] But what about proposition (4)? What sort of greater significance are human interests given over animal interests in the U.S. regulations?

In fact, that question is never directly addressed. This stands in sharp contrast to the U.S. regulations on human subjects in research. These regulations require the minimization of risks, but they also require that the minimized ris sonable in relation to anticipated benefits, if any, to subjects, and the of the knowledge that may reasonably be expected to result."[13] Nothing like these strictures occurs in the U.S. principles and regulations governing animal research.

Something else can be inferred from the wording of the U.S. principles on animal research. Discomfort, distress, or pain of the animals should be minimized "when consistent with sound scientific practices." The number of animals used should be minimized to "the number required to obtain valid results." Unrelieved pain necessary to conduct the research is acceptable so long as the animal is euthanized after or during the procedure.[14] What this amounts to in the end is that whatever is required for the research is morally acceptable; the 3R principles are to be applied only as long as they are compatible with maintaining scientifically valid research. There is never the suggestion that the suffering of the animal might be so great—even when it is minimized as much as possible while still maintaining scientific validity—that its suffering might outweigh the benefits from the research. Even when these benefits are modest, the U.S. principles never morally require the abandonment of a research project.

This is a position that gives very strong priority to human interests over animal interests, especially to the human interests that are promoted by scientific research using animals as subjects. Given the wide variety of such animal research projects, which range from developing and testing new life-saving surgical techniques to developing and testing new cosmetics, the human interests that are given this strong priority over animal interests are very diverse. It is not clear if there are any human interests that are not given this priority. Whether or not this strong and broad priority is compatible with the adoption of the 3R principles is a question to which we will return later.

The European approach to these issues is quite different. It is not that the Europeans do not believe in the 3R principles; their regulations embody these principles. Rather, the Europeans find these principles incomplete and augment them with additional principles that give greater significance to animal interests by disallowing some research because the costs to the animal subjects are too great.

The 1986 Directive from the Council of the European Communities (now called the European Community) provides us with one example of this approach, directed to cases in which animals suffer severe, prolonged pain that cannot be relieved. The directive stipulates that the relevant authority "shall take appropriate judicial or administrative action if it is not satisfied that the experiment is of sufficient importance for meeting the essential needs of man or animal."[15] This is a limited provision, as it involves animal interests outweighing human interests only in the case of severe and prolonged pain. The provision does not clearly specify what the "appropriate" actions in such cases are, and it implies that even severe and prolonged pain is acceptable if the research is of "sufficient importance." Nevertheless, it goes beyond anything in the U.S. principles and regulations by giving somewhat greater significance to animal interests.

This approach is developed in national legislation in several European countries. In Great Britain, for example, the British Animals (Scientific Procedures) Act of 1986, which requires each project involving animal research to get a project license, stipulates that "in determining whether and on what terms to grant a project licence the Secretary of State shall weigh the likely adverse effects on the animals concerned against the benefit likely to accrue as a result of the programme to be specified in the licence."[16] This provision is broader than the provision in the E.C. directive because the British legislation is not limited to the case of severe prolonged pain. Furthermore, it is also more explicit in specifying that when animal interests are unduly affected, the appropriate regulatory action is to forbid the research from proceeding at all. A similar provision is found in a German statute that requires that "experiments may be carried out on vertebrates only if the pain, suffering, or harm which they can be expected to inflict upon the animals is ethically justifiable in relation to the purposes of the experiment."[17]

While these national provisions are both broader in application and more explicit in their implications than is the E.C. directive, they still leave a crucial question unanswered. Let me explain. All the European regulations assume that animal interests in avoiding the harmful consequences of being in a research project have enough moral significance—in comparison to human interests in conducting research—that in some cases the proposed research is ethically unacceptable. All involve a balancing of animal interests against human interests in a way that allows the protection of animal interests to be given priority in some cases. In this way, they all reject the American pro-research position, in which human interests seem to have priority in all cases. This may be due to European acceptance of the very strong animal-advocacy position that animal interests count equally with human interests. But one need not accept this extreme position, and I see no evidence for such a strong claim. To justify the European positions as found in their regulations, it would be sufficient to maintain that animal interests and human interests are comparable enough so that very significant animal interests can outweigh minimal human interests. Exactly how comparable these interests are is left unanswered by each of the European regulations.

Let me put this point another way. Consider a whole continuum of positions, ranging from the claim that animal interests and human interests count equally (the *equal-significance position*) to the claim that even though one may attend to animal interests, human interests always take precedence (the *human-priority position*). In moving from the first position to the second, the significance of animal interests in comparison to human interests is gradually discounted. The intermediate positions move from those that discount animal interests modestly (and are therefore increasingly close to the equal-significance position) to those that discount them significantly (and are therefore increasingly close to the human-priority position). The U.S. position is the human-priority end of this continuum, and the animal rights movement's rejection of proposition (4) of the pro-research position puts that movement at the other end. The European positions are somewhere in-between, but there is no way to tell from their regulations where they are on the continuum. This could best be ascertained by examining how their systems actually operate in practice. What sorts of research projects have they rejected that might have been acceptable in the United States? Unfortunately, no comparative study of this sort has been conducted on the actual operation of the various national systems of review of animal research. Therefore, at this point, one cannot tell from European practices where various nations stand on the continuum.

A country's position on the continuum is not merely of theoretical interest. Your place on the continuum determines which research you would disallow because of its adverse impact upon animal interests. My impression is that the very limited balancing in the E.C. directive—which rules out animal research only in cases of severe, prolonged pain, and then only when the research is not "of sufficient importance for meeting the essential needs of man or animal"—means that the E.C. position is pretty close to the U.S. end of the continuum. In contrast, the broader language in the British and German statutes suggests that they are further away from the American end of the continuum, that is, they discount animal interests to a lesser degree. But how far their positions are from the human-priority position is totally undetermined. In this respect, their positions are in need of much further articulation.

In short, we have seen that proposition (4) of the pro-research position, the principle of giving greater significance to human interests than to animal interests, is understood very differently in the United States and in Europe. For the United States, the proposition means that human interests in conducting research always take lexical priority over animal interests. This lexical priority is not characteristic of the European positions, which allow for some balancing of interests. But there is no evidence that the Europeans have rejected proposition (4) and adopted the equal-significance position that is characteristic of the animal-advocacy position. They seem, instead, to have adopted some discounting of animal interests in comparison to human interests, with the crucial discount rate being undetermined.

Are there any reasons for supposing that a lexical-priority approach is a more plausible articulation of proposition (4) than is a discounting approach (or vice versa)? This is the question I will examine in the next section of this essay.

III. Lexical Priority versus Discounting

There are two arguments I will consider in this section. The first argument, in favor of a lexical-priority approach to proposition (4), argues that the cross-species comparison of interests that is presupposed by the discounting approach is meaningless, and that the discounting approach must, therefore, be rejected in favor of a lexical-priority approach. The second argument, in favor of the discounting approach, asserts that lexical priority is incompatible with significant components of the 3R program, and that pro-research adherents of that program must, therefore, adopt the discounting approach.

The first argument begins by noting that there are three steps to the discounting approach. The first step is to identify and quantify the impact of the research on the animal subjects and on the human beneficiaries of the knowledge that might be gained. The second step is to discount the impact on the animals by whatever discount rate is adopted by the particular version of the discounting approach. The final step is to decide whether to allow the research to proceed, taking into consideration the full impact on the humans and the discounted impact on the animals. The quantification involved in the first step and the discounting involved in the second step must be on a common metric, or the third step becomes meaningless. It is the existence of this common metric that is challenged by the first argument.

This challenge of the first argument thus has two components. The first component is the claim that there is no basis for placing animal pain and pleasure (if one defines 'interests' hedonistically) or the satisfaction of animal preferences (if one defines 'interests' in terms of preference-satisfaction) on a common metric with human pain and pleasure or human preference-satisfaction. I will refer to this first component of the challenge as the *incommensurability claim*. The second component is the claim that even if there were such a basis, we do not know enough about the sensations or preferences of animals to make such comparisons; I will call this component the *cross-species ignorance claim*.

It should be noted that this two-pronged challenge, if sound, is as much an objection to the animal-advocacy equal-significance position as it is to the pro-research discounting approach. Both involve quantifying, on a common metric, the pains and pleasures or the preference-satisfactions of humans and animals; the two only differ on whether or not the animal quantifications should be discounted before we draw any conclusions about the total impact of the research on all the interests involved. If there is something problematic about performing the initial quantification, that casts doubt upon both approaches.

It is also important to note that even if one accepts this two-pronged challenge, it does not necessarily follow from this that we should adopt the lexical-priority approach to proposition (4). Those who oppose the lexical-priority approach on the intuitive grounds that it does not give sufficient significance to animal interests can simply conclude that some other approach, one which captures those intuitions, must be developed. All that does follow from the first argument's two-pronged challenge is that the lexical-priority approach to proposition (4) is more plausible than is the discounting approach (which, if the incommensurability claim is correct, has no plausibility at all).

But should we grant the challenge's components? I see no reason to accept the incommensurability claim. Human pain and pleasure is quantified on the basis of dimensions such as duration and intensity; animal pain and pleasure can also be quantified on those dimensions. Duration is certainly not conceptually different for different species, and no reason has been offered for why we should treat intensity as differing conceptually for different species. Thus, there is a basis for a common metric for hedonistic comparisons of the impact of research on human and animal interests. I think that the same is true for preference-satisfaction comparisons of the impact of research on human and animal interests, but it is hard to say that with the same degree of confidence, since we still have little understanding of the dimensions on which we quantify preference-satisfaction. The duration dimension is certainly the same, and the dimension of the importance of the preference may be the same as well, but that is the dimension we do not really understand. In short, then, the premises of the incommensurability claim are questionable.

The cross-species ignorance claim is more serious. We are not particularly good at measuring *human* pains, pleasures, and preference-satisfaction on the same metric, even for one person let alone many. These uncertainties can only be magnified when we do cross-species comparisons. How does the discounting approach intend to deal with this problem?

This issue has been faced most directly by a working party of the British Institute of Medical Ethics (an unofficial but respected interdisciplinary group of scholars) in a report published in 1991.[18] The working party's members took note of the fact that the quantification of interests on a common metric seems to be required by the British Animals Act, and that there are doubts as to whether this can be done. In response to these concerns, they make two observations, which seem to me to be the beginning of a good answer to these concerns. First, they note that not every reliable judgment must be based upon a mathematically quantifiable balancing of values: it is often sufficient to have confidence in "the procedures which have been used to arrive at that judgment, . . . upon whether [researchers] have taken into account all the known morally relevant factors, and whether they have shown themselves responsive to all the relevant moral interests."[19] Second, the working party claims that it is possible to identify the moral factors relevant to the assessment of animal research and the degree to which they are present in a given case; this knowledge would allow for reliable judgments about the moral acceptability of proposed protocols for animal research. In fact, the working party goes on to create such a scheme and to show by examples how it might work in a reliable fashion.[20]

I say that this is only the beginning of a good answer because the working party does not really note the issue of discounting and its implications for the approach that they are adopting. Thus, more work needs to be done on their approach in order to incorporate this crucial component of the pro-research position. Moreover, more work is needed in defense of this view that reliable judgments need not be based on mathematically quantifiable balancing. I have provided some of this defense in my own writings on pluralistic casuistry.[21] I believe, however, that those who support the discounting approach to proposition (4) of the pro-research position can feel confident that they need not abandon it and adopt the lexical-priority approach.

This brings me to the second argument of this section. There are, this second argument suggests, reasons for doubting that the lexical-priority approach is compatible with even the 3R approach to the reasonable pro-research position. Satisfying the 3R principles, even if done in a way that allows the proposed research to proceed, involves considerable costs. These costs mean that other human interests, in research or otherwise, will not be satisfied. If human interests truly take precedence over animal interests, this seems inappropriate. A lexical-priority approach, then, cannot support even the now widely accepted 3R approach to protecting animal interests; this, it seems to me, makes the lexical-priority interpretation of proposition (4) an implausible version of the pro-research position.

Consider, for example, that aspect of the 3R program's refinement plank that calls for modifications in the environment in which research animals live in order to make those environments species-appropriate and not a source of distress or discomfort. Those modifications, now widely required throughout the world, are often quite costly, and these costs are passed on to the researchers as a cost of doing research. Some poorly funded research never takes place because these extra costs cannot be absorbed. Other, better funded, research projects go on, but require extra funding. This extra funding may mean that other research projects are not funded, or that the funded research will not be as complete as originally envisioned. To avoid these outcomes, extra funding would have to be provided to research efforts in general, but this would compromise funding for other human interests. In these ways and others, the adoption of this aspect of the 3R program is not compatible with maintaining the full research effort and/or with meeting other human interests. Hence, human interests are not being given full priority, contrary to the basic premise of the lexical-priority position.

None of this, of course, is a problem for the discounting approach unless the discounting of animal interests is so significant that it approaches the lexical-priority position. If the discounting is not this extensive—if animal interests count a lot, even if not as much as the interests of humans—then it seems reasonable to suppose that the interests of the animals in living in a species-appropriate environment are sufficiently great to justify imposing these burdens on the research effort.

There are components of the 3R program that do not raise this problem for the lexical-priority approach. The most obvious of these is the requirement to reduce the number of animal subjects to the minimum necessary to maintain the scientific validity of the research. This demand may often be cost-saving, and is unlikely to ever be cost-increasing. The impact of the 3R program's replacement component is the hardest to be sure about, because the cost comparison between using animals and using other models will vary.

In short, then, those who want a reasonable pro-research position to incorporate the widely adopted 3R program should find the discounting approach more plausible than the lexical-priority approach. But what could possibly justify such a discounting of animal interests? We turn to that question in the next section.

IV. The Rationale for Discounting

Before attempting to develop an approach to justifying discounting, it is important to be clear as to exactly what is claimed by discounting. I shall develop this point by using a hedonistic account of interests; the same point could be developed using other accounts of interests.

Consider a human being experiencing pain for a certain duration of time and at a certain level of intensity. Now suppose that an animal experiences pain of the same intensity for the same duration of time. Some will say that the animal's experience may count less, morally, because the human being anticipates the pain beforehand and remembers it afterwards in ways that the animal does not; these factors allegedly add to the total quantity of pain or distress experienced by the human being. This may or may not be true, but it is not what is at stake in the claim of discounting. To see this, suppose further that the pain is totally unanticipated and that both the human being and the animal are immediately given amnesiac drugs so that neither remembers anything about the painful experience. The claim of discounting is that the animal's pain would still count less, morally. Others may attempt to find additional associated mental states in the human being that add to the badness of the human pain and make it count more. Suppose further that none of these associated mental states is present in the case in question. The claim of discounting is that the animal's pain would *still* count less, morally. Discounting, then, is the claim that the same unit of pain counts less, morally, if it is experienced by an animal than it would if it is experienced by a human being, not because of the human's associated experiences but simply because of the species of the experiencer. Discounting directly denies the equal consideration of interests across species.

I am emphasizing this point to make it clear that *discounting* of animal interests is radically different than the *preference* for human interests that even animal advocates such as Peter Singer accept:

> There are many areas in which the superior mental powers of normal adult humans make a difference: anticipation, more detailed memory, greater knowledge of what is happening, and so on. These differences explain why a human dying from cancer is likely to suffer more than a mouse.[22]

But for Singer and other supporters of the equal-significance position, all that follows from this is that humans may suffer more and that this quantitative difference in the amount of suffering is morally relevant. What discounting affirms, and what they deny, is that even when there is no quantitative difference in the amount of suffering, the human suffering counts more morally.

With this understanding of the claim of discounting, we can easily understand why many would find its claims ethically unacceptable. Why should the moral significance of the same amount of suffering differ according to the species of the sufferer if there are no associated additional differences?

There have been many attempts to answer this question, and I certainly do not intend to review and critically analyze them here. I do want to note just a few points. Some of these attempts deny moral status to animals on the ground that they lack certain capacities. That approach is unavailable to adherents of the reasonable pro-research position who concede that animal interests count morally, and may even (in the discounting approach) outweigh human interests. Other attempts to justify the preference to human interests do so on religious/metaphysical grounds. Whatever the merit of such claims, they are unavailable to adherents of the reasonable pro-research position who want to use this position as the foundation of public policy on animal research.

I see no reasonable alternative for the adherent of the discounting position except to challenge the whole idea that we are, in general, morally committed to an equal consideration of interests. This is a plausible move, since equal consideration of interests has come under much challenge in contemporary moral philosophy, totally independently of the debate over the moral significance of the interests of animals. I would trace the beginning of the idea that we should not accept equal consideration of interests to W. D. Ross's contention, as early as 1930, that we have special obligations to ourselves, our family members, our friends, our fellow citizens, etc.[23] Recognizing these special obligations means, of course, giving higher priority to the interests of some (those to whom we have special obligations) than to the interests of others (those to whom we do not). Equally important is the emphasis in the 1980s on the idea that we have a morally permissible prerogative to pay special attention to our own interests in the fulfillment of some of our central projects.[24] Recognizing this prerogative means giving a higher priority to at least some of our interests over the interests of others. Each of these ideas, in separate ways, presupposes a denial of equal consideration of interests, and both are best understood as forms of the discounting of certain interests.

How should we understand the special obligations that we have? One good way of understanding them is that we have special obligations to some people to give a higher priority to their interests than we do to those of others. This may call upon us to promote their interests even at the cost of not promoting the greater interests of strangers. Note, by the way, that it is implausible to see this as a form of lexical priority favoring the interests of those people to whom we have special obligations. When their interests at stake are modest, and when the conflicting interests of strangers are great, we are not obliged to put the interests of those to whom we are specially obligated first; we may not even be permitted to do so. It would appear, then, that special obligations might well be understood as involving a requirement that we discount the interests of strangers when they compete with the interests of those to whom we have special obligations.

The same approach sheds much light upon our prerogative to pursue personal goals even at the cost of not aiding others (or even hindering them) in the pursuit of their interests. This is, once again, hardly a lexical priority. No matter how important a goal may be to me, I may be morally required to put it aside if the competing interests of others are especially great. Our prerogative may best be understood as involving only a permission to discount the interests of strangers when they compete with our interests in attaining our goals.

Note, by the way, that this means that we really have a whole family of theories about special obligations and about personal prerogatives. Different theories will differ on the acceptable discount rate.

Looked at from this perspective, the discounting approach to the animal research position no longer seems anomalous. Rather than involving a peculiar discounting of the interests of animals, in violation of the fundamental moral requirement of the equal consideration of interests, the approach represents one more example of the discounting of the interests of strangers, a feature that is pervasive in morality.

We can see another way of developing this point if we consider the difference between the following two questions:

1A. Why should the interests of my children count more than do those of others?

1B. Why should the interests of my children count more for me than do those of others?

The former question, asked from an impersonal perspective, is unanswerable. The latter question, which is asked from the personal perspective, is answerable. The same needs to be said about the following pair of questions:

2A. Why should the interests of humans count more than do those of animals?
2B. Why should the interests of humans count more for human beings than do those of animals?

As with the previous pair of questions, what is unanswerable from one perspective may be very answerable from the other perspective.

There is, of course, an important difference between special obligations, even to oneself, and personal prerogatives. The former *require* you to give certain interests priority, while the latter just *permit* you to do so. This difference is helpful in explaining a certain ambiguity in the reasonable pro-research position. While its adherents often seem to be attempting to justify only the permissibility of animal research, they sometimes talk as though they are arguing that such research is required. Consider, for example, the standard Food and Drug Administration requirement that new drugs be tested on animals before they are tested on humans. I would suggest the following: when adherents justify the permissibility of animal research, they are invoking the analogy to prerogatives, but when they want to require this research, they are invoking the analogy to special obligations. On the latter view, we have an obligation to human beings, as part of our special obligations to members of our species, to discount animal interests in comparison to human interests by testing new drugs on animals first.

This defense of animal research on the ground of species solidarity has been developed elsewhere by the British philosopher Mary Midgley, although her emphasis seems to me to be more on psychological bonds and less on the logical structure of the consideration of interests in moral thought.[25] It may be that the discounting of interests, which I endorse, is grounded in differential psychological and social bonds, but it may not be. For now, it is sufficient to note that the discounting version of the pro-research position fits in with the general structure of the consideration of interests in moral thought. It will not do, as many have tried, to assert that the very definition of "thinking morally" requires that we count all interests equally and that, therefore, the discounting of animal interests is morally unacceptable. Any definition of morality or conception of moral thinking that requires this conclusion is suspect for just that reason.

V. Further Issues

My argument until now has been that a reasonable pro-research position should be formulated in terms of discounting animal interests rather than in terms of giving a lexical priority to human interests. The discounting approach is better able to incorporate the complete 3R program, and it allows for some balancing of human interests against discounted animal interests (as called for in some European regulations). While discounting does not accept the equal consideration of interests, that by itself is not problematic since much of common morality rejects that postulate anyway. There remain, of course, several aspects of the discounting approach that require fuller development. An appropriate discount rate is yet to be determined; the process of cross-species comparisons of gains and losses in interests must be refined; and the conditions under which discounting is merely permissible as opposed to when it is mandatory need to be defined.

In addition to these necessary developments, there is a fundamental challenge that still needs to be confronted. It is a variation on the issue of equal consideration of interests, and it requires much further theoretical reflection.

Recall that the basic objection to the discounting approach was that it violated the principle of the equal consideration of interests. That objection was met by the observation that this principle is not necessarily correct, because we seem to accept the permissibility of violating it in some cases and the requirement to violate it in others. However, there seem to be some violations of the principle that are clearly wrong. Discounting the interests of members of other races or of the other gender seems to be part of the wrong of racism and sexism. Might one not argue that discounting the interests of the members of other species is equally wrong? That is the wrong of "speciesism."

This point can also be put as follows: The charge of speciesism might just be the charge that discounting animal interests is wrong because it violates the principle of equal consideration of interests. This charge is severely weakened by the challenge to the legitimacy of the equal-consideration principle. But the charge might be the very different claim that discounting animal interests is wrong because it is a *discriminatory* version of discounting; this charge is not challenged by the general challenge to the principle of the equal consideration of interests. This version of the charge is articulated by DeGrazia in a critique of Midgley:

> Can appeals to social bondedness in justifying partiality towards humans be convincingly likened to family-based preferences but contrasted with bigotry? Why are racism and sexism unjustified, if species-based partiality is justified?[26]

It is of interest and importance to note that the examples DeGrazia invokes are of partiality toward family members, on the one hand, and toward members of our race or gender, on the other hand. Left out are partiality toward fellow citizens, fellow believers, and fellow members of an ethnic group. All of these seem, *as long as they are not excessive,* to be within the bounds of acceptable partiality toward our fellows and of acceptable discounting of the interests of others. This is why it is appropriate that so much charitable giving is organized by religions and national groups. This is, also, why it is appropriate that nearly all redistribution is done at the individual-country level rather than at the international level. These examples are important in reminding us that the rejection of the equal consideration of interests principle in common morality is very broad, and covers large-scale groups that are more analogous to species than to family members. Of course, this by itself is not a refutation of the discrimination charge leveled against the pro-research position. It does, however, place the position in the company of partialities and discountings that are widely accepted in moral theory and in public policy.

What my arguments foreshadow is the need for further ethical reflection on these controversial issues. We have seen that morality can legitimately involve the discounting of even other people's interests when one acts from a prerogative or a special obligation. A question that requires much more exploration is what differentiates legitimate discounting from discrimination? Only an answer to this question can fully justify the discounting-based, reasonable pro-research position that I have articulated in this essay.

NOTES

1. David DeGrazia, "The Ethics of Animal Research," *Cambridge Quarterly of Healthcare Ethics* 8, no. 1 (Winter 1999): 23–34.
2. For summaries of the extensive literature, see, for example, Tom Beauchamp, "The Moral Standing of Animals in Medical Research," *Law, Medicine, and Health Care* 20, nos. 1–2 (Spring/Summer 1992): 7–16; and David DeGrazia, "The Moral Status of Animals and Their Use in Research: A Philosophical Review," *Kennedy Institute of Ethics Journal* 1, no. 1 (March 1991): 48–70.
3. DeGrazia, "The Ethics of Animal Research," 23–24.
4. For a discussion of Descartes's position on these issues, see F. Barbara Orlans, *In the Name of Science: Issues in Responsible Animal Experimentation* (New York: Oxford University Press, 1993), 3–4.
5. This is in opposition to the position articulated in Tom Regan, *The Case for Animal Rights* (Berkeley: University of California Press, 1983).
6. This is in opposition to the position articulated in Peter Singer, *Practical Ethics,* 2d ed. (New York: Cambridge University Press, 1993).
7. National Institutes of Health—Office for Protection from Research Risks (NIH-OPRR), *Public Health Service Policy on Humane Care and Use of Laboratory Animals* (Bethesda, MD: NIH-OPRR, 1986).
8. National Commission for the Protection of Human Subjects of Biomedical and Behavioral Research (USNCPHS), *The Belmont Report: Ethical Principles and*

Guidelines for the Protection of Human Subjects of Research (Washington, DC: USNCPHS, 1978).

9. NIH-OPRR, *Policy on Humane Care and Use of Laboratory Animals,* i.

10. W. M. S. Russell and R. L. Burch, *The Principles of Humane Experimental Technique* (London: Methuen, 1959).

11. *National Institutes of Health Revitalization Act of 1993,* 42 U.S.C.S. sec. 283e(a) (Law. Co-op. 1999).

12. NIH-OPRR, *Policy on Humane Care and Use of Laboratory Animals,* principle 2, p. i.

13. 45 C.F.R. sec. 46.111 (1999).

14. NIH-OPRR, *Policy on Humane Care and Use of Laboratory Animals,* principles 3, 4, and 6, p. i.

15. Council Directive of November 24, 1986, art. 12, sec. 2, reprinted in Baruch Brody, *The Ethics of Biomedical Research: An International Perspective* (New York: Oxford University Press, 1998), 237–40.

16. *British Animals (Scientific Procedures) Act of 1986,* sec. 5(4), reprinted in Brody, *The Ethics of Biomedical Research,* 321–25.

17. Federal Republic of Germany, *Law on Animal Protection,* art. 7(3), reprinted in Animal Welfare Institute, *Animals and Their Legal Rights,* 4th ed. (Washington, DC: Animal Welfare Institute, 1990), 336–52.

18. Jane A. Smith and Kenneth M. Boyd, eds., *Lives in the Balance: The Ethics of Using Animals in Biomedical Research—The Report of a Working Party of the Institute of Medical Ethics* (Oxford: Oxford University Press, 1991).

19. Ibid., 141.

20. Ibid., 141–46.

21. See, most recently, Brody, *The Ethics of Biomedical Research,* chap. 10.

22. Singer, *Practical Ethics,* 60.

23. W. D. Ross, *The Right and the Good* (Oxford: Oxford University Press, 1930), chap. 2.

24. Samuel Scheffler, *The Rejection of Consequentialism* (Oxford: Oxford University Press, 1982), chap. 3.

25. Mary Midgley, *Animals and Why They Matter* (Hammondsworth, Middlesex: Penguin Books, 1983).

26. David DeGrazia, *Taking Animals Seriously: Mental Life and Moral Status* (New York: Cambridge University Press, 1996), 64.

A Darwinian View of the Issues Associated with the Use of Animals in Biomedical Research

Charles S. Nicoll and Sharon M. Russell

I. Introduction

We humans have used animals in various ways for our own benefit for countless millennia. Although statements of concern about animal welfare were occasionally made by philosophers and others in the classical literature, the exploitation of animals by humans was not widely considered to have moral significance until the nineteenth century, when organizations were formed in Europe and North America that were concerned about the prevention of cruelty to animals. The historical record indicates that some of the members of these "humane" societies felt that the use of animals for experimental purposes was particularly objectionable. Consequently, they formed associations or societies that were *antivivisectionist* (i.e., opposed to conducting surgical procedures on animals).[1]

Moral justification for opposition to animal exploitation in general, and to animal experimentation in particular, was initially supported by the belief that animal suffering and human suffering should have equal moral significance. This belief was crystallized by the following statement of British utilitarian Jeremy Bentham: "The question is not, Can they *reason*? nor, Can they *talk*? but, Can they *suffer*?"[2] This statement is a fundamental part of the basic credo of the animal liberation/animal rights movement (hereafter referred to as the ALARM).

Some contemporary philosophers have argued that because animals share a number of qualities with humans (besides being able to feel pain and to suffer), their lives also have moral worth and significance. Accordingly, we cannot justify causing animals to suffer or using them in the various ways that we do. Some of these philosophers, such as Tom Regan, contend that because animals have qualities of life comparable to those of humans, they deserve the rights that we normally accord to ourselves (i.e., to life, liberty, and the pursuit of happiness).[3] Others, such as Peter Singer (who claims to be a utilitarian), believe that although animals are not entitled to have rights in the same way that people are entitled to have them, animals are nevertheless deserving of equal moral consideration, particularly when we contemplate exploiting them for our own purposes. Singer argues that if humans are justified in exploiting other animals for any reason, we should be willing to exploit humans in the same ways for the same purpose.[4]

Counterarguments to the belief that animals and humans are morally equal have been published by several scholars.[5] In essence, they argue that even though humans and animals share a number of features in common, there are large qualitative and/or quantitative differences between us and other creatures with respect to these features. Therefore, the quality of human life is much greater than that of any other animal, and so we are justified in denying rights or equal moral consideration to nonhuman animals.

Another type of counterargument is called *contractualism,* which was elaborated by Peter Carruthers,[6] who was influenced by political philosopher John Rawls.[7] As applied by Carruthers, contractualism refers to entering into a moral understanding with another being in which both parties agree not to harm each other or other members of their kind. In effect, then, they agree to abide by moral behavior that would be in accord with the "Golden Rule." Only rational beings (i.e., those with the capacity to reason) who have an understanding of the concepts of morals and rights could enter into such a contractual agreement. Therefore, if we ever encounter advanced space aliens, we could establish a mutual agreement with them to do no harm. However, we could not establish such an agreement with any nonhuman species on our planet, even those that are the most intelligent.

As biologists, we view the arguments of the ALARMists[8] to be without merit. As for the arguments of philosophers who believe that humans are morally superior to animals,[9] we think the thrust of these arguments is correct, but that they are somewhat beside the point in terms of providing justification for our exploitation of animals. By contrast, contractualism is consistent with the realities of biology, as we shall attempt to explain. Different individuals or groups of humans can enter into moral agreements not to harm or exploit each other; these agreements serve the function of mutual protection. We cannot, however, enter into such agreements with nonhuman animals, nor can they do so between or among themselves.

The human animal is a product of evolution, as are all other living things on Earth. All existing creatures have been sculpted by the forces of natural selection that operate to weed out the unfit (or unlucky) individuals and species. These forces of natural selection are extremely effective; it is estimated that more than 99.9 percent of the species that ever existed on Earth have become extinct.[10] To ensure our survival as individuals and as a species, humans must do what other species do. What follows in this essay is our interpretation, from the perspective of biological evolution, of the issues surrounding the use of animals in medical research.

II. Human Characteristics

All species of organisms have some heritable characteristics that distinguish them from other species. These features are often related to the adaptive advantage(s) possessed by the species. Human beings have several distinctive physical, physiological, behavioral, and cognitive characteristics. The distinctive physical characteristics of *Homo sapiens* include bipedality, sparse body hair, exceptional manual dexterity, and an unusually large brain. Physiological features that are distinctly human include breeding unconfined to a particular season, concealed ovulation, and the lack of an estrous period in the female reproductive cycle.

Evolutionary psychologists John Tooby and Irven DeVore[11] have listed fifteen "divergences" that they considered to be "zoologically unique" to humans, and five others that are not zoologically unique to humans but do differentiate them from other apes.[12] All fifteen "unique" features involved behavioral adaptations (e.g., controlled use of fire, manufacture of complex tools) or cognitive abilities (e.g., language, an expanded system of kin recognition). These behavioral and cognitive adaptations allowed for the development of distinctive social characteristics, such as monogamous pair-bonding and extensive paternal care and provisioning.

The physical, physiological, and behavioral changes that occurred during hominid evolution were accompanied by the emergence of the concepts of morality and rights. We will never know when humans began to develop these concepts, but scholars in various disciplines agree that significant cognitive and linguistic capacities would have been prerequisites.[13] Anthropologists estimate that the complex linguistic abilities of modern humans were in place at least 30,000 to 40,000 years ago, coincident with the appearance of paintings on cave walls.[14] However, humans almost certainly had high levels of cognitive and linguistic skills well before this. The cranial capacity of modern *Homo sapiens* was acquired about 250,000 years ago.[15] Thus, it seems likely that early members of the line of hominids that gave rise to modern humans would have had relatively highly developed cognitive and communicative skills as early as a quarter of a million years ago. This conclusion is supported by the fact that chimpanzees, our closest living relatives among the great apes, have a relatively well developed ability to communicate by vocalizations and gestures, even though their cranial volume is only about one-third that of ours.[16] Furthermore, some chimps and at least one gorilla have been taught to communicate using sign language or symbols.[17]

III. Hominid Evolution

The selective pressures that caused protohumans to evolve distinctly human characteristics are the subject of speculation by anthropologists. Figure 1 shows the approximate sequence of development of some of these characteristics during hominid evolution.

As the figure shows, bipedality was followed by the appearance of improved manual dexterity, the production of crude stone tools, and evidence of scavenging. These developments preceded the onset of brain enlargement.[18] The evolution of bipedality may have been driven by competition among males to provide food for females and their young in exchange for mating.[19] Bipedal competence would have freed the hands for more effective carrying of foodstuffs, and may have led to the development of tools in the form of trays, baskets, or other simple carrying devices, and the use of sticks and stones as weapons or scavenging implements.

Competition among males to excel at provisioning, and among females to attract the most skillful male providers, may have been important selection pres-

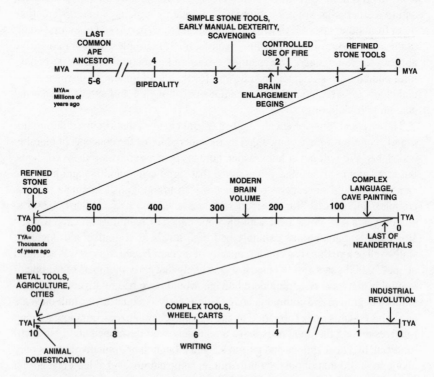

Figure 1. Approximate Times of Major Developments in Human Evolution

sures that promoted cranial enlargement. The smarter males and females would have been more successful in the "mating game," and improved intelligence accompanies brain enlargement. This competition could have involved the formation of alliances between or among males to improve their scavenging and/or hunting success, which would also be favored by improved communication skills. Females may also have formed alliances for mutual protection of young and for food gathering. These activities would also be facilitated by improved intellectual and linguistic competence.

Chimpanzees seem to have the rudiments of the idea of using weapons, but they are not quite "clear on the concept." When displaying aggressive behavior, they often throw objects about and use branches and sticks to beat on various things, but they do not direct their weapons effectively at other chimps or other animals.[20] It probably would not require much of an increase in brain size, with an associated increase in intelligence, for early hominids to realize the lethal potential of throwing stones or bashing animals with sticks. The use of sharpened sticks for stabbing or throwing as spears would easily follow the first use of clubs and stone projectiles. Good evidence indicates that early hominids practiced scavenging before they acquired hunting skills.[21] Bipedality and the use of weapons would have made early hominids more adept at competing with other scavengers (e.g., hyenas, jackals, vultures, etc.) for the carcasses of large animals that had been killed by more successful predators (e.g., lions), and would have greatly improved the hunting success and nutritional status of the protohumans. It has been suggested that increased meat consumption was an important factor contributing to brain enlargement in early hominids because animal flesh has a greater caloric density than plant foods, and a high caloric intake is required to support the growth of a large brain over a relatively short time, as occurs in humans.[22]

IV. Weapons, Morals, and Rights

The development of the effective use of weapons by early hominids must have had a profound effect on their social fabric and their subsequent social evolution because they would then have had the ability to injure severely or even kill one another. Thus, disputes that previously would have resulted in minor injuries or bruised egos could become deadly. The small bands of hominids that, until very recently, constituted the basic social group in hominid evolution would not have been able to survive in the face of this new technology without appropriate changes in behavior. It would have been necessary for them to devise means of reducing or avoiding conflicts between weapons-bearing members of the tribe, and when conflicts did occur, nonlethal means of resolving them would need to be developed. Some animals that are equipped naturally with lethal weapons (e.g., fangs, talons, horns, or antlers) have evolved behaviors that generally allow

them to avoid fatal outcomes in conflicts;[23] such behaviors include the use of sub-
missive or appeasement gestures by combatants who concede defeat. Hence, the
hominids would have adopted the same kind of survival strategy as did other
species with lethal weapons. Bands that were not able to adapt such compen-
satory behavior would not have survived. In addition, fighting among different
weapon-using hominid bands over resources may have provided an additional selection pressure (i.e., interband competition) that promoted brain enlargement,
improved intelligence and linguistic skills, and weapons technology. The smarter
hominids, with their larger brains, would have prevailed over those who were less
well endowed. Accordingly, weapon use may have served as a major driving
force for improved communication skills, and may have inspired the emergence
of codes of morality and the concept of rights; the development of these moral
mechanisms would have helped to ensure the survival of small bands consisting
of a few mutually interdependent individuals. This speculative scheme of hominid evolution is depicted diagrammatically in Figure 2.

Some anthropologists and animal ethologists have suggested that many social
species show behaviors toward conspecifics (i.e., their own kind) that are interpreted as moral behaviors when practiced by humans. For example, Frans de
Waal and Jane Goodall have reported that chimpanzees show altruism, empathy,
indignation, community concern, mutual tolerance, and retribution for transgres-
sions.[24] De Waal also suggests that the evolution of moral-like behavior requires
that animals live in groups in which there is mutual interdependence for resource
acquisition and defense, and that the members of the group be cooperative even
though they have conflicting individual interests. It seems likely, therefore, that
the concepts (and subsequent codification) of morality and rights that emerged

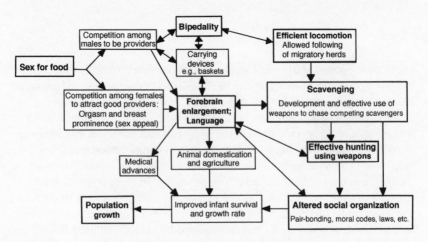

Figure 2. Speculative Scheme of Human Evolution

during human evolution had their foundation in behaviors that appeared early in the evolution of social species, including the social primates.

Codes of morality similar to those embodied in the Ten Commandments or in the "Golden Rule" are essentially universal among human cultures.[25] These codes and the concept of rights promote the welfare and ensure the survival of the "naked ape"[26] as individuals and as a species. Until very recently in human history, moral consideration was extended only to kin and to other members of one's clan, most of whom would be at least distantly related. Members of other clans in the same tribe were also regarded as "moral agents," but the strength of moral concern decreased with the distance of kinship. Members of other tribes, being potential competitors for resources, were considered to be "them" as opposed to "us," and were thus unworthy of moral concern.

V. Kinship Preference and Xenophobia

Preference for kin and for other members of one's own group is an innate tendency in all social animals, including insects. Favoring members of one's social group encourages various behaviors that help to promote bonding among the group members. These behaviors include cooperation, reciprocity or mutualism, care and concern, and reciprocal altruism.[27] Such behaviors have obvious survival value. Social species that were deficient in kinship preference would have experienced reduced reproductive fitness, which would have doomed them to extinction.

Another inherent inclination among social species is xenophobia, which reinforces the tendencies of showing preferences for one's own kind.[28] An instinctive fear of or caution toward strangers (i.e., members of other groups) is an adaptation that protects animals and their kin from being overrun by potential competitors: "Do not trust strangers, because they may steal your resources." Xenophobic sentiments lead to discrimination by humans against other humans on the basis of race, nationality, ethnicity, religion, clan affiliation, etc.; based on kinship preference, these types of discrimination find their root in humans' evolutionary history. In contrast, other forms of discrimination, such as on the basis of age, sex, or physical abilities, are probably not inherent human tendencies.

The natural inclinations of xenophobia and preference for members of one's own group have been superseded in humans, at least to some extent, by cultural evolution. The development of agriculture and animal domestication about 10,000 years ago fostered the emergence of communities that grew to encompass varying numbers of previously competing tribes (see Figure 1). Groups that remained as hunter-gatherers were either absorbed or exterminated in this process. This change from hunting and gathering to an agrarian lifestyle is called the *first demographic transition*.

Successful agriculture allowed for a rapid increase in population size, which resulted in armed conflicts between larger tribes or tribal groups over territory and other resources. With improved weapons technology, these conflicts became increasingly brutal and devastating. Therefore, it became in our own mutual and enlightened self-interest to expand the membership in our realm of moral concern so as to eventually include all of humankind. This expansion of concern gave rise to the ideas of the "brotherhood of man" and the "sanctity of human life," and eventually led to the codification of these ideas in documents such as the United Nations' Declaration of Human Rights (imperfectly followed though it is), the Geneva Convention, and the Nuremberg Code.

VI. Cultural Evolution and the Progress in Medical Science

The development of successful food-crop cultivation and animal domestication allowed for an accelerating rate of cultural evolution. City-states, which gave rise to early civilizations, emerged because it was no longer necessary for all the members of these early agricultural communities to be fully engaged in food production; some community members could devote time and energy to other pursuits. Thus, the communities could support craftsmen, artisans, and scholars. This last group included philosophers, teachers, scientists, and physicians. Although advances in technlogy and the arts occurred relatively rapidly in these early civilizations, the acquisition of knowledge in the biomedical and other sciences progressed very slowly during the first several millennia of recorded history (beginning about 5,000 or 6,000 years ago). However, the rate of technological progress began to increase rapidly about four centuries ago, and it has subsequently become exponential.[29] Thus, more than 80 percent of our current knowledge in the biomedical sciences has been acquired since 1800, and more than half our total knowledge in the field has accrued during the twentieth century.

This rapid gain in progress was to a large extent dependent upon the increase in the use of animals for experimental purposes. For example, during the first quarter of the nineteenth century, animal studies contributed to fewer than one-third of the major biomedical advances. By contrast, during the twentieth century, studies on animals have contributed significantly to about three quarters of the major advances.[30] This estimate of the extent of the contribution of animal research to our biomedical knowledge is supported by a report by biomedical scientists Robert Leader and Dennis Stark stating that of the seventy-six Nobel Prizes for Physiology or Medicine awarded between 1901 and 1982, 71 percent were given for research that depended upon studies with animals.[31] Since then (i.e., between 1983 and 1998), at least eleven of the sixteen prizes awarded (i.e., nearly seventy percent) also involved the use of animals.[32]

The improved understanding of how living organisms function when they are healthy, and of what causes them to become unhealthy or diseased, has resulted in a dramatic improvement in the health, well-being, and survival of humans and domestic (and some nondomestic) animals. For example, in the ancient civilizations of the Mediterranean and the Middle East, the average life expectancy was about twenty years because of the very high death rates of infants and of young women during their first childbirth. By 1900, the average life span in Europe and North America had increased to forty-seven years, and by 1990 it had risen further, to seventy-six years.[33]

The striking increase in average life span during the past century is due primarily to the implementation of various public health measures, including the regulation of the purity of air and drinking water, the covering of open sewers, the processing of sewage wastes, and the prevention and control of infectious diseases by immunizations and antibiotic treatments.[34] The establishment of such public health measures came about because the *germ theory of disease* was proven to be valid by the research of Louis Pasteur and Robert Koch in the late nineteenth century. Prior to this work, the "medical establishments" in Europe and North America thought the idea that microbes could cause large, healthy animals or humans to become sick and die was ludicrous. However, Pasteur and Koch proved that anthrax in sheep and cholera in chickens were each caused by a bacterium. Thus, the role of microbes in infectious diseases was established.[35]

VII. The Second Demographic Transition

The rapid technological progress during the past several centuries was accompanied by major demographic changes in the Western world. The population shifted from being overwhelmingly rural and agricultural to being urbanized and employed in industries. This shift to an urban environment separated a growing segment of the population from regular contact with wild and/or domestic animals. Thus, they lost their awareness of the relationships between humans and animals and between different species of animals, relationships that were known to humans for at least a quarter of a million years.[36]

Technological progress and urbanization also caused the emergence of a growing middle class, many of whom were freed from concerns about obtaining the necessities of life from day to day. Social anthropologist Susan Sperling has concluded that animal-welfare sentiments arose from the growing ranks of the middle class during the nineteenth century—particularly in the United Kingdom—and that some of these animal-welfare advocates developed sentiments of opposition to animal experimentation, especially when it involved surgical manipulations (i.e., they became antivivisectionists).[37]

Antivivisectionist sentiments developed in reaction to the increased use of animals in biomedical research, and the present-day animal rights and animal liberation organizations are derived from the antivivisectionist groups that formed as a result of these sentiments.[38] Although the current advocates of animal rights and animal liberation do not always identify themselves as antivivisectionists, they use the same arguments and tactics—and have the same objectives—as their Victorian-era predecessors.[39] Three kinds of "persuasion" are used by animal activists to win converts to their cause. First, a large proportion of the ALARM literature is devoted to promoting the moral or ethical basis of their philosophy; this tactic, however, has not succeeded in winning over many converts.[40] Accordingly, animal advocates often resort to a second tactic, namely, to misrepresenting, in various ways, the history and the utility of animal-based research, as well as how such research is conducted and regulated.[41] Third, some of the more extreme activists have resorted to threats, vandalism, and violence in an attempt to halt animal research. This last tactic is particularly virulent in the United Kingdom.[42] The remainder of this essay will be devoted to addressing the moral or ethical arguments of the ALARM from an evolutionary perspective.

VIII. The Moral Argument for Animal "Protection"

The moral justification of the philosophical position of the leading advocates of the ALARM have been well summarized by Andrew Rowan and Bernard Rollin (a veterinarian and philosopher, respectively) as follows:

1. Animals should not be regarded as mere objects for human use, because they have an interest in living and in avoiding discomfort and pain. Thus, they have value in their own right.
2. In dealing with animals, we must consider their interests and the moral implications of our behavior toward them.
3. Humans do not differ from other animals in ways that meet the "test of moral relevance."[43]

We believe that most people would essentially agree with the first two points, because they are consistent with the "humane" treatment of animals. However, the third point is not widely accepted.

Although the leading animal moralists differ in the criteria that they emphasize for the "test of moral relevance," they generally agree that animals and humans have certain qualities in common that should be considered, such as the following:

1. The ability to feel pain and to suffer
2. An interest in living and in avoiding pain, discomfort and death
3. Self-awareness, self-control, beliefs, and desires
4. Intentionality and purposiveness, and a sense of the past and of the future
5. Kinship awareness and the capacity to relate to and show concern for others
6. Curiosity and an ability to communicate

Although many social species may have these "shared qualities" to some degree, it is doubtful that any, except possibly the great apes, have all of them. On the basis of these criteria, however, animal rights/liberation moralists conclude that there are no "morally relevant" differences between us and nonhuman animals. Because we grant ourselves certain rights (e.g., to life, liberty, and the pursuit of happiness), then animals should be similarly awarded, especially since they have the same "morally relevant" characteristics, particularly the ability to feel pain and to suffer. Thus, we cannot justify exploiting animals for our own benefit. This argument, however, merely makes an association between the possession of certain characteristics that we share with animals and the possession of rights. This association is comparable to arguing that since both humans and animals reproduce sexually, and humans have moral codes regulating their sexual activity, then animals should have similar codes.

IX. The Concept of Rights

Simply defined, rights are just and fair claims (to anything—life, liberty, power, privilege, etc.) that belong to persons, as groups or individuals by law or tradition. Understanding rights in their various manifestations is not simple, however. As philosopher Carl Cohen has cogently written:

> The differing targets, contents, and sources of rights, and their inevitable conflict, together weave a tangled web. Notwithstanding all such complications, this much is clear about rights in general: they are in every case claims, or potential claims, within a community of moral agents . . . [i.e.,] among beings who actually do, or can, make moral claims against one another.[44]

Thus, it is clear that animals cannot have rights: they cannot claim them. The concept of "rights" is a creation of the human mind that was invented to promote harmony and/or to reduce conflict in complex social, political, economic, and legal interactions. Accordingly, there are no "natural" or "God-given" rights.

The granting or claiming of rights has significant ethical ramifications that can be understood only by beings with the capacity to reason and to make moral judgments. When persons claim the rights to which they are entitled, they must accept the associated obligations. For example, individuals who claim the right to freedom of expression must refrain from abusing that right by slandering other people. People who do not meet their moral obligations can lose their rights. In our society, they may lose their property, their freedom, and even their life. Thus, the claiming of rights is not without cost. Obviously, animals cannot have rights of the kinds that are accorded to normal human beings. Animals can neither claim rights nor accept the responsibilities that are associated with having them. The concept of rights has meaning only in a community of moral agents. Therefore, only humans can have rights.[45]

These conclusions are supported by considering how rights and moral codes might be applied to animals. Contributors to a recent anthology, *The Great Ape Project: Equality Beyond Humanity,* argue that all species of the great apes should be given moral standing equal to that of human beings.[46] If this suggestion were to be implemented, then nonhuman apes would need to be given special status because their behavior cannot be judged by the moral standards that apply to normal human beings. For example, Goodall reported in a 1977 article that adult male and female chimpanzees have been observed killing and eating infant chimps on numerous occasions in different reserves in Central Africa.[47] Should these animals have been tried for infanticide and cannibalism? If they had, would they have been entitled to a trial by a jury of their peers? What would those peers be? Could a nonchimpanzee ape (i.e., a human) have served as the presiding judge at such a trial? How could we have communicated with the animals to inform them of their rights? Obviously, if apes or other animals were given rights or considerations equal to those we accord to normal human beings, we could not hold them accountable to the same moral standards to which we hold humans.

Singer and other advocates for animals argue that we should give special consideration to animals that lack the cognitive capacities of normal adult and subadult humans because we give such consideration to classes of humans whose physical and/or mental abilities are no greater than those of many mammals, such as chimpanzees, pigs, or dogs.[48] Such classes of humans, often referred to as "marginal cases," include normal infants and mentally retarded or mentally disabled (i.e., brain-damaged) individuals. Including these groups in this category runs counter to the innate inclination of all social animals, and of many or most nonsocial animals, to protect their young and to favor their own kind over other species. Any social species that did not show such a preference for its own kind would soon become extinct, because the survival of such species is strongly dependent on mutual support.

Mentally retarded or disabled individuals have suffered a tragedy because they cannot realize the full potential in life that normal human beings can experience. By contrast, apes, dogs, or pigs with cognitive capacities comparable to those of a mentally retarded or disabled human are not tragic beings. The families of retarded or brain-damaged individuals also suffer from the tragedy that befell their loved ones. To regard retarded or disabled persons as subhuman, as some animal activists suggest, would compound this tragedy. Furthermore, what degree of mental retardation would a person have to display before being consigned "equal-to-animals" status? Crossing the gap that we maintain between our own species and others would place this judgment on the proverbial slippery slope. Cohen addresses the issue of rights and the mentally impaired in this way: "The capacity for moral judgment that distinguishes humans from animals is not a test to be administered to human beings one by one. Persons who are unable, because of some disability, to perform the full moral functions natural to human beings are certainly not for that reason ejected from the moral community."[49]

X. "Speciesism"

Some advocates for animals, including Singer, do not believe that animals deserve to have rights in the same sense that we accord them to humans.[50] Instead, they argue that because animals meet their criteria of "moral relevance," they are entitled to equal moral consideration with human beings. If we are willing to exploit animals in any way, we should be willing to do likewise to people since humans are not more "morally relevant" than animals. When we regard animals to be less than our moral equals, we are practicing a kind of interspecies discrimination that these advocates call "speciesism," an attitude they analogize to types of intraspecies discrimination such as sexism and racism. Richard Ryder claims credit for coining the term "speciesism" in 1970.[51] In 1985 the term was defined in the *Oxford English Dictionary* as "[d]iscrimination against or exploitation of certain animal species by human beings, based on an assumption of mankind's superiority."[52] Singer has stated that "[s]peciesism . . . is a prejudice or attitude of bias in favor of the interests of members of one's own species and against those of members of other species."[53]

To support the correctness of their opinion about the immorality of speciesism, animal activists claim that it is comparable to discrimination on the basis of sex or race. We object strongly to this kind of equation. To quote Cohen again, "[t]his argument is worse than unsound: it is atrocious."[54] Sexism and racism are not justifiable because normal men and women of all racial and ethnic groups are, on average, intellectually and morally equal, and their behavior can be judged against the same moral standards. Animals do not have such equivalence with humans. To deny rights or equal consideration on the basis of sex or race is immoral because all normal humans, regardless of sex, ethnicity, or race, can claim the rights and considerations that they deserve, and they know what it means to be unjustly denied them. No animals have these abilities. Speciesism, as defined by Ryder and Singer, is a normal kind of discrimination displayed by all social animals, but racism and sexism are widely considered to be morally indefensible practices. By equating racism and sexism with speciesism, Ryder and Singer degrade the struggle to achieve racial and sexual equality.[55] In addition to having this ethical problem, the concept of speciesism is also biologically absurd; we consider this below.

XI. The Double Standard of Animal Advocates

According to animal rightists, only the human animal is immoral for exploiting other species, because we do not need to do so and we are moral agents. They also allege that we could use so-called "alternatives to animals" for biomedical research and that we do not need to consume animals for food or clothing, or to satisfy our other needs. Thus, we could choose to live a "cruelty-free" lifestyle if we had the proper moral fiber. The fact that the so-called cruelty-free lifestyle is an illusion has been discussed by us previously.[56] Animal advocates also argue that when predators kill and eat other species, they are justified in doing so because, unlike us, they have no alternative food sources.[57] However, these beliefs—that only human behavior toward other animals should be judged morally, and that we are the only natural predator that could abandon a predatory lifestyle—contradict the central tenet of the ALARM philosophy, the claim that we are "just like other animals." In fact, virtually all human behavior is judged against moral standards, particularly our treatment of our own kind and other animals. In contrast, no one can rationally judge the behavior of any nonhuman species against any moral standards. This difference between other creatures and us nullifies the argument of ALARMists that there are "no morally relevant differences between humans and nonhuman animals."

Animal activists also maintain that we are especially cruel and destructive to our own kind and to other species. For example, Singer stated:

> We rarely stop to consider that the animal who kills with the least reason to do so is the human animal. . . . Throughout their history they [human beings] have shown a tendency to torment and torture both their fellow human beings and their fellow animals before putting them to death. No other animals show much interest in doing this.[58]

This undocumented, sweeping condemnation of humanity shows an obvious (possibly willful) ignorance of biology. Numerous examples of cruelty by animals toward other animals can be cited. For example, even when well fed, the domestic cat is notoriously ruthless to the small mammals and birds that it kills; it often does so after tormenting them and inflicting increasingly serious injury. In fact, it has been estimated that the "recreational" hunting by domestic cats in the United Kingdom kills about 100 million small birds and mammals each year.[59] In the United States, cats are estimated to kill at least 4.4 million songbirds *each day*.[60] The U.S. figure alone amounts to more than 1.6 billion songbirds each year, which exceeds the current number of animals used each year for biomedical research in the United States (about 25 million) by several orders of magnitude.[61] Thus, it would seem that if ALARMists were genuinely interested in minimizing animal suffering, they would advocate the extermination of the domestic cat.

Shrikes, or "butcherbirds," capture small animals and impale them, often while they are still alive, on thorns and barbs in their territory to display their hunting skills to females.[62] The great horned owl and wild mink are both known to kill, in a murderous frenzy, more animals than they can eat.[63] Orcas, or killer whales, have been observed tormenting and brutalizing (seemingly "playing with") sea-lion pups until they are dead before eating them.[64] Walter Howard has reported other examples of animal brutality to animals.[65] Female cougars and mountain lions often injure several sheep in a flock so that their cubs can learn to kill prey animals. The death of these sheep is not swift or merciful. Like such cubs, canids such as wolves or coyotes are not efficient killers of large prey animals. Hence, they usually begin to consume their prey while it is still alive and conscious. Similar acts of cruelty, when committed by humans, are considered to be grossly immoral, but animal advocates are largely silent about these examples of cruelty to animals by animals.

Some interspecies exploitation does not involve predation. Many species of animals, including numerous types of birds and fish, practice a form of nonconsumptive exploitation called *brood parasitism,* whereby the parental instincts of a foreign species are exploited to raise the young of the exploiting creature.[66] This form of exploitation often occurs at the expense of the exploited species' young. Cuckoos and cowbirds are the most commonly known examples of species that practice brood parasitism, "victimizing" various species of songbirds such as reed warblers.[67]

To try to judge the behavior of these animals by our moral standards would be ludicrous. They are simply acting out their instinctive behaviors. Brood parasitism, for example, is an adaptation that gives its practitioners a significant reproductive advantage. By exploiting unwitting foster parents, they can produce more offspring during each breeding season than they could if they were obliged to care for their own young. This is clearly behavior that is advantageous from an evolutionary standpoint, though beyond the pale of moral consideration.

XII. Some "Morally Relevant" Human Characteristics

From our perspective as biologists, we do not believe that proving the moral superiority of humans over other animals is necessary to justify our exploitation of them. Nevertheless, we do acknowledge that there are some uniquely human characteristics that tend to be ignored by the ALARMists. The human animal is unique in showing concern for the welfare of other species, and this concern extends beyond the realm of domestic animals. Consider the effort and resources being expended to prevent many species of animals—and even plants—from becoming extinct. Although many species live in *symbiotic relationships*—that is, the living together of two dissimilar organisms in a mutually beneficial relationship—there are no societies of nonhuman predators that promote the minimizing of the suffering of prey animals when they are killed. Human concern for animal welfare probably arose when the symbiotic relationship between humans and canids was first established some 12,000 years ago.[68] People in agrarian cultures, as well as those who remained in hunter-gatherer societies, were not only dependent on animals for their survival, but they also had a high regard, or even a reverence, for them. Evidence for this respect is seen in the earliest human artwork and in the totemic figures of virtually all primitive human cultures.[69]

As we stated above, the human animal is the only species whose behavior is (or can be) judged against moral standards, especially in our treatment of our own kind and of other animals. We are also alone in being the judges of such behavior. More differences between other animals and ourselves are discussed below.

XIII. The Human Adaptive Advantage

The adaptive advantage of the "naked ape" is his large brain, with its associated cognitive capacities that greatly exceed those of any other species. Although many species are inquisitive, we are the only one with an insatiable curiosity that extends well beyond the desire to find food, shelter, and mates. Evolution has endowed us with a need to know as much as we can about the universe around us, in both its living and nonliving aspects. We use that knowledge to improve the quality of our lives and to protect ourselves from various forces that threaten our survival as individuals and as a species. Accordingly, the ability to acquire knowledge and to use it, to be technologically creative, and to have the capacity for cultural evolution (i.e., *behavioral plasticity*) constitutes our major adaptive advantage.

We believe there are five major threats to human survival, as follows:

1. Microbes, including bacteria, viruses, and protozoans
2. Parasites, such as malaria and schistosomiasis

3. Insects and arachnids, which destroy food crops and act as vectors for diseases
4. Natural catastrophes, such as impact by a comet like the one that apparently caused the extinction of the dinosaurs
5. Ourselves—through pollution, environmental destruction, and possibly via annihilation by nuclear holocaust

At this time we cannot deal with the fourth problem, and coping with the fifth will require concerted efforts on an international scale. The first three dangers to human survival are ones that we will always have to battle, because these organisms evolve rapidly. Thus, when we devise means of controlling these threats—with drugs, immunizations, or pesticides—the organisms often change to escape from these controlling agents. For example, new strains of the tubercle bacillus and of the microbe that causes cholera have recently emerged, resistant to the antibiotics that killed their evolutionary predecessors. Furthermore, new viral agents, such as HIV, Hanta, and Ebola, are always emerging.

The only way that we can cope with these ever-changing and newly emerging threats is to use our adaptive advantage to its fullest extent. If our cognitive abilities, including our incessant drive to acquire new knowledge, were to be curtailed, we would face the likelihood of decimation, or even extinction. As noted above, it is estimated that over 99.9 percent of all animals and plant species that have ever existed on Earth have become extinct. They were unable to cope indefinitely with the forces of natural selection that operate relentlessly to exterminate species. However, we may be the only species that has a chance to avoid that fate, because only we know that extinction is virtually an inevitable outcome, and perhaps our intellect will enable us to avoid it. Within the next century, humans will probably colonize at least one other planet (Mars), and possibly our own moon and one or more of the moons of Jupiter. Thus, if catastrophic events do occur on Earth, some of our species surviving at these outposts could eventually repopulate our planet.

XIV. Animal Rightsism: A Maladaptive Philosophy

Because it is an evolutionary necessity to regard one's own kind as more important than members of other species (especially for social species), the philosophy of the ALARMists takes on an even more bizarre countenance. What could motivate a few members of the species *Homo sapiens* to adopt such an un-Darwinian attitude? Demographic data collected by Wesley Jamison and William Lunch shed some light on this question.[70] These investigators distributed questionnaires to participants in the "March for the Animals" that was held

Table 1. Demographics of Participants in the National "Rally for the
Animals," June 10, 1990, Washington, D.C.

95% Caucasian	50% Professional
89% Had pets	50% Liberal
80% Had no children	50% Vegetarian
77% Women	48% Held bachelor's
77% Urban or suburban	degrees or higher
71% Born after 1950	28% Vegan

on June 10, 1990 in Washington, D.C. Their data, based on a total of 412 interviews, are summarized in Table 1.

Clearly, the vast majority of the activists are white urban or suburban women, and a large percentage of them are highly educated and have pets. Large numbers of them are professionals, describe themselves as vegetarians or vegans, and/or have a liberal political inclination. It is also noteworthy that 71 percent of the respondents were born after 1950.[71] Thus, they did not experience the fear of the dreaded infectious diseases—such as polio, diphtheria, or tuberculosis—that prevailed during the earlier decades of this century. By the mid-1950s, such killers were largely eliminated by vaccination programs and antibiotics. These developments were strongly dependent on animal research.[72]

Perhaps the most revealing statistic from the data in Table 1 is the fact that only 20 percent of those interviewed had children. In a group with similar demographics in the general population, at least 80 percent would have children. It seems, therefore, that animal activists are very fond of animals but not so fond of children, which is consistent with the fact that they do not favor their own kind over other species. From a Darwinian perspective, this attitude shows that these animal advocates are adaptively unfit. Inasmuch as only a small percentage of them have children, and children generally adopt the sentiments of their parents, it seems unlikely that animal activists will become a dominant proportion of modern society.

XV. Antiscience and Misanthropic Sentiments

The survey by Jamison and Lunch revealed some additional important insights into the sentiments of the marchers.[73] More than half of the respondents believed that science has done more harm than good, whereas only about one quarter of them held the opposite view. One can contrast these data with the results of a survey conducted by the National Science Foundation, of U.S. residents' attitudes toward science. Only 5 percent of the general public believes that science has done more harm than good, while almost 60 percent agrees that science has done more good than harm.[74] Obviously, skepticism about the benefits of science is a prevalent sentiment among animal activists—they are ten times more likely to have such an attitude than is a member of the general population.

Another significant finding of the Jamison-Lunch survey was that more than half of the marchers would not approve of animal research that would be beneficial to humans, *even if the animals were not harmed by it.*[75] This datum illustrates that antiscientific and misanthropic sentiments were held by a majority of the animal activists whose opinions were gathered at the 1990 "March for the Animals." Statements made by the leading figures in the movement also show the prevalence of these sentiments. For example, Ingrid Newkirk, national director and cofounder of People for the Ethical Treatment of Animals (PETA), one of the largest animal rights organizations in the United States, has made several revealing statements, including her claim that "[m]ankind is the biggest blight on the face of the Earth."[76] Criticisms of basic research with animals (that is, research done simply to acquire knowledge) appear frequently in Singer's publications, and his portrait of animal experimentation in the second edition of *Animal Liberation* is grossly distorted and unbalanced, a serious mischaracterization of such research. He makes no attempt to compare the true costs and benefits of animal research; one would expect that a quantitative comparison of this sort would be essential to a professed utilitarian.[77] The fact that Singer regards his own species with something less than great regard is revealed by the following statement: "[I]f . . . children [were given] a pleasant year before being humanely slaughtered, it would seem that the gourmet who wished to dine on roast human child would have as good a defense of his practice as those who claim that they are entitled to eat pork because the pig would not otherwise have existed."[78] As a final example of the true sentiments of animal rights activists, consider PETA member Dan Mathews's answer to a question, put to him by a newspaper reporter, about PETA's solution to fighting diseases: "Don't get them in the first place, schmo."[79]

XVI. Conclusions

From an evolutionary perspective, attempts to find moral justification for the use of animals on the basis of our "moral superiority" or otherwise are unnecessary, and the arguments against such justifications are nonsensical. We are essentially like all other organisms whose fundamental goals in life are to eat, survive, and reproduce. Our adaptive advantage—our intellect, with all that it entails—has enabled us to be exceptionally successful at realizing these fundamental goals. It has also enabled us to achieve many things that no other animal can even imagine, including science, technology, the arts, and so on.

Because of their idiosyncratic philosophical beliefs, animal advocates would deny us the ability to use our adaptive advantage in certain ways: namely, to use animals for our benefit, particularly in pursuits that involve acquiring knowledge about the functions and malfunctions of living creatures, including ourselves. Animal advocates have an unbalanced obsession with the use of animals in biomedical research. This is illustrated by our content analysis of twenty-one of the major books on animal rights that are devoted to describing how humans exploit animals. Nearly two-thirds of the total pages of these books emphasize concern about animals' use in research and teaching, even though only about 0.3 percent of the animals used by humans are employed for this purpose.[80]

The relationships that develop between or among different species (e.g., symbiotic or parasitic) are a result of evolution. Since these relationships are based in biology, it is nonsensical to moralize about them and to advocate "rights" for animals, or even for equality among the species. Accordingly, the only code of morality that could be rationally applied to relationships between other species and ourselves is that of contractualism, as we discussed in Section I. However, given that animals are not capable of understanding the moral concepts needed to engage in a contractual agreement with humans, approaching human-animal interactions from a contractualist perspective leads to the conclusion that moral theorizing about human duties to animals is a pointless enterprise.

The foregoing arguments in this essay illustrate that, from the perspective of Darwinian theory, the exploitation of some species of animals by others is not an appropriate topic for moral concern, especially when the exploiting animals need to engage in this activity in order to survive. This generalization applies to the human animal as well as to other predatory species. However, although the evolutionary viewpoint would hold that the human use of animals per se is not worthy of moral consideration, the humane perspective requires that *how* we use animals is of moral concern. The unnecessary or unjustified suffering of animals, including humans, should always be avoided.

NOTES

1. Susan Sperling, *Animal Liberators: Research and Morality* (Berkeley: University of California Press, 1988), 25–75.
2. Jeremy Bentham, *An Introduction to the Principles of Morals and Legislation,* ed. J. H. Burns and H. L. A. Hart (London: Athlone Press, 1970), 282–83 n. b. (In fairness to Bentham, it should be noted that though the *Introduction to the Principles* contains 311 pages of text, animals are mentioned exactly three times. The most substantive mention is the one quoted, which appeared, as indicated, in a footnote.)
3. Tom Regan, *The Case for Animal Rights* (Berkeley: University of California Press, 1983).
4. Peter Singer, *Animal Liberation: A New Ethics for Our Treatment of Animals* (New

York: Random House, 1975); Peter Singer, *Animal Liberation,* 2d ed. (New York: New York Review of Books, 1990). Singer has objected to being called an advocate for animal "rights." See Peter Singer, "Postcommentary: Ethics and Animals," *Behavioral and Brain Sciences* 13, no. 1 (March 1990): 46. However, in a more recent interview with an animal rights activist, he appears to be supportive of the concept, at least for apes. See Kim W. Stallwood, "A Conversation with Peter Singer," *Animals' Agenda,* March/April 1994, 25–29.

5. For example, see Michael Allen Fox, *The Case for Animal Experimentation: An Evolutionary and Ethical Perspective* (Berkeley: University of California Press, 1986); Carl Cohen, "The Case for the Use of Animals in Biomedical Research," *New England Journal of Medicine* 315, no. 14 (October 2, 1986): 865–70; Michael P. T. Leahy, *Against Liberation: Putting Animals in Perspective* (London: Routledge, 1991); and John U. Dennis, "Morally Relevant Differences Between Animals and Human Beings: Justifying the Use of Animals in Biomedical Research," *Journal of the American Veterinary Medical Association* 210, No. 5 (March 1, 1997): 612–18.

6. Peter Carruthers, *The Animals Issue: Moral Theory in Practice* (Cambridge: Cambridge University Press, 1992).

7. John Rawls, *A Theory of Justice* (Oxford: Clarendon Press, 1972).

8. See the references in notes 2–4.

9. See the references in note 5.

10. David M. Raup, *Extinction: Bad Genes or Bad Luck?* (New York: W. W. Norton, 1991), 4.

11. John Tooby and Irven DeVore, "The Reconstruction of Hominid Behavioral Evolution Through Strategic Modeling," in Warren G. Kinzey, ed., *The Evolution of Human Behavior: Primate Models* (Albany: State University of New York Press, 1987), 183–237.

12. Although anthropologists and taxonomists have classified humans in a separate family (*homo*) from the pongids or great apes (e.g., chimps, gorillas, and orangutans), this separation is arbitrary and anthropocentric. The fact that humans are members of the great ape family is now widely accepted, as evidenced by our being referred to as "the naked ape" by Desmond Morris in his *The Naked Ape: A Zoologist's Study of the Human Animal* (New York: McGraw-Hill, 1967), and as "the third chimpanzee" by Jared Diamond in his *The Third Chimpanzee: The Evolution and the Future of the Human Animal* (New York: HarperCollins, 1992).

13. Gunther S. Stent, ed., *Morality as a Biological Phenomenon—Report of the Dahlem Workshop on Biology and Morals* (Berlin: Dahlem Konferenzen, 1978), 53–74.

14. Constance Holden, "No Last Word on Language Origins," *Science* 282, no. 5393 (November 20, 1998): 1455–58.

15. Terrence W. Deacon, "The Human Brain," in Steve Jones, Robert Martin, and David Pilbeam, eds., *The Cambridge Encyclopedia of Human Evolution* (Cambridge: Cambridge University Press, 1992), 115–23.

16. Jones, Martin, and Pilbeam, eds., *The Cambridge Encyclopedia of Human Evolution,* 108; Elke Zimmerman, "Vocal Communication by Non-Human Primates," in Jones, Martin, and Pilbeam, eds., *The Cambridge Encyclopedia of Human Evolution,* 124–27; Jared Diamond, *The Third Chimpanzee,* 141–67.

17. Sue Savage-Rumbaugh, "Language Training of Apes," in Jones, Martin, and Pilbeam, eds., *The Cambridge Encyclopedia of Human Evolution,* 139–41.
18. Lewis R. Binford, "Subsistence—A Key to the Past," in Jones, Martin, and Pilbeam, eds., *The Cambridge Encyclopedia of Human Evolution,* 365–68; Jean de Heinzelin, et al., "Environment and Behavior of 2.5-Million-Year-Old Bouri Hominids," *Science* 284, no. 5414 (April 23, 1999): 625–29.
19. C. Owen Lovejoy, "Modeling Human Origins: Are We Sexy Because We're Smart or Smart Because We're Sexy?" in D. Tab Rasmussen, ed., *The Origin and Evolution of Humans and Humanness* (Boston: Jones and Bartlett, 1993), 1–28.
20. Jane Goodall, "Unusual Violence in the Overthrow of an Alpha Male Chimpanzee at Gombe," in Toshisada Nishita et al., eds., *Human Origins,* vol. 1 of *Topics in Primatology* (Tokyo: University of Tokyo Press, 1992), 131–42.
21. Binford, "Subsistence"; de Heinzelin et al., "Environment and Behavior of Bouri Hominids."
22. Ann Gibbons, "Solving the Brain's Energy Crisis," *Science* 280, no. 5368 (May 29, 1998): 1345–47.
23. Konrad Lorenz, *On Aggression* (New York: Bantam Books, 1967), 109–38.
24. Frans de Waal, *Good Natured: The Origins of Right and Wrong in Humans and Other Animals* (Cambridge, MA: Harvard University Press, 1996); Jane Goodall, *The Chimpanzees of Gombe: Patterns of Behavior* (Cambridge, MA: Harvard University Press, 1986).
25. Stent, *Morality as a Biological Phenomenon.*
26. Morris, *The Naked Ape.*
27. Dennis L. Krebs, "The Evolution of Moral Behaviors," in Charles Crawford and Dennis L. Krebs, eds., *Handbook of Evolutionary Psychology: Ideas, Issues, and Applications* (Mahwah, NJ: Lawrence Erlbaum Associates, 1998), 337–68; J. Philippe Rushton, "Genetic Similarity, Human Altruism, and Group Selection," *Behavioral and Brain Sciences* 12, no. 3 (September 1989): 503–59.
28. Garrett Hardin, "Population Skeletons in the Environmental Closet," *Bulletin of the Atomic Scientists* 28, no. 6 (June 1972): 37–41; Carl Sagan and Ann Druyan, *Shadows of Forgotten Ancestors: A Search for Who We Are* (New York: Ballantine Books, 1992), 241–56.
29. Gerhard Lenski, *Human Societies: A Macrolevel Introduction to Sociology* (New York: McGraw-Hill, 1970); Charles S. Nicoll and Sharon M. Russell, "Mozart, Alexander the Great, and the Animal Rights/Liberation Philosophy," *FASEB Journal* 5, no. 14 (November 1991): 2888–92.
30. Nicoll and Russell, "The Animal Rights/Liberation Philosophy."
31. Robert W. Leader and Dennis Stark, "The Importance of Animals in Biomedical Research," *Perspectives in Biology and Medicine* 30, no. 4 (Summer 1987): 470–85.
32. Extracted from press releases and biographies of the prize's awardees provided by the Nobel Foundation, which are available at http//www.nobel.se/prize/lists.html.
33. Edward Shorter, *The Health Century* (New York: Doubleday, 1987), 2–3.
34. Ibid.
35. Albert S. Lyons and R. Joseph Petrucelli, *Medicine: An Illustrated History* (New York: Abradale Press, 1987), 556–59. See also Kenneth F. Kiple and Kriemhild

Connè Ornelas, "Experimental Animals in Medical Research: A History," in this volume, 23–48.

36. See Stephan Budiansky, *The Covenant of the Wild: Why Animals Chose Domestication* (New York: W. Morrow, 1992); and Juliet Clutton-Brock, "Domestication of Animals," in Jones, Martin, and Pilbeam, eds., *The Cambridge Encyclopedia of Human Evolution,* 380–85.

37. Sperling, *Animal Liberators,* 25–75.

38. Ibid., 77–102.

39. Larry Horton, "Commentary: The Enduring Animal Issue," *Journal of the National Cancer Institute* 81, no. 10 (May 22, 1989): 736–43.

40. Charles S. Nicoll and Sharon M. Russell, "Analysis of Animal Rights Literature Reveals the Underlying Motives of the Movement: Ammunition for Counter Offensive by Scientists," *Endocrinology* 127, no. 3 (September 1990): 985–89.

41. Charles S. Nicoll and Sharon M. Russell, "Animal Rights, Animal Research, and Human Obligations," *Molecular and Cellular Biosciences* 3, no. 4 (August 1992): 271–77; Sharon M. Russell and Charles S. Nicoll, "A Dissection of the Chapter 'Tools for Research' in Peter Singer's *Animal Liberation,*" *Proceedings of the Society of Experimental Biology and Medicine* 211, no. 2 (February 1996):109–38; Adrian R. Morrison, "Biomedical Research and the Animal Rights Movement: A Contrast in Values," *American Biology Teacher* 55, no. 4 (April 1993): 204–8.

42. David Henshaw, *Animal Warfare: The Story of the Animal Liberation Front* (London: Fontana, 1989).

43. Andrew N. Rowan and Bernard E. Rollin, "Animal Research—For and Against: A Philosophical, Social, and Historical Perspective," *Perspectives in Biology and Medicine* 27, no. 1 (Autumn 1993): 1–17. Rowan and Rollin would both be classified as "moderates" in the animal rights/research debate by some individuals. However, they both favor more restrictions on animal research than are currently in practice.

44. Cohen, "The Case for the Use of Animals," 865.

45. Readers interested in a more extensive discussion of this point should see ibid., 865–67.

46. Paola Cavalieri and Peter Singer, eds., *The Great Ape Project: Equality Beyond Humanity* (New York: St. Martin's Press, 1996).

47. Jane Goodall, "Infant Killing and Cannibalism in Free-Living Chimpanzees," *Folia Primatologica* 28, no. 4 (1977): 259–89.

48. Singer, *Animal Liberation,* 2d ed.; James L. Nelson, "Marginal Cases" and Evelyn Pluhar, "Marginal Cases: Categorical and Biconditional Versions," both in Marc Bekoff, ed., *Encyclopedia of Animal Rights and Animal Welfare* (Westport, CT: Greenwood Press, 1998), 237–38 and 239–41, respectively.

49. Cohen, "The Case for the Use of Animals," 866.

50. Singer, *Animal Liberation* and *Animal Liberation,* 2d ed. See note 4.

51. Richard D. Ryder, *Victims of Science: The Use of Animals in Research* (London: National Anti-Vivisection Society, 1975).

52. *Oxford English Dictionary,* s. v. "speciesism."

53. Singer, *Animal Liberation,* 2d ed., 6.

54. Cohen, "The Case for the Use of Animals," 867.

172   **Charles S. Nicoll and Sharon M. Russell**

55. As we mentioned in Section V, there is a biological basis—an "ancient call"—for an inherent distrust of, or discrimination against, "other" humans that are of a different race, nationality, etc.; this is not the case for sexism. To anyone familiar with contemporary world events, race-, nationality-, and sex-based hatreds are all clearly maladaptive for life in the modern-day "global village."
56. Charles S. Nicoll and Sharon M. Russell, "The Unnatural Nature of the Animal Rights/Liberation Philosophy," *Proceedings of the Society for Experimental Biology and Medicine* 205, no. 4 (April 1994): 269–73. In that paper, we argue that it is not possible for humans to live without harming and killing animals. Modern agricultural practices (even those that are "organic") deprive animals of their natural habitat, and the harvesting of crops kills animals (e.g., field mice) that had adapted to life in the cultivated fields. In addition, one may shun leather, wool, or fur garments, but many of the alternatives are made from petroleum products, and the petroleum industry has had devastating impacts on the environment and its plant and animal inhabitants.
57. Steve F. Sapontzis, "Predation," in Bekoff, ed., *Encyclopedia of Animal Rights and Animal Welfare,* 275–77.
58. Singer, *Animal Liberation,* 2d ed., 222.
59. Robert M. May, "Control of Feline Delinquency," *Nature* 332, no. 6163 (March 1988): 392–93.
60. Rich Stallcup, "A Reversible Catastrophe: Cats: A Heavy Toll on Songbirds," *Observer: Quarterly Journal of the Point Reyes Bird Observatory,* Spring/Summer 1991, 8–9.
61. See U.S. Department of Agriculture, *Animal Welfare Report, Fiscal Year 1998: Report of the Secretary of Agriculture to the President of the Senate and the Speaker of the House of Representatives* (Washington, DC: The Service, 1998), appendix, table 2. The total number of laboratory animals used in research from October 1, 1997 to September 30, 1998 was 1,213,814. This number does not take into account rodents and mice, which are not counted by the USDA but are estimated to comprise well over 90 percent of the research animals used. See U.S. Congress, Office of Technology Assessment, *Alternatives to Animal Use in Research, Testing and Education* (Washington DC: U.S. Government Printing Office, 1986), 5.
62. Sarah Sloane, "The Shrike's Display Advertising," *Natural History* 6 (June 1991): 32–38.
63. Richard Conniff, "Fuzzy-Wuzzy Thinking about Animal Rights," *Audubon* 92, no. 6 (November 1990): 120–33.
64. David Attenborough, *Hunting and Escaping,* vol. 4 of *The Trials of Life* (Alexandria, VA: Time-Life Video, 1991).
65. Walter E. Howard, *Animal Rights vs. Nature* (Baker City, OR: available from W. E. Howard, 1990), 27.
66. Richard Dawkins and John R. Krebs, "Arms Races Between and Within Species," *Proceedings of the Royal Society of London,* series B, 205, no. 1161 (September 21, 1979): 489–511.
67. Bruce E. Lyon and John M. Eadie, "Mode of Development and Interspecific Avian Brood Parasitism," *Behavioral Ecology* 2, no. 2 (Summer 1991): 309–18.
68. Budiansky, *The Covenant of the Wild*; Clutton-Brock, "Domestication of Animals."

69. Paul G. Bahn, "Ancient Art," in Jones, Martin, and Pilbeam, eds., *The Cambridge Encyclopedia of Human Evolution,* 361–64.

70. Wesley V. Jamison and William M. Lunch, "Rights of Animals, Perceptions of Science, and Political Activism: Profile of American Animal Rights Activists," *Science, Technology, and Human Values* 17, no. 4 (Autumn 1992): 438–58.

71. These data, as well as the other demographic data shown in Table 1, are very similar to those provided by other more extensive polls of animal activists, such as the report of Rebecca T. Richards and Richard S. Krannich, "The Ideology of the Animal Rights Movement and Activists' Attitudes Toward Wildlife," *Transactions of the 56th North American Wildlife and Natural Resources Conference* (1991): 363–71. Richards and Krannich surveyed 1,020 subscribers to the animal rights magazine, *The Animals' Agenda,* from a list generated randomly by the magazine's subscription-office personnel. They received 853 completed questionnaires. Of the respondents, 78 percent were female, 97 percent were Caucasian, and 71 percent were childless. Only 16 percent reported having children living in their home, but 89 percent had pets.

72. Leader and Stark, "The Importance of Animals in Biomedical Research"; Nicoll and Russell, "The Animal Rights/Liberation Philosophy."

73. Jamison and Lunch, "Profile of American Animal Rights Activists."

74. Richard Barke, *Science, Technology, and Public Policy* (Washington, DC: Congressional Quarterly Press, 1986), 127–28.

75. Jamison and Lunch, "Profile of American Animal Rights Activists," 448.

76. Ingrid Newkirk, quoted in Katie McCabe, "Beyond Cruelty," *The Washingtonian* 25, no. 5 (February 1990): 191.

77. Russell and Nicoll, "A Dissection of the Chapter 'Tools for Research.'"

78. Singer, *Animal Liberation,* 255–56. Although it can be argued that Singer is merely making a strong case for pigs, rather than dismissing the importance of children, the equation of a human child with a pig strikes us as an example of his disdain for his own kind. A similar sort of quotation from PETA's Ingrid Newkirk makes the same point: "Six million people died in concentration camps, but 6 billion broiler chickens will die this year in slaughterhouses." (Chip Brown, "She's a Portrait of Zealotry in Plastic Shoes," *Washington Post* (November 13, 1983, B10). Does this statement elevate the moral worth of chickens, or does it simply trivialize the horrors of the Holocaust?

   Robert Nozick, chairman of the Department of Philosophy at Harvard University, had this to say in a review of Regan's *The Case for Animal Rights:* "Our view of what treatment severely retarded people are owed surely in part depends on their being human, members of the human species. Sweeping away that consideration as morally irrelevant can only result in society's treating severely retarded people like animals, not the other way around." Robert Nozick, "About Animals and People," *New York Times Book Review,* November 27, 1983, 11.

   Simply put, equating people—be they infants, the mentally retarded, the persecuted, or anyone else—with animals demeans people. We believe that Singer (and Newkirk, and Regan) does this intentionally.

79. Dan Mathews, quoted in Ann Oldenburg, "Animals' Best Friends: PETA Plays Hardball for its Cause," *USA Today,* July 27, 1994, 1D.

80. Nicoll and Russell, "Analysis of Animal Rights Literature."

Animals: Their Right to Be Used

H. Tristram Engelhardt, Jr.

I. Introduction: How Animals Become Morally Important

Animals acquire their moral significance from humans because morality—that is, secular morality—is articulated by humans. In a number of obvious and straightforward ways, morality is human-centered. It does not descend from the heavens, but is constructed from the perspective of human persons within the epistemic capacities of finite, human moral agents. Morality offers an account, developed by humans, of how humans should regard right- and wrong-making conditions; it is a human account of the right and the good.[1] As such, morality provides an understanding of the good that humans ought to pursue regarding animals. Even when it concerns the good of animals from an "animal point of view," morality always provides a human moral account. The morality of everyday life is human in its origin and is justified in terms of human concerns. It must motivate humans, not animals. It is not just that it is humans alone who write books on morality and moral philosophy, or who discuss the morally appropriate uses of animals. It is humans alone who are held to be blameworthy if they do not act in accordance with morality, giving humans (at least those humans who are moral agents) a moral status not possessed by animals.

Because morality is an account defended in discursive rational terms,[2] it can be regarded from a perspective that need not be human: the perspective of self-conscious rational beings who are moral agents.[3] However, humans are the only known animals who can act as *persons* by engaging in the practice of morality in the strong sense. That is, only humans can make judgments as to when actions are praiseworthy or blameworthy, and only humans reflectively advance grounds to justify one view of the good in preference to others. This moral superiority of humans is therefore morally decisive, but because it does not give an unjustified priority to humans, it is not improperly "speciesist."[4]

Animals are inevitably at the disposal of humans because as persons, humans have the authority to put animals in their moral place, a place that is appropriately one of subservience to humans. In this essay, I develop three clusters of arguments for this conclusion. The first explores the moral centrality of persons, which arises from the challenge of resolving moral controversies in a world marked by moral pluralism. Against an irresolvable pluralism of religious and secular views regarding the nature of the good and the ordering of right- and wrong-making conditions, moral authority is, by default, drawn from persons. This moral pluralism is not just a fact; more significantly, it is a function of the limitations of our moral knowledge. Content-full, canonical, morally normative conclusions cannot be secured from sound rational arguments unless one grants initial premises or moral perspectives that can only be secured by engaging in question-begging or in an infinite regress. Given these circumstances, general secular moral authority must, by default, be drawn from the consent of persons, from their agreement as to how they will collaborate. There is no other generally available source of secular moral authority. This gives persons the authority to construe the moral worth of animals in terms of their contributions to humans. In general secular moral terms, there are no higher moral judges than persons.

Second, I will argue that the self-conscious experience of pleasures and pains by humans achieves a richness and depth not available to animals. This argument involves a quasi-phenomenological defense of the qualitative priority of human pleasures, pains, and experiences over those of animals; by a "quasi-phenomenological defense," I mean a defense based on a description of the greater moral significance and complexity of the pains and pleasures experienced by moral agents. By being placed not just within the self-conscious memory of a moral agent, but also by being nested within moral life projects and within narratives generally, human experiences take on a depth and undergo a qualitative transformation. Through this transformation, human pains and pleasures are reflectively anticipated, recalled, interpreted, placed within moral contexts, and given a quality of significance unavailable to animals. This transformation finds its full realization when all pains and pleasures are regarded within the perspective of a culture. Insofar as this culture is sustained by and/or derives goods from the use of animals, that use will have a positive significance. This leads to a presumptively positive moral assessment of all nonmalevolent uses of animals, whether as experimental subjects, objects of the hunt, or as denizens of wildlife areas. The embrace of a culture also makes it licit to affirm what will appear to many to be a form of speciesism. One can give preference to humans simply because they are humans. One can give preference to humans who are not moral agents (e.g., human fetuses and infants) over animals that are cognitively more able (e.g., adult great apes) simply because the members of the former group are human, because of their role in human culture, and because of their importance for humans who are moral agents.

Finally, I will develop the argument for the special status of humans as moral agents by using a quasi-Kantian exposition of the centrality of moral agents; this centrality, I argue, provides humans with a moral priority not enjoyed by animals. Persons are ends in themselves, in the sense that they are able, by use of consent, to ground a general practice of secular morality. Because of this, persons may not be used merely as means—that is, one may not use them, without their free choice, in order to realize a good. Since animals are not ends in themselves, using them as mere means does not violate the Kantian wrong-making condition of using them without their consent. Furthermore, the dignity of humans as moral agents would be violated if they were forbidden to use their own animals in nonmalevolent ways. It is not simply that humans, as moral agents, are the only definitive secular moral judges. In addition, moral agents constitute a moral domain grounded in the authority of consent, in which it is possible to act with common agreement and to hold those who act against this possibility as blameworthy. In this domain, only moral agents can be ends in themselves.

To summarize, humans have a radical lexical moral priority over animals: this is the case thrice over. First, humans as persons are the source of moral authority for general secular morality, so they have the authority to use animals nonmalevolently for the good, as defined and understood by humans. Second, human moral experience is not simply richer than that of animals: all of moral experience is placed *within* human culture. Thus, the significance of animals (and of their pains, pleasures, and experiences) can only be understood in the context of human concerns. All animal rights claims lead back to a human perspective. This is the case whether the right is to be hunted or to be protected in a wildlife preserve. To have moral value, significance, and standing in secular moral terms is to have significance for humans; this reflects the cardinal secular moral truth: "Man is the measure of all things, of things that are that they are, of things that are not that they are not."[5] In the absence of attending to God's revelation, humans, as self-conscious moral agents, become the standard for morality. In this office of moral agent, a categorial gulf between humans and animals is revealed. Third, only humans are ends in themselves—only they can choose freely and be held accountable, in the sense of being blameworthy or praiseworthy, for their decisions. They alone are self-conscious members of a moral practice grounded in mutual respect for each other's moral agency. In short, the use of animals has a prima facie morally positive character because secular morality is unavoidably anthropocentric: the use of animals gains a positive moral significance through its contribution to the welfare and concerns of humans, who are the only moral agents.

Next, in anticipation of the results of these arguments, I shall advance their conclusions as rights claims that highlight appropriate uses of animals for human benefit. By recognizing animals as having these rights, one respects animals through acknowledging that they gain their cardinal moral significance by contributing to human welfare. These rights are shorthand expressions for the goods supported by the relevant practices and for the human-centered character of morality. Given that only humans are moral agents, only humans have the standing to waive any of these "animal rights". In an age when moral concerns are encapsulated as rights, as prima facie markers in favor of certain claims, the following rights should be acknowledged for all animals as a way of indicating how animals can take on a moral significance by contributing to the welfare and culture of humans.[6]

1. The right to be hunted. Animals have a right to be the objects of sport, pursuit, and the chase.
2. The right to be eaten. Animals have a right to be consumed by humans. The more this consumption is nested in the realization of complex human goods, the greater the strength of this right. Thus, animals have a special right to be the object of the culinary arts of Chinese and French chefs.[7]
3. The right to be domesticated. This right is possessed not just by those animals currently used as pets and livestock, but by all animals that can potentially be brought from the wild and made to support human needs and interests.[8]
4. The right to be bred and genetically transformed so as better to contribute to human welfare and enjoyment.
5. The right to be skinned. This right is possessed not just by animals whose hides can produce boots, belts, and purses, but by all animals whose pelts can be transformed into fur coats, trimmings on hats, etc.
6. The right to be harvested. By producing milk, eggs, wool, and feathers, animals contribute to the fullness of human culture.
7. The right to be used as beasts of burden and draft animals.
8. The right to be used for amusement. This right compasses:
   a. The right to be used in circuses, bullfights, cockfights, rodeos, etc.
   b. The right to be maintained in various wildlife preserves and sanctuaries for the delight of ecologists, wildlife enthusiasts, etc.
9. The right to be used for education. This right involves not just the dissection of dead animals, but also the use of living animals (by manipulating them or operating upon them) in order to teach biology, physiology, anatomy, etc. more effectively.
10. The right to be used to develop new knowledge. This right encompasses four general subsidiary rights:
    a. The right to be used to produce knowledge of interest to humans, even if it will not have any practical application.
    b. The right to be used to produce information that is likely to protect humans or give them advantages in their various activities (e.g., animals being used in crash simulations).

  c. The right to be used in the testing of cosmetics. Here animals aid humans in two ways, by protecting humans from harm and by contributing to human beauty and charm.
  d. The right to be used in medical research, in order to develop new ways to treat human diseases, disabilities, discomforts, and deformities.

These rights express the recognition that in general secular terms, the full moral significance of animals can be understood only with reference to their contributions to human contemplation, delight, amusement, welfare, and culture.

II. Humans as the Authors of Morality: Putting Animals in Their Place

Moral philosophy explores what it means to act rightly and to pursue the good. It must determine how one can be sure that one knows rightly what one ought to do. In approaching such challenges, it is persons as moral agents who must determine the appropriate balancing of goods and harms, pleasures and pains. Due to the plurality of visions of the right and the good, and because of the need to reflect on how appropriately to weigh competing moral sentiments, intuitions, appeals, visions, and projects (including different approaches to the proper use of animals), a general secular morality that is rationally justified has an unavoidably second-order character. Philosophical moral reflection addresses, criticizes, and arranges the various claims of the various competing moralities. It reflectively determines which moral claims govern, when, and how. The results of such reflections about morality are grounded in moral agents as final adjudicators of competing moral understandings. Persons have their cardinal place in secular morality, in part because of the controversies at the roots of secular morality.

These moral controversies include disputes regarding the moral standing of animals as well as the comparative standings of various species. For instance, how does one compare the moral standings of gorillas, dolphins, whales, pigs, rattlesnakes, and roaches? Humans, and humans alone, can assess all arguments and reflections concerning the moral comparability of humans and animals. Human primates have the capacity, self-consciously, to advance arguments about the moral life and to act on an examined understanding of moral probity. In contrast, other animals (such as nonhuman primates, whales, dolphins, etc.) may in some sense be self-conscious, but nevertheless give no clear evidence of the ability to frame a reflectively articulated understanding of moral probity. Morality is articulated from the perspective of reflective, self-conscious moral agency, a perspective that even higher-order animals cannot realize. It is from this perspective, enjoyed by humans, that the use of animals must be assessed.

Consider the issue of testing cosmetics on animals. Such testing offers the prospect of enhancing human safety by protecting humans from pain—pain being an evil that, all things being equal, should be minimized. Thus, when assessing the consequences of cosmetics testing, one will need to balance the pain and suffering that testing causes animals against both the human pain and suffering prevented by testing and the pleasure that humans get from the final cosmetic products. This will require a comparison of the quality and significance of human pain and suffering versus that of animals. One will not only need to take into account those who will be directly harmed, but will also have to consider the general reaction of other humans and animals to this suffering. On the one hand, one will need to consider the reactions (i.e., displeasure) of those who oppose making animals suffer for the sake of safer cosmetics. On the other hand, one will need to take into account the reactions of the parents, spouses, friends, and associates of those who may be injured by inadequately tested cosmetics. Also, one will need to consider the enhanced human beauty provided by cosmetics whose release would be delayed, or even prevented entirely, if not for animal testing.[9] Beyond such consequentialist concerns is the right-making authority of humans to act to protect other humans, even if this causes suffering for animals and displeasure for those disturbed by the fact that such research occurs.

Assessments of moral claims can occur either within particular religious and ideological moral communities, or from a general secular moral perspective, one open to all independently of particular religious, cultural, or ideological commitments. Such a secular moral point of view is inevitably one of self-conscious critical reflection: responsible moral action requires responsible assessment of competing moral claims. These assessments are somewhat like counting change in different currencies. If one is carrying, say, American dollars, Australian dollars, Canadian dollars, and Taiwanese dollars in one's pocket, determining the total value of the money requires knowledge of not just how many units of each one has, but also their relative worth. Anyone who takes seriously the moral standing of animals, as well as the moral significance of their pains, pleasures, and suffering, must do more than advance the claim that animals have moral standing or worth (e.g., claims about the moral standing of gorillas and roaches). He must also indicate how to *compare* the standing of different animals, as well as how to compare the significance of their well-being (e.g., how ought one to compare the discomfort of gorillas with that of roaches). Furthermore, he must describe what constitutes the standing of animals and how it should be compared to the standing of humans; this is necessary for assessing the relative moral significance of human and animal pains, pleasures, suffering, projects, etc. Returning to the metaphor of money in one's pocket, one will gladly spend a Taiwanese dollar to gain an American dollar. Such a judgment does not indicate that the Taiwanese dollar is worthless, only that it is of much less significance in the market than is the American dollar, so that it is fully appropriate to forgo a Taiwanese dollar in order to gain an American dollar. *Mutatis mutandis,* one should consider oneself justified in causing pain to roaches in order to aid gorillas, and in causing pain to gorillas in order to aid humans. To determine when it is appropriate—indeed, good and praiseworthy— to cause pain and suffering to animals in order to benefit humans, one must know how to compare the standing of humans with that of animals, as well as how to compare the moral significance of human and animal pains, pleasures, and suffering.

Consider the different ways in which some might regard the abundance of deer in a particular locality. On the one hand, certain sects of ecologists might consider it ennobling to establish environmental conditions such that there is a balance between the deer and their natural nonhuman predators. They might find the existence of such a balance to be a good that one should celebrate and enjoy. They might even hold that allowing the deer to be killed by nonhuman predators rather than by humans is a good in itself. These views may be sustained by background premises regarding the goodness of nature when undistorted by human intervention, and regarding the moral evil of human enjoyment of the chase and the kill. There are also crucial assumptions involved regarding what counts as evidence as well as which claims are supported by a given piece of evidence.

On the other hand, those who understand the nobility of the hunt may see the satisfaction of the hunter as evidence in favor of justifying the chase. Also, hunters with a disposition to enjoy venison will understand that a surplus of deer offers an additional ground to pursue the joys of the hunt, the kill, the preparation of a fine meal, and the consumption of that meal with good wines. They will recognize that deer, in order to survive naturally, must face predators. They will consider humans as much of a natural predator as any other to which deer might be subject. In addition, they will observe that humans, as predators, can savor the hunt and the kill within stories that will enrich their lives and the lives of others who join in the hunt and the meal made from the hunted. No other animal has such a culture of the hunt. Humans can even appreciate the hunt as an appropriate cultural mediation of aggressive passions.

In the absence of a foundational agreement about the comparability of humans and animals, disagreements like those between the hunter and ecologist perspectives will not be resolvable by sound rational argument. This is not to deny an intrinsic worth or significance to the pains, pleasures, interests, and projects of animals. It is, rather, to recognize that there are, and unavoidably will be, competing accounts about how properly to understand and acknowledge this intrinsic worth. The intrinsic worth of animals must be placed within a framework of argument and philosophical discourse, a framework which is integral to the self-consciously reflective character of human culture. It is this self-consciously reflective character of morality as a cultural endeavor that defines the space within which secular moral concerns are placed. To recognize this cultural space of morality is to acknowledge something like Hegel's sphere of *objective spirit*: a cultural domain, defined by persons in community, of concern about the right and the good.[10] This cultural space (or category of cultural existence) is the ongoing creation of humans, not animals, though animals do constitute part of its subject matter. Moreover, this cultural space is the object of self-conscious reflection about the claims and commitments that frame the domain of objective spirit. It is the matrix of laws, moral obligations, and customs created and sustained by humans. This self-conscious moral reflection, this thinking about moral thought, is the endeavor of *absolute spirit,* the viewpoint of philosophy.[11]

In all of this, humans are central and animals peripheral. It is only humans who, as a cultural task, reflect and debate about morality: all moral philosophy is human. Humans are also the *only* moral philosophers: monkeys, dolphins, gorillas, and roaches cannot enter into this class of cultural and moral arbiters. It is not simply that humans get to impose their views regarding the relative worth of animals on the objects of moral interests and concerns. Much more importantly, all moral concerns are embedded in a context that gives priority and (most significantly) authority to the self-consciously reflective moral life of humans. This is not just a matter of the order of justification or of knowledge, but of the *ordo essendi* (that is, the very order of being) of secular moral claims. Secular moral philosophy is constructed from the perspective of moral agents who are rational stakeholders in moral controversies, and it is these stakeholders who have the dignity of being the cardinal arbiters of morality. This grants a plausible but not conclusive priority to human concerns, interests, and projects over and against considerations of the pains, pleasures, and lives of animals. It is humans who incarnate the fullness of the moral life, suggesting that the health, quality, and extension of human life should have priority over concerns regarding animal life. From this it follows that it is good to use animals to advantage human well-being. Like the premises that ground it, this claim may be persuasive, but it is not conclusive. What is unqualifiedly the case is the radical moral standing of persons as the source and arbiters of secular morality.

III. Persons as the Source of Moral Authority

Morality is marked by disagreements and foundational difficulty in resolving them. Any intuition can be met with a contrary intuition. Nor can this situation be remedied by bringing moral intuitions, judgments, principles, and theories into reflective equilibrium. Any claim asserting that one can normatively balance competing moral intuitions or judgments can be met by contrary claims. The insistence on an ability to balance moral claims, appeals, or intuitions is itself, at best, an intuition followed by an exclamation point. For arguments on be-half of a special moral standing for animals to go through to a definitive, canon-ical normative conclusion, there must be initial concurrence regarding basic moral premises and the rules of moral evidence.[12] In the absence of such con-currence over animal standing, debates will beg the question or engage in an infinite regress, especially insofar as the debates involve the balancing of conse-quences for animals and humans. In such circumstances, the moral authority of any resolution of debates regarding the comparable moral standing of humans and animals — as well as the relative moral significance of human versus animal pain, pleasure, suffering, and mental life — cannot be drawn from the force of in-tuitions or the soundness of particular philosophical arguments. This is the case because one cannot definitively dismiss one set of foundational intuitions with a contrary set of intuitions without granting the normative superiority of a higher set of intuitions that can warrant such a definitive judgment. This, though, would be to beg the question or to engage in an infinite regress. Moreover, history shows that the plausibility of claims to the right moral intuitions, or to the nor-mative facility that can properly balance competing moral claims, is inevitably hostage to the fashions of time and circumstance.

In order to choose among competing moral intuitions, determine how to rank consequences, or give content to the decisions of a hypothetical chooser, one must always have a perspective that supplies content in the sense of right-making principles or a guiding ranking of goods. The same difficulty emerges as one attempts to choose among moral rationalities, game-theoretic understand-ings, or content-full[13] construals of natural law. To sort moral information from "noise," in order to determine the right way to balance moral appeals, compare consequences, rank preferences, or select a moral rationality, one must already have a moral perspective. Otherwise, one cannot balance appeals or choose among different consequences or select the right moral rationality. But how does one secure this perspective? To answer, one must again either beg the question or engage in an infinite regress. The resolution of content-full moral disputes de-pends on the granting of crucial initial premises and rules of moral evidence.

In the absence of a common experience of God's revelation and in the face of a plurality of moral rationalities, a general secular morality can only be drawn from the authority of moral agents able to agree regarding how they will collaborate. Insofar as one wishes to appeal to a general secular resolution of moral controversies, one must inquire after the possible foundation for such resolutions. This is equivalent to asking after the proper general secular moral-ity in these matters. In the face of a perennial pluralism of moral visions — a content-full pluralism that is, in principle, irresolvable by sound rational argu-ment — secular moral authority is, by default, grounded not in God nor in ra-tionality, but in consent, that is, in the authorization of persons. This secular moral authority is derived not from intuitions, the balancing of claims, or sound rational arguments, but from the consent of persons. By default, consent becomes the linchpin of a general secular morality that can be justified to all, despite disagreements over what intuitions should be morally guiding and what content-rich moral premises should lie at the foundations of a content-full, canonical moral vision.

This way of grounding general secular morality has implications for matters involving animals and their standing, as well as matters involving the moral significance of animals' pains and pleasures. Because sound rational arguments are inconclusive without at the onset granting particular moral premises (and thus begging the question), if we cannot agree as to God's wishes in these matters and our moral intuitions are divergent, then we must draw general moral authority in these matters from the consent of persons, that is, from humans. Humans, as persons, thus have an unavoidable moral centrality that distinguishes them as the arbiters of secular morality and places them in authority over animals. It is persons who must agree regarding the use of animals. Moreover, because persons are the source of authority over themselves, and because there is a diversity of moral views involving animal use, persons will, by default, be at liberty to do with their own animals as they wish, as long as their projects are not malevolent. To be malevolent, to wish to do evil, is to reject morality itself. Malevolence has a fundamental wrong-making character because it contradicts the practice of morality, which includes the pursuit, *ceteris paribus,* of the good.[14]

In the face of moral pluralism and within the limits of secular moral reason, the centrality of persons as the source of moral authority is expressed in the ubiquity of free and informed consent, contracts, markets, and limited democracies as procedures for gaining moral authority; all of these practices recognize humans as the source of secular moral authority. The role of humans vis-à-vis moral authority is also expressed in the existence of privacy rights or spheres of privacy, which mark the limits of others upon that which belongs to each of us. Where sound rational argument cannot resolve moral controversies, people are, by default, at liberty to act nonmalevolently with themselves, their property (e.g., entities that are not moral agents, such as animals), and consenting others, even if many may argue from a particular religious or secular ideological perspective that such activity is wrong. For example, because neither fetuses nor animals are moral agents who can give or withhold consent, in general secular moral terms women will have a secular moral right to have abortions and hunters will have a secular moral right to chase, kill, and cook their prey (thus honoring the right of animals to be useful to humans). This consistent secular morality will disappoint all. On the one hand, pro-choice vegetarians[15] will decry hunters; on the other hand, morally insightful hunters will understand pro-choice vegetarians as murderers of unborn humans.[16] The permissibility of hunting and abortion are matters of real, substantive, and impassioned disagreement.

These disputes will not be resolvable in general secular terms. They reflect the deep gulfs that separate moral visions, and they erupt in the battles of the cultural wars that cannot be settled by sound rational argument without prior agreement regarding basic premises. Insofar as general secular authority for common moral action in these matters must be derived from the consent of the governed, space should be available both for abortionists and hunters.[17] Those who appreciate human embryos as persons regard the destruction of such embryos with great horror (i.e., as morally equivalent to murder), but must nevertheless acquiesce in a secular society that allows women to procure abortions. Anyone who understands this should recognize as well a similar right of humans to use their own animals as they wish, though some may think this to be the equivalent of torture and murder. Moral diversity in the face of the limited character of secular moral knowledge should lead to moral space for different nonmalevolent uses of animals. This establishes the moral necessity of acquiescing in a diversity of approaches to animal use in research and elsewhere, and of strongly condemning systematic, universalist aspirations to regulate the use of animals. In this regard, conflicts among legal and regulatory approaches in America—and between America and Europe, as well as other countries—are only to be applauded.

IV. Pains, Pleasures, Experience, and Culture

Not only are persons in secular moral authority over animals, but a plausible account can be given of why human welfare should be acknowledged as counting for more than animal welfare—indeed, as having a qualitatively higher moral status. As already indicated, this argument can be plausible, but not conclusive, given our inability to resolve content-full moral controversies decisively. An account of the good requires a ranking of goods, a comparison of costs, benefits, pleasures, and pains by persons. A comparison of the quality of pleasures and pains also involves a comparison of the subjects of the experiences. It is only self-conscious moral agents who can gauge and experience the good and the bad, pleasure and pain, within a reflective self-conscious sphere of experience. Only self-conscious moral agents can reflectively decide how to measure and compare harms and benefits, pleasures and pains. They must do all of this from the perspective of their experience: human experience. In short, moral agents have a metric and they provide phenomenological centrality in the moral universe. Additionally, if one grants that it is wrong to cause unnecessary pain,[18] one must then determine when pains are necessary, that is, when the inflicting of pain is justified by the good being pursued. Such weighing, such judging can only be done by self-conscious moral agents. This does not give a centrality to self-conscious moral agents simply as a matter of special pleading, but rather as a function of such agents' special capacities.

It is not just that persons have the opportunity to weight things to their advantage, while animals, being incapable of making self-conscious, rational comparisons, do not. In addition, self-conscious rational agents give their pains and pleasures a context of experience unavailable to animals. As self-conscious beings, humans can place their pains and pleasures within complex narratives of meaning. In this way, experience is enhanced in its force and refined in its character through anticipation, remembrance, reflective judgment, and narrative composition. Humans construct complex narratives based on their experiences of dread and longing that expand and enrich the meaning of pains and pleasures. In this way, their experiences are grasped, comprehended, and elaborated.

The recognition that pains and pleasures are enriched by being placed within nuanced, reflective narratives and understandings of life lies at the core of the Greek notion of *philanthropia* and the Roman understanding of living *humaniter*.[19] The term *philanthropia* compasses not just a charitable or humane disposition toward others. Most significantly, it involves a commitment to a developed appreciation of the richness of the truly human, which can be achieved through an education (indeed, a *paideia*[20] or a *Bildung*[21]) and which places pleasures and pains within a reflective and self-conscious appreciation of the human condition. To live *humaniter* is to live in the deliberate development of those virtues that distinguish humans from other sentient creatures. Within the framework of a culture, persons may also convey special standing and consideration to humans who are not persons (i.e., not moral agents), simply because they are humans. Persons may licitly bestow a special standing to humans as such because of their place in human culture. Humans who are not moral agents have a special moral significance for the lives of humans who are moral agents; "speciesism" reflects this legitimate special significance. Animals are denied nothing that is rightfully theirs. Instead, within particular moral understandings or narratives, a special standing for humans is recognized and protected. Within human culture, persons have a centrality as the source and arbiters of secular morality.

This observation has perfectionist and humanist implications. The achievement of that which is most fully human, of that which is *humanissimus,* and of that which is most to be valued by humans depends on cultivation, self-consciousness, self-reflection, and the premeditated, disciplined development of good taste. Such depth of appreciation of pain, pleasure, and experience is available only to humans. However, animals can participate in this richness of culture by serving as objects of sacrifice, or by being consumed in meals that take on a religious or cultural significance. In this way, the significance of animals becomes their contribution to the cultural life of humans. This appreciation of culture serves as an invitation to value animals because of their contribution to the refinement of human experience. The value of animals can only be fully appreciated insofar as they contribute to the richness and diversity of human culture. This diversity and richness compasses numerous ways of using animals, including keeping them not only as pets and as inhabitants of zoos, but also as denizens of those special large-scale gardens designed as national parks and wildlife preserves.[22] In wildlife preserves, animals may be enjoyed, observed, or perhaps only contemplated in the wild in the mode of a deep ecologist.

Such care and preservation of animals can be a goal to celebrate along with the use of animals in education, research, and as objects of the hunt.[23] Moreover, such uses of animals, even when they involve pain, need not violate the prohibition against malevolence. As the hunters approach to kill the hunted, for example, the hunters may understand themselves as appropriately completing the life of the hunted, as assuring that the full good and significance of the animal is realized in—and through—its being the object of a successful hunt. They may also recognize the hunt as providing a culturally mediated expression to a deep human aggressive drive, an expression that allows the prey to die meaningfully rather than as a result of disease or at the hands of a nonhuman predator. Consider a party of hunters who enjoy a weekend of drinking beer and killing deer. When killing the deer, the hunters do not will that there be more evil, but that there be more good. They recognize that the hunt and the kill, on sum, will add to the good. As long as a project that involves animal suffering is not directed simply toward harming animals, it will not involve malevolence. A hunter who acknowledges that the significance of animals is primarily achieved in their contribution to the delight and experience of humans acts benevolently when savoring not just the chase, but the kill. One can also recognize an important difference in kind between a bull dying at the hands of a matador and the ways in which one might leave various animals to die or be killed, without the intervention of humans, in wildlife preserves. In the cases of the hunt and the bullfight, the animals' deaths are endowed with a rich significance and completion by being placed in human art, ceremony, celebration, and culture.[24]

Kant is correct when he argues that "[v]ivisectionists, who use living animals for their experiments, certainly act cruelly, although their aim is praiseworthy, and they can justify their cruelty, since animals must be regarded as man's instruments."[25] The vivisection of animals, when done for education or research, can contribute to the good of humans. Such vivisection can be willed nonmalevolently. Without willing to do evil, one can will to accomplish a good that unfortunately, but not unfairly, involves pain and suffering for an animal. The good to be achieved must be willed nonmalevolently. Note that the use of animals in sport can be willed nonmalevolently, a matter that Kant fails to appreciate when he says that "sport cannot be justified."[26] Kant understands, correctly, that pain for pain's sake would involve malevolence. However, the suffering caused to animals as part of the hunt, the bullfight, etc. is not pursued for its own sake as an act of cruelty. Instead, it is lodged within a complex cultural mediation of human aggressive drives articulated within a cultural achievement that uses no person merely as a means.

The variety of human interests should support the flourishing of a diversity of cultural practices aimed at savoring the animals around us. Where liberty is restricted in these matters, uniformity of law and regulation regarding the use of animals should be resisted with great vigor in order to preserve space for the diversity of human understandings regarding the proper use of animals. Diverse and inconsistent regulation has the virtue of inadvertently creating such space.

V. Why Kant Was Right about Both Animals and Utilitarians

It is not simply that the appropriate use of animals can only be judged from the perspective of self-conscious moral agents, and that all moral narratives, visions, and theories are produced by human moral agents. It is also the case that, as the core of moral responsibility, self-conscious moral agency is theoretically primary to morality. Only moral agents may be justifiably blamed or praised because only they are worthy of blame or praise. Only self-conscious moral agents can be held to be blameworthy or praiseworthy, because only they can make free choices, for which they can then be held accountable. This centrality of reflective, self-conscious moral agents to the practice of morality privileges humans as moral agents over all other sentient beings.

The point here is that, by default, deontology is for humans (i.e., their use is properly judged with reference to obligations that govern independently of their consequences), and utilitarianism is for animals (i.e., their use is properly judged in terms of its consequences, especially the consequences for humans).[27] *Pace* Robert Nozick, who suggests that animals may have deontological claims,[28] such claims are only for humans, for only moral agents can have claims that cannot be reduced to the pursuit of the good. Deontological rights can only be possessed by self-conscious moral agents. Deontological right- and wrong-making conditions are grounded in the practice of never treating ends in themselves as if they were merely means (that is, without their permission), because ends in themselves are the source of the authority that supports general secular morality. Entities that cannot be reflective and self-conscious are irremediably means: they are placed within the moral concerns, projects, and narratives of those entities who can self-consciously choose and affirm their own moral perspective. Thus, only moral agents can be the subject of a duty that specifically protects them from being used without their consent. All of this gives humans central place in the moral world, and makes the moral significance of animals dependent on their relationship to humans.

This point is more than the recognition that persons are the source of authority as derived from consent, or that a reflectively self-conscious experiencer of pains and pleasures has a depth and quality of life that is not open to animals. It is the recognition of the radical moral status of those entities that can (1) self-consciously recognize their moral projects; (2) attempt to define these projects' content and character; and then (3) resolve to act in conformity with these projects or in violation of them, thus rendering themselves praiseworthy or blameworthy. In order to be an end in itself, a being must be able to recognize itself as a responsible moral agent, as being free and therefore morally accountable in the sense of being able to be judged as blameworthy or praiseworthy. More than mere self-consciousness is required. There must be the recognition of oneself as a morally responsible agent so that one is not just at risk of blame and praise, but can be *worthy* of them as well; there must be moral self-consciousness in which one can recognize oneself as accountable for one's choices. This requires recognizing moral projects as moral, as well as understanding oneself as self-consciously able to act on these projects in a way that entails accountability. These accomplishments are possible only for moral agents who can think of themselves as free. This condition of being able to think of oneself as free is necessary to being an end in itself, and is not met by any animals save humans.

This self-reflective ability of humans, as persons, to regard themselves as free not only distinguishes humans from animals, but gives humans, as moral agents, a standing unavailable to animals. It places humans in a domain of rights and obligations (a deontological realm) not reducible to concerns with pains, pleasures, or the pursuit of the good (a utilitarian realm). Kant construes this domain of rights and obligations in terms of the sphere of rational autonomous choice in order to resolve the tension that he perceived between recognizing humans as determined when they are regarded as objects of empirical scientific investigation and recognizing them as free when they are regarded within the practice of morality.[29] In a departure from Kant, I argue that general secular morality is by default grounded in the authority derived from the consent of persons; as a result, reflective free choice becomes central for the domain of moral agency. Insofar as such an account of morality is successful, there will be a moral domain that can sustain claims about right and wrong action that are independent of concerns about goods and values, thus setting constraints to teleological or utilitarian goals. This domain will constrain the pursuit of these goals by imposing the side-constraint that persons, as the source of secular moral authority, may be used only with their consent. Furthermore, it will also set constraints as to how far one may act on sympathies for animals or concerns about their well-being.

Kant underscores the importance of this domain of morality when he argues that, strictly speaking, one cannot have duties to animals, but only duties to persons regarding animals.[30] One may have sympathies, concerns, and interests directed toward animals, but one cannot share with animals the fundamental bond that obliges persons to persons as part of the very fabric of secular morality. Only persons can give authorization through consent by reflectively and self-consciously recognizing themselves as part of a practice of morality. The obligation to use persons only with their consent is integral to deriving moral authority from the consent of moral agents, the core right-making condition of secular morality.[31] Since animals cannot consent, humans as moral agents must agree *regarding* animals, not *with* animals.

VI. Taking Moral Differences Seriously: From Pro-Choice Vegetarians to Aficionados of the Bullfight

The moral commitment never to cause animals unnecessary pain leads to justifying, if not requiring, the infliction of pain when this is integral to endeavors sufficiently useful for or enjoyable to humans. Insofar as one wishes to achieve important goals for humans that involve the suffering of animals, it will be, at the very least, licit, if not obligatory, to cause that suffering. It will surely be appropriate to distinguish between those practices that aim at cruelty and those that involve suffering as part of an important human project or cultural practice. Such distinctions will lead to condemning certain uses of animals, but will not count against those that are a part of sport, culinary arts, agriculture, education, or research, as long as reasonable steps have been taken to avoid inflicting unnecessary pain.

The very logic of these reflections also requires that one not engage in needless concerns about avoiding unnecessary pain and suffering for animals when the welfare of persons and those about whom persons are concerned (i.e., humans who are not moral agents) is at stake. Where the costs of such concerns will unduly burden sport, culinary arts, agriculture, education, or research, they can be dismissed as inordinate and inappropriate. This is most clear where concerns for the welfare of research animals impose burdens on research that are likely to retard the advancement of science and technology, to the detriment of humans. It is surely reasonable to insist that concerns for animal welfare never lead to research being conducted on humans rather than on animals, and that animal welfare should never be protected at the expense of not acquiring or developing treatments that would benefit humans. Therefore, one should always attempt to replace research on humans with research on animals. Where this is not possible, one should reduce the role of humans in research through the use of animals, and refine all medical procedures, safety measures, etc. through the use of animal research subjects.

There are ways in which compromises can be fashioned. Those concerned about animal welfare should contribute to the costs borne by researchers in providing enhanced amenities to animals kept for research purposes. Enhanced reviews of research are performed sometimes in order to determine whether a project could be done without using animals; to avoid significant burdens on human welfare, those concerned about animal welfare should pay for any and all costs involved in doing these reviews. In a world in which there are substantial moral differences, those who think that others' conduct with animals is insufficiently protective of animal welfare should either acquiesce in a diversity of approaches or make whole those who are forced to expend additional resources to care for animals. Here one may draw an analogy from debates between pro-life and pro-choice advocates. Those who are pro-life can provide funds to women who, were they not given the money, would have abortions for financial reasons. If such compromises can be made in an area where many consider that the choice is between murder and preserving the life of a human, one would judge that similar compromises should be possible regarding the appropriate use of animals. This would leave persons free to use their own animals as they wish (as long as they do not act malevolently), while also defraying the costs of animal welfare—costs that, if unsupported, may have adverse effects on the welfare of persons.

VII. A Conflict between Moral Visions: Another Battle in the Culture Wars

Disagreements about how properly to use animals reflect conflicts between foundationally different views of how animals are appropriately to be used. These disagreements presuppose different moral premises, so that those who disagree will speak past each other. In particular, any account of the moral significance of animals that does not accord a lexical priority to persons and their welfare reflects an antihumanistic turn of foundational proportions, a proposed moral revolution that seeks to deny the moral centrality of persons. Thus, much more is at stake in these debates than how one should treat animals. Seemingly innocent compromises meant to indicate goodwill toward those who wish to establish uniform obligations for the use of animals may inadvertently signal a radical discounting of the centrality of persons, and may set at risk the liberty to give special significance to humans who are not moral agents. For this reason, among others, one should firmly oppose a global animal rights ethics that would discount the lexical priority of persons and their interests or jeopardize the space for divergent, nonmalevolent uses of animals in the pursuit of human flourishing.

NOTES

1. In this essay, morality is identified with *secular morality,* which is used to identify that fabric of rights, obligations, and concerns with values that can be articulated without appeal to revelation, special moral insight, or particular moral assumptions. It is the morality that can bind moral agents when they are deaf to God's guidance and disagree about the content of moral rationality. For a further exploration of this

account of morality, see H. Tristram Engelhardt, Jr., *The Foundations of Bioethics,* 2d ed. (New York: Oxford University Press, 1996), especially chaps. 1–4.

The author of this essay recognizes that there is a canonical, content-full morality, though it cannot be disclosed through discursive rational argument: he is, after all, an Orthodox Christian. The traditional Christian understanding of the rights of humans over animals is grounded in the covenant between God and Noah. This covenant reestablishes human authority in a world broken by sin, and, unlike the covenant for the Garden of Eden, does not require vegetarianism. "And God blessed Noah and his sons, and said unto them, Be fruitful, and multiply, and replenish the earth. And the fear of you and the dread of you shall be upon every beast of the earth, and upon every fowl of the air, upon all that moveth upon the earth, and upon all the fishes of the sea; into your hand are they delivered. Every moving thing that liveth shall be meat for you; even as the green herb have I given you all things." Gen 9:1–3 New King James. Indeed, Christians have traditionally been forbidden to be vegetarians on moral principle. "If any Bishop, or Presbyter, or Deacon, or anyone at all on the sacerdotal list, abstains from marriage, or meat, or wine, not as a matter of mortification, but out of an abhorrence thereof, forgetting that all things are exceedingly good, and that God made man male and female, and blasphemously misrepresenting God's work of creation, either let him mend his ways or let him be deposed from office and expelled from the Church. Let a layman be treated similarly." "85 Canons of the Holy Apostles," canon 51, in SS. Agapius and Nicodemus, eds., *The Rudder of the Orthodox Catholic Church* (New York: Luna Printing, 1983), 91. Christians also have traditionally recognized an obligation of loving stewardship toward animals. It is very important to note that many of the projects that use animals in order to satisfy human passions, although permissible in secular morality, must also be understood, within traditional Christianity, as being seriously misdirected. Games or spectacles that involve the mutual slaughter of animals are one sort of project exemplifying this.

2. Discursive rational moral reflection is here contrasted with a kind of intellectual intuition that lies at the root of traditional Christian morality: noetic knowledge. For an account of *noesis,* that is, an immediate, nondiscursive experience or knowledge, see, for example, I. M. Kontzevitch, *The Acquisition of the Holy Spirit in Ancient Russia* (Platina, CA: St. Herman of Alaska Brotherhood, 1988). See also H. Tristram Engelhardt, Jr., *The Foundations of Christian Bioethics* (Lisse, The Netherlands: Swets and Zeitlinger, 2000), esp. chap. 4.

3. The class of self-conscious rational beings includes all the bodiless powers (e.g., angels and devils), as well as any extraterrestrials who might be moral agents. Since this essay explores secular morality, it does not address the case of angels and devils, who know noetically, not discursively. After all, these beings do not simply believe in God; they know Him. Since we know of no extraterrestrial beings, it is simply acknowledged that insofar as secular morality would touch them, it would be as outlined in this essay.

4. From a secular moral point of view, humans are important first and foremost not because they are humans, but because they can be persons and because humans are of special interest to humans, *pace* Peter Singer, *Animal Liberation,* 2d ed. (New York: Avon Books, 1990).

5. This phrase is attributed to Protagoras (ca. 480–410 B.C.), who according to Diogenes Laertius (ca. late-second or third century A.D.) opened a work with this assertion. Diogenes Laertius, *Protagoras* IX, 51, in Laertius, *Lives of Eminent Philosophers,* trans. R. D. Hicks (Cambridge, MA: Harvard University Press, 1980), 2:463, 465. There is considerable dispute regarding the actual opinions of Protagoras. See, for example, John M. Rist, *Human Value: A Study in Ancient Philosophical Ethics* (Leiden, The Netherlands: E. J. Brill, 1982), 21.

6. This list of animal rights can be regarded as a further elaboration and correction of Georges Chapouthier and Jean-Claude Nouët, eds., *The Universal Declaration of Animal Rights* (Paris: Ligue Française des Droits de l'Animal, 1998).

7. When one considers the deplorable character of much of indigenous British cuisine, the strength of vegetarian movements in the United Kingdom and certain former British dominions, such as Australia, becomes only too understandable. Authentic British fare is often so deplorable that it is difficult to imagine how even the British could, with good conscience, slaughter an animal for such a kitchen. In contrast, given the quality of meat dishes in France and Italy, one can understand why principled vegetarians in those countries should be regarded with deep horror and revulsion, as reflecting a perversion of human sentiments. Perhaps the higher truth of British imperialism is realized in the establishment in London of restaurants with decent food whose cuisine is derived from Britain's former colonies.

8. For an interesting study of the virtues of the domestication of animals, see Stephen Budiansky, *The Covenant of the Wild: Why Animals Chose Domestication* (New Haven, CT: Yale University Press, 1999).

9. These considerations show why it is appropriate to blind rabbits for beauty's sake, not to mention the importance of better knowledge regarding the safety of cosmetics, *pace* Singer, *Animal Liberation,* 58. This knowledge is especially important for the discharge of the parental obligation to ensure that one's children will not be harmed by cosmetic use.

10. This construal of Hegel can be characterized as a nonmetaphysical, categorial understanding of the main thrust of his work. See H. Tristram Engelhardt, Jr., and Terry Pinkard, eds., *Hegel Reconsidered: Beyond Metaphysics and the Authoritarian State* (Dordrecht, Germany: Kluwer, 1994).

11. Here I invoke Hegel's understanding of absolute spirit as the community of philosophers through history.

12. For an exploration of the role of epistemic and nonepistemic values in scientific controversies that have a heavy political and ethical overlay, see H. Tristram Engelhardt, Jr., and Arthur L. Caplan, eds., *Scientific Controversies* (New York: Cambridge University Press, 1987).

13. With regard to morality, the term "content-full" is employed to identify a particular understanding of the appropriate ranking of values or right-making conditions.

14. Engelhardt, *The Foundations of Bioethics,* chap. 3.

15. The phrase "pro-choice vegetarian," I understand, was coined by Richard Wasserstrom.

16. As an Orthodox Christian, the author of this essay recognizes the very great evil of abortion, which is equivalent to murder. For a further elaboration of this point, see H. Tristram Engelhardt, Jr., "Moral Content, Tradition, and Grace: Rethinking the

Possibility of a Christian Bioethics," *Christian Bioethics* 1, no. 1 (March 1995): 29–47.

17. I have provided a detailed account of the character that secular morality must take by default, given our moral epistemological limits and the centrality of permission as the source of moral authority. See Engelhardt, *The Foundations of Bioethics,* chap. 2.

18. In the world in which we live, our concern cannot be to avoid pain; it must be to avoid *unnecessary* pain, as well as to avoid directly causing pain to moral agents without their consent. See, for example, F. Barbara Orlans et al., *The Human Use of Animals: Case Studies in Ethical Choice* (New York: Oxford University Press, 1998), 5. For a critical assessment of the shortcomings of *The Human Use of Animals,* see Adrian R. Morrison, "Choosing to Favor Animals," *Science* 283, no. 5399 (January 8, 1999): 181.

19. For a detailed examination of these points, see H. Tristram Engelhardt, Jr., *Bioethics and Secular Humanism: The Search for a Common Morality* (Philadelphia: Trinity Press International, 1991). See also Franz Beckmann, *Humanitas* (Münster, Germany: Aschendorff, 1952); and Heinz Haffter, "Die römische Humanitas," in Hans Oppermann, ed., *Römische Wertbegriffe* (Darmstadt, Germany: Wissenschaftliche Buchgesellschaft, 1983), 468–82.

20. *Paideia* originally identified the rearing of children. It came to take on a rich sense of education and formation in the culture and learning of the Greco-Roman world. In particular, the concept focused on *philanthropia,* the love for and development of that which is most truly human in grace, culture, deportment, and refinement. See, for example, Werner Jaeger, *Paideia: The Ideals of Greek Culture* (Oxford: Oxford University Press, 1943–45), 3 vols.

21. *Bildung* is a complex German term that for well over a quarter of a millennium has included not merely education or training, but the development of refinement, humane sensibilities, and an understanding of one's culture. Even in the early eighteenth century, it carried the sense of the "formation of a genteel character." Friedrich Kluge, *Etymologisches Wörterbuch der deutschen Sprache,* 20th ed. (Berlin: Walter de Gruyter, 1967), 77.

22. I am indebted to Hans-Martin Sass for this understanding of the scope of gardens.

23. In celebrating the cultural significance of the hunt, it is important to avoid affirming only European accounts. Such accounts support the European ceremony of venery, but are adverse to the American and Texan celebration of the hunt with good friendship and cheap beer.

24. The argument in this essay is developed in general secular moral terms. There would surely be special religious grounds from which one might oppose bullfights. See, for example, Tertullian's *De Spectaculis.*

25. Immanuel Kant, *Lectures on Ethics,* trans. Louis Infield (New York: Harper and Row, 1963), 240. For Kant, animals are beings that have neither rights nor duties. See Kant, *The Metaphysical Elements of Justice,* AK 6.241.

26. Kant, *Lectures on Ethics,* 240.

27. John Rawls defines deontological theories as follows: "By definition, a deontological theory [is] one that either does not specify the good independently from the right, or does not interpret the right as maximizing the good. It should be noted that

deontological theories are defined as non-teleological ones. . . ." John Rawls, *A Theory of Justice* (Cambridge, MA: Belknap Press, 1971), 30. On Rawls's account, a teleological theory is one that is grounded in the pursuit of the good.

28. Robert Nozick, *Anarchy, State, and Utopia* (New York: Basic Books, 1974), 39. While recognizing that humans have rights of a Kantian sort, that is, rights that are not reducible to concerns regarding the good, Nozick is ill-disposed to deny them to animals. However, the side-constraints cardinal to his account in *Anarchy, State, and Utopia* depend on the importance of freedom, and animals do not possess self-conscious, reflective, moral freedom.

29. In his *Critique of Pure Reason,* Kant reviews four antinomies generated by reason when it attempts to stray beyond the bounds of possible experience. The third antinomy is the one I discuss in the text. It involves the contradiction between empirical knowledge, within which humans must be treated as determined, and morality, within which humans must be treated as free. For Kant's discussion of the third antimony, see Kant, *Critique of Pure Reason,* A444–51=B472–80 and A538–58=B466–86.

30. As Kant puts it, "Our duties towards animals are merely indirect duties towards humanity." Kant, *Lectures on Ethics,* 239.

31. Although this account of moral agency is grounded in the ability to give permission or consent, it does not coincide with Kant's distinction between heteronomy and autonomy, which is grounded in an account of rational choice. For Kant, one acts autonomously when acting in accordance with the moral law; one acts heteronomously when one does what one wants, as determined by one's inclinations and desires. Kant embeds his notion of moral obligation in a rational account of a universally legislative will. Nevertheless, the account of moral agency that I present does draw on the same fundamental recognition that Kant's account expresses—that morality is a fabric binding the "kingdom of ends," the community of moral agents.

Justifying Animal Experimentation: The Starting Point

R. G. Frey

I. Introduction

If the use of animals in scientific and medical research is justified, it seems reasonably clear that it is justified by the benefits that this research confers upon humans. The benefits involved here are understood to include such things as advances in knowledge as well as things more commonly regarded as benefits, such as improvements in disease diagnosis and treatment. Even were we to concede in a particular case that we may be unclear whether something is a benefit or whether the extreme costs we propose to exact from some animal are worth an envisaged benefit, some version of this *argument from benefit* appears to underlie all attempts to justify animal experimentation in science and medicine. This is not to ignore the fact that many of our efforts in fact benefit animals themselves, but I take it that no one would dispute the claim that the vast bulk of research has human benefit, not animal benefit, as its goal. Moreover, we must not think only of the short term: much research does not lead to immediate benefit. Often, it is only later, when the results of the research are put together with the results of other pieces of research (usually done by other researchers), that their long-term import can be detected. More often than not, science and medicine work by accretion rather than by individual instances of dramatic breakthrough.

II. Benefit and Abolitionism

The argument from benefit is a consequentialist argument: it maintains that the consequences of engaging in animal research provide clear benefits to humans that offset the costs to animals involved in the research.[1] This is an empirical argument and so could be refuted by showing that the benefits of research are not all that we take them to be. This is not the place to undertake an examination of the costs and benefits of the myriad uses that we make of animals in science and medicine, nor am I the person to undertake such an examination. Instead, I want to look at another aspect of the argument from benefit. Therefore, I shall simply assume that, either in the short or long term (or both), the benefits of research are substantive, an assumption that is quite compatible with it also being true that some alleged benefits of research are spurious.

I myself accept some version of the argument from benefit, as do, I think, most people. Those who favor the abolition of animal experiments may dispute that the benefits of these experiments are all that substantial, but I often encounter in argument "abolitionists" who do not dispute this fact. They simply maintain that human gain can never be used to justify animal loss, while conceding that many human advances in medicine have come at the cost of animal suffering and loss of animal life.

There is another position, the *3R approach,* that shares some of the abolitionists' concerns about animal research, but still accepts the argument from benefit, at least at our current state of scientific knowledge. Those who favor the 3R approach to animal research usually support a pro-research position, suitably qualified.[2] The 3R approach seeks (1) to *refine* experiments in order to diminish animal suffering and/or loss of life; (2) to *reduce* the number of animals used and the number of experiments performed to obtain or confirm a particular result; and, ultimately, (3) to *replace* animal subjects with nonanimal models or replace "higher" animals with "lower" ones. In fact, the 3R approach typically is thought today to help define a humane research position, even if and when adopting the approach might require that some piece of research be curtailed on the ground that it is incompatible with one strand or more of the 3R approach.

A humane research position is not an abolitionist position. While abolitionists may themselves be concerned with refinement, reduction, and replacement in animal experimentation, so long as present practices continue, abolitionists cannot be satisfied. They will still object that the 3R approach permits animal research to continue.

Moreover, an abolitionist will not be concerned with exactly how far along a piece of research is, or how likely we are to be able to come up with a nonanimal model for conducting this research in the immediate future. The thought that we may be able to replace animal models with nonanimal models for studying certain diseases is a pro-research thought, if it is also held that this replacement must await the development of nonanimal models for these diseases. Abolitionists reject this conditional approach because it would hold replacement hostage to scientific advances that may lie a considerable period into the future.

If an abolitionist had the opportunity to shut down all animal research now — whatever the potential for human benefit, however far along the research, and whatever the state of development of nonanimal models — I take it that the abolitionist would do so. Why a complete shutdown now? Why not a progressive shutdown over a much longer period, during which some experiments would be allowed to run their course, realize some benefit, or evolve into a nonanimal model? The abolitionist's reason is that a progressive shutdown of animal research would perpetuate animal suffering and/or loss of life. Therefore, a progressive shutdown, while it may appeal to those of a more practical disposition, is not typically proposed by abolitionists.

While it is obvious that abolitionists oppose the argument from benefit, it is not evident that many others do so. It is ironic, to say the least, that abolitionism has received so much attention in the media of late at the very time that scientific and medical research seems on the threshold of revolutionary discoveries that will greatly alleviate human suffering. Genetic research involving animals promises new treatments for diseases that previously were thought to be intractable defects in the human condition. AIDS research proceeds apace, with animal research playing a crucial role. One aspect of genetic engineering that is likely to have an impact in the near future involves transforming animals to become carriers of human organs for human transplants. Cross-species transplants—xenografts—that should result from these efforts will benefit the thousands of people who die each year while waiting on queues for human organs. Cloning of animals is another scientific breakthrough that holds out the prospect of genetic replacement as the solution to some presently incurable medical disorders. An enormous amount of genetic engineering in animals is presently underway with the goal of advancing human health care (quite apart from any genetic engineering in animals that has to do with food or meat-eating).

With the prospect of such remarkable discoveries on the horizon, I do not think it likely that very many people will embrace abolitionism. The benefits, real and potential, of animal research appear too considerable for us to turn away from them. Yet, lab break-ins, disturbances, and assaults upon scientists by abolitionist fringe groups are already of grave concern to researchers, and these incidents may increase. It is unlikely that such acts will win many converts to the abolitionist cause. In fact, it seems likely that acts of intimidation may well alienate moderates who strive for observance of the 3R approach, who otherwise might see themselves as allies of the abolitionists on some policy proposals. On the whole, then, I doubt that abolitionism is going to capture the day. The argument from benefit will continue to predominate.

III. Animals or Humans?

The argument from benefit requires closer philosophical scrutiny. For example, with many uses of the argument, the individual who bears the costs is also the individual who benefits; this is not true in the case of animal experimentation. Yet there are plenty of instances in which we impose costs on some to benefit others, as in the cases of conscription or the progressive income tax.

The feature of the argument from benefit that I want to discuss is this: Whatever benefits animal experimentation is thought to hold in store for us, those very same benefits could be obtained through experimenting upon humans instead of animals. Indeed, given that problems exist because scientists must extrapolate from animal models to humans, one might hold that there are good scientific reasons for preferring human subjects.

Accordingly, any reliance upon the argument from benefit, however hedged and qualified that reliance may be, has to be accompanied by a further argument establishing that while we may use animals as means to the ends of scientific and medical inquiry, we may not use humans to these ends. I do not mean that we may never use humans as research subjects; obviously, a good deal of research involves experiments on humans. I mean, rather, that we may not do to humans all the things that we presently do to animals. For example, we may not induce amyotrophic lateral sclerosis in a perfectly healthy human in order to study the pathology of the disease. Furthermore, we may not do this even if the human in question were to consent to be treated in this way.

The argument from benefit, then, needs to be supplemented by a further argument, one that strikes a deeper note than any obvious appeal to discernible benefit. This further argument must answer the question: what justifies using animals in science and medicine in ways that would be considered improper to use humans, even humans who consented to the treatment? This question can be asked regardless of whether the research is applied or pure (that is, whether or not the research has practical use), whether the techniques involved in it are invasive or noninvasive, or whether it involves pain or is entirely painless. In fact, what this question is asking of us is how we distinguish the human from the animal case. I have discussed this issue in a number of other places.[3] In this essay, I want to distill from these other discussions how it is that this issue of separating humans from animals forms the starting point of any justification of animal experimentation.[4]

IV. The Appeal to Similarity

The appeal to similarity between ourselves and animals (or, in any event, the "higher" animals) has come to be thought of as one important barrier to animal experimentation. In its general form, this appeal is as follows:

1. It is agreed on all sides that there are features characteristic of human beings, such as intelligence, sentiency, and self-direction of one's life, that bar the use of such beings in invasive or noninvasive research without

their consent. Indeed, certain types of research may not be done even on humans who have consented.

2. These features are present in a great many animals, including the main types of research animals.

3. Therefore, we are barred from using such animals in much, if not all, scientific/medical research.

What this argument is really about is not consent (after all, many humans, as well as animals, cannot consent to what would be done to them), but rather the very idea of using creatures who have the characteristics noted in the argument's first step. The appeal to similarity thus raises this question: what must be shown in order to justify using animals in research, especially those animals that possess intelligence, sentience, and self-direction?

One can, of course, simply insist that these animals do not share in the relevant characteristics, or do not share in them to the same degree as do human beings. It might be held that we humans are just more intelligent; have greater capacities for pain, distress, and suffering; and are much more able to direct our lives according to our own choices. The problem with this reply to the appeal to similarity is that not all human beings share in these characteristics to the same degree. What, then, do we do about these humans? If animals lose protection because they fall below the requisite standard of sharing in these characteristics, then what about those humans who fall below this standard?

One answer here—and a consistent answer at that—is to say that, side effects apart, we may use those humans who fall below the requisite standard exactly as we use animals in scientific/medical research. (By "side effects," I mean such things as the effects on others of our using these human beings in such ways.) Plainly, however, most people would be outraged by our using these humans in the ways that we use animals; talk of the Nazi camps, the ubiquitous example of humans experimenting upon and killing humans, would not be far from the lips of many. Therefore, I think it is a certainty that most people would oppose using such humans in scientific research. However, I assume that many of these very same people do not find it wrong to use animals in research. What, then, is the difference? What can make it wrong to use (certain) humans but acceptable to use animals? An answer to this question is ultimately what the appeal to similarity demands from us.

In short, the argument from benefit cannot stand alone as a justification of animal experimentation; alone, it would also justify human experimentation, or at least experimentation on certain humans. It must be accompanied, therefore, by a further argument, one that has the effect of explaining and justifying why it would be wrong to use humans—any humans—in order to obtain the benefits in question. This in turn demands that we have some answer, other than the consistent response noted above, to the appeal to similarity. This, I submit, is the starting point from which any justification of animal experimentation must begin if it relies, even in part, on the argument from benefit. This starting point has to do not with animals, but with humans. Even someone who has no interest in animal-welfare issues at all must nevertheless begin here if he relies upon the argument from benefit and accepts that both humans and animals share in the characteristics around which one may generate some claim of nonuse.

V. An Assumption about Humans

It is true, of course, that the appeal to similarity depends upon a crucial assumption, an assumption that those who make use of the appeal nevertheless seem justified in making. This is the assumption (which might be called the *characteristics claim*) that, for any characteristic around which one formulates the appeal, humans will be found who (1) lack the characteristic altogether, (2) lack it to a degree such that they are not protected from being used in scientific/medical experiments, or (3) lack it to a degree such that some animals have it to a greater degree. For example, it seems undeniably true that chimps give evidence of being more intelligent than many severely mentally subnormal humans, more sentient than anencephalic infants (infants born without a brain), and more able to direct their lives than humans in the final stages of Alzheimer's disease or senile dementia. Indeed, depending upon the characteristics selected and the humans under consideration, many animals, of many different species, will display levels of the characteristics higher than those found in some humans.

The only characteristic that seems unquestionably to favor humans, no matter what their condition or quality of life, is that of having had two human parents (in the near future, cloning may well call this characteristic into question). It is unclear, however, why this characteristic would be relevant. Having human parents could matter in one sense, at least if they objected to what was to be done to their offspring, but it is hard to see why having human parents matters in any deeper sense. The nature of one's parentage says nothing about one's present quality of life; one's intelligence; one's capacity for pain, distress, and suffering; one's ability to direct one's own life; etc. These characteristics seem more like the things that could serve to distinguish a human life as something that may not be treated in the way that we presently treat animal lives. This is because these characteristics say something not about what produced a life, but rather about the life being lived, about the nature and quality of that life. Thus, while it is true that anencephalic infants have human parents, the nature and quality of their lives nevertheless seem, by all reasonable standards, to be far worse than the lives of numerous ordinary animals. The same seems true of people in the final throes of AIDS, Alzheimer's disease, Lou Gehrig's disease, Huntington's disease, and so on.

In short, the appeal to similarity depends upon an assumption that, though it can be overturned, nevertheless appears to be very plausible. If we pick any characteristic around which to formulate the appeal, we seem inevitably doomed to come across some humans who lack that characteristic and some animals who, to a greater or lesser degree, have it. The result is a dilemma of a painful, unhappy kind: either we use humans as well as animals in order to obtain the benefits of research—since some humans fall outside the class of those having the relevant characteristic—or we use neither humans nor these animals that possess the characteristic and fall into the class of the protected. Given this dilemma, the case for opposing experimentation in science and medicine that uses the typical animal subjects is stronger than usually imagined, and it is salutary to be aware of this. However, if the benefits of scientific/medical research are everything we think them to be, then we can see how the first option, allowing the use of some humans as well as animals, is bound to seem the lesser of the two evils to some people. Those to whom this occurs are not Hitlers in the making; rather, they are simply those who employ the argument from benefit but are unable to separate human cases from animal cases in a morally significant way.[5]

It should be obvious now why the search for distinguishing characteristics that are very strongly cognitive, such that their use would exclude all animals from the class of protected beings, is doomed to failure. If such criteria were identified, the number of humans who would fall outside the protected class seems certain to increase, depending upon how sophisticated a set of cognitive tasks one selects as the screening characteristics. Making the cognitive task less sophisticated, in order to protect as many humans as possible, creates the risk that some animals will be included within the protected class, even as some humans fall outside it.

Notice, in turn, why the answer cannot be simply to grant that *some* animals fall within the protected class and so are unavailable for experiments. On the one hand, this extends the reach of antivivisectionism, thus compromising what the argument from benefit contends are the substantial benefits of research. On the other hand, and more importantly, we would be placed in the unenviable moral position of arguing for the protection of some animals from experimentation while leaving some humans unprotected.

Thus, if we go down the path of trying to find some characteristic or set of characteristics, including cognitive ones, that separates us from animals and provides a ground for treating us differently from them, we find a problem that has nothing per se to do with animals. Do we use the humans who fall outside the protected class in the same way that we use animals, side effects apart? Or do we protect these humans on some other ground, one that bars the inclusion of any animals within the protected class and that can plausibly be maintained to anchor a difference in treatment? What, then, is this ground?

VI. The Appeal to Abstractions and the Judeo-Christian Ethic

At this point, it is very tempting, in order to avoid the apparent dead end of manipulating the characteristics claim as a way of escaping the seeming grip of the argument from similarity, to opt for something more abstract. For example, one such abstraction is the claim that humans possess moral rights not to be treated in certain ways, but animals do not. Another is the claim that our cultural, social, and moral traditions just do not allow us to use humans as we use animals, no matter what characteristics those humans may have or lack. Yet another claim is that we may permissibly show partiality toward our own kind, including members of that kind whose lives are radically deficient both in quality and in the abilities and capacities that are characteristic of human life.

Each of these claims has its own difficulties, which I shall briefly identify in a moment, but the really interesting point is that in each case this move toward abstraction does not in fact move us away from appealing to some preferred characteristic (or set of characteristics) at all. For example, the appeal to rights cannot get off the ground until one specifies the characteristic(s) in virtue of which humans, but not animals, have moral rights. Here again, one must indicate how we are to regard the cases of those humans who lack the characteristic(s) in question. Moreover, an appeal to specifically "human rights" is no improvement, since if this does not mean that the operative characteristic is simply that of having two human parents, then one needs to specify what will count as the desideratum by which we have specifically "human" rights. It cannot be the case, for example, that we have a specifically "human" right not to be tortured, because if the possession of that right depends even in part upon the ability to feel pain, then animals that possess this characteristic would qualify for the right.

The appeal to our cultural, social, and moral traditions is also problematic, though in a slightly more complicated way. It makes perfect sense to say that our cultural, social, and moral traditions bar us from using humans as we use animals. What underlies this claim, I think, are two ideas: that animals are not members of the moral community, and that their lives have little or no value. It is quite clear that these two ideas would indeed mark off a sharp moral difference between humans and animals. Behind these two ideas, of course, lies the Judeo-Christian ethic, which traditionally has held that there is a sharp difference between humans and animals.

If animals are not members of the moral community, then what we do to them, including using them in invasive research and inflicting pain and suffering upon them, is of little moral concern. (Using animals in malevolent ways would still be morally objectionable, but for reasons to do with what such treatment shows about the person treating animals in this way.) If the lives of animals have little or no value, then the destruction of those lives in the course of research cannot be of great moment. This idea of a sharp difference between humans and animals, however, leads us directly back to the characteristics claim. In virtue of *what* do humans belong in the moral community? In virtue of *what* are human lives of more value? Again, we find ourselves in a search for that characteristic or set of characteristics that distinguishes all humans from all animals such that it can plausibly be held to be the basis for treating humans and animals differently.

Moreover, as we learn more about animals, whether in captivity or in the wild, any sharp break between them and ourselves becomes more questionable. Especially (though not exclusively) in primates, the picture that seems more in order is one that portrays a continuum of abilities and capacities. Worse yet, as we learn more about the massive and progressive deterioration in the quality of some human lives, and as we find humans in conditions in which they can do little, if any, of what a chimp can do, a sharp break between ourselves and animals becomes even more doubtful. Besides, there is the sheer convenience of it all, of how our religious ethic has advantaged ourselves.

Distinguishing humans from animals through the use of tradition is not problematic merely due to concerns raised by the characteristics claim. Today, we cannot take the religious underpinning of the ideas underlying our "tradition" as common ground. In our pluralistic society, in addition to people of different religious faiths—some of whom include animals within the moral community and believe that their lives have value—we find people of no religious faith whatsoever. This latter group has grown larger, and even those who proffer a religious ethic tend to do so today in terms that are less eschatological than humanistic: by focusing less on divine judgments and more on distinctly human goods and human flourishing.

The idea that all humans but no animals are made "in the image and likeness of God" just does not seem as persuasive today as it used to be. The idea that all humans but no animals possess an immortal soul is not even agreed to by all religions, and the thought that all human but no animal life is sacrosanct has similar problems.

Though it is ultimately untenable, the attempt to invoke the Almighty to salvage the benefit argument does have its attractions. Since the characteristics claim does not work as a refutation of the similarity argument, it is tempting to appeal to the Almighty. This appeal has the effect of including all humans and excluding all animals from the protected class of those who cannot be used in scientific experiments. Since absolutely all humans were made "in the image and likeness of God," possessed of an immortal soul, all had lives that were held sacrosanct. Precisely what God did, then, was to provide a ground for the nonuse of humans in experiments by showing that all humans, whatever their condition and quality of life, shared in a characteristic that animals did not possess. Humans were, if I may put it this way, God's preferred creature. In our more secular age, any such assumption of our preferred status is precisely what has been thrown into question.

As for showing partiality to "our own kind," this in essence leaves up to each of us the determination of "our own kind," and if I were to pick the characteristics "white," "heterosexual," and "male" to define my own kind, presumably there would be many who object. So why is it any more justifiable to identify "our own kind" with characteristics specifically preferred for their potential ability to exclude animals?

VII. Use and Quality of Life

I have argued elsewhere that these ideas underlying the Judeo-Christian ethic must be rejected: animals are indeed members of the moral community, they have moral standing in their own right, and their lives do indeed have significant value (though not the value of normal adult human life).[6] If it is thought that the argument in favor of experimentation starts by denying animals moral standing or by denying that their lives have value, then I think that this strategy must be rejected. I see no way of denying either proposition. How, then, does the argument for experimentation get underway?

As I noted in the previous section, in our secular age, our problem is that we can find nothing that ensures that all human life (whatever its condition and quality), but no animal life (whatever its condition and quality), falls into the preferred class of nonuse. Secular attempts to replace God as the guarantor of the preferred status of humans have not proved successful. They inevitably involve us, yet again, in the search for some magical characteristic that can both separate humans from animals and be a plausible candidate upon which to hang a difference in treatment.

Suppose one can save either one's faithful dog, who has rendered long and valuable service, or some human whom one does not know. If one saves the dog, has one done something wrong? Is there a sense in which one *must* prefer human beings over animals, if one is to be moral? Suppose further that the human being suffers from a series of terrible maladies that give him a very low quality of life and a prognosis of a much-reduced life span: must one still prefer him to the dog? What if the human were an anencephalic infant? In these latter two cases, the questions seem to be asking us for the characteristic or set of characteristics upon which we can decide which life to save, whether human or animal, in circumstances in which it may be the dog, rather than the human, who best exemplifies that characteristic or set of characteristics.

Our central problem should now be obvious. Suppose someone were to claim that all human lives, whatever their condition or quality, possess equal worth. This comforting thought, which encapsulates the claim that two lives of massively different quality are nevertheless of the same worth, lies, I am sure, at the base of many attempts to provide a secular analog to the religious claim that all human lives are equal in the eyes of God. But if not in its condition or quality, in what does the worth of a life consist? How do we assess and recognize the worth of a life? What criteria do we use to determine such worth?

It is obvious that not all human lives are of the same quality: no one in the final stages of amyotrophic lateral sclerosis or pancreatic cancer would say otherwise. From the Judeo-Christian perspective, however, such lives are equal in worth to ordinary human lives because they are held to be equal in the eyes of God. If God is taken out of this picture, then what underpins the claim that all human lives are of equal worth? The notion of worth here does not pick out any actual features of the lives in question. Rather, what we are left with is simply the *quality* of the lives being lived, whether human or animal, and the implicit recognition that, in some cases, an animal will have a higher quality of life than a human.

VIII. Similarity Reconsidered

To summarize so far, I think that those who hold that we may permissibly use animals in scientific/medical research and simultaneously hold that we may not permissibly use humans in such research, face a problem from the outset. This stance raises the issue of what it is that creates the difference between the human and animal cases. The idea that we can sharply distinguish these cases by using a characteristic or set of characteristics that encompasses all humans and excludes all animals encounters problems. The retreat to more cognitive tasks and abilities will not work. The retreat from characteristics to abstractions that would place all humans into the preferred class also has difficulties.

However, implicit in the similarity refutation of the benefits argument for animal experimentation is a possible route out of our dilemma. The appeal to similarity does uncover something of a metric; it reveals that humans and animals have a *quality of life,* a quality that can vary between humans. But this route of escape quickly proved chimerical: if only humans are to be in the preferred class of nonuse, then there must be something that ensures, always and without exception, that any human life has a higher quality than any animal life. But there appears to be no such "something."

What, then, is the driving idea, so far as the question of use is concerned, behind recognizing that both humans and animals have a quality of life? It is that if we have to experiment, we should experiment upon the creature that has the lower quality of life, just as, by analogy, if we have a choice of lives to save, we should save the life of the higher quality. This proposition would get experimentation off the ground, if it had to be done. It would also dictate using whichever creature has the lower quality of life, even in conditions in which there appears to be nothing that ensures that human life is always of higher quality than animal life.

IX. Experience and Quality of Life

As far as I can see, then, defending animal experimentation by means of the argument from benefit, which I think most people want to do, leaves us with a problem not about animals, but about humans. If there is nothing that shows that humans always, without exception, have a higher quality of life than any animal, then the cost of permitting experiments upon animals may have to be a preparedness to envisage similar uses of humans. For it seems inevitable, given that we know of nothing that always gives human life a higher quality, that on some occasions an animal will have a higher quality of life than a human to whom it is compared. To avoid the conclusion that humans may be used we might be forced to accept one of two claims: that we just do not know what an animal's quality of life is, or that animals have no quality of life whatsoever.

The claim of not knowing what an animal's quality of life is, while an important claim, does not seem to be a decisive refutation of the human-use conclusion. It might simply dictate that we should make greater efforts to learn about the quality of life of the animal. To say that we can never really know what it is like to be a rat is not to say that we can never know a good deal about what a better quality of life is like for a rat. Indeed, veterinary textbooks are filled with discussions of subjects that directly refer to or imply something about the inner states of animals. Difficulty is not the same thing as impossibility, and in the case of the higher primates, I think that we have already begun to overcome the difficulties of assessing quality of life. Moreover, to say that we do not know what an animal's quality of life is may well be taken as a reason for *not* using the animal, on the basis of some "play-safe" principle. The second claim then becomes crucial. But the claim that animals do not have a quality of life seems to me to be simply false.

Animals are *experiential subjects,* with an unfolding series of experiences that, depending upon their quality, can make an animal's life go well or badly. A creature of this sort has a welfare that can be enhanced or diminished by what we do to it; with this being the case, such a creature has a quality of life. To deny that rats, rodents, rabbits, and chimps are experiential subjects is to deny that they have subjective experiences at all. It is to deny that their lives are lived, just as ours are, in terms of unfolding sets of experiences, of a kind such that what we do to these animals can affect the quality of those experiences. Today, however, it is increasingly the case that scientific journals, peer review committees, Institutional Animal Care and Use Committees, and government funding agencies demand that it be clearly stated what sorts of techniques will be used on research animals and what sorts of impacts these techniques are likely to have on them. The scientists involved do this regularly. It cannot be the case, therefore, that these groups and scientists think that they are dealing with nonexperiential creatures, creatures that do not register anything at all with respect to what is done to them. So I doubt very much whether any party to the experimentation debate will argue that animals do not have a quality of life.

X. Moral Standing and Valuable Lives

There will still be those who want to deny that a human's quality of life can ever be lower than an animal's. I think the most likely fallback position for these individuals is to allow that animals are experiential creatures with a quality of life, but claim that animals' experiences are not themselves relevant to the issue of moral considerability. In humans, this position asserts, the very same experiences would be relevant to the issue of moral considerability.

The view I have argued for elsewhere in response to this claim has two parts.[7] First, I argue that membership in the moral community is a matter of whether a creature is an experiential subject with an unfolding series of experiences that, depending upon their quality, can make that creature's life go well or badly. A creature of this sort has a welfare that can go up or down depending upon what sorts of experiences we inflict upon it; this being the case, it has a quality of life. Pigs, rodents, and chimps are all such creatures, and this is true of them whether or not they are creatures with moral rights or are capable of moral agency. Accordingly, a creature falls within the moral community even if we ultimately conclude that it is not the sort of creature that has moral agency and moral rights or that thinks it is part of a moral community. All that is required is that the creature have a welfare and a quality of life; pigs, rodents, and chimps meet these conditions.

Moreover, these creatures are members of the moral community in exactly the same way that we are. All have unfolding experiences in which their lives consist, experiences that comprise their mental lives, and while it is difficult to uncover and identify these experiences in the cases of animals, it is also difficult to uncover and identify them in the cases of many humans. This difficulty does not mean, however, that animals do not have such experiences; because they have such experiences, creatures have a welfare and a quality of life that are affected by what is done to them.

Notice that on my view, then, however important pain and suffering may be so far as their effect on a life is concerned, they are simply part of experiential lives, on a par with the other subjective experiences of creatures. Inquiry into the nature of a creature's subjective experiences becomes, then, an important part of the inquiry into who or what is a member of the moral community and, hence, into how various creatures may be treated.

The second part of my view is the claim that with a welfare and a quality of life, animal life has value, where the value of a life is a function of its quality; I will call this the *quality-of-life view*. Human lives are not the only lives that can go well or badly: all experiential creatures have a welfare and a quality of life that our actions can affect, positively or negatively. Given this, I think quality of life determines the value not only of human lives, but also of animal lives. In my view, quality of life is itself a function of a creature's scope and capacities for different kinds of experiences. I suggest that normal adult humans outstrip animals in these regards, but it is also true that some perfectly healthy animals outstrip some humans in these regards. Hence, the quality-of-life view of the value of a life denies (1) that all human lives have the same value; (2) that all human lives have more value than animal lives; and (3) that there is something that ensures that no animal life, however high its quality, will be more valuable than any human life, however low its quality. Obviously, in the end, the quality-of-life view does not function as God did in the traditional argument for nonuse. Whereas Judeo-Christian beliefs were used as a way to distinguish human from animal life, the quality-of-life view suggests that sharp distinctions between the two sorts of lives cannot be drawn.

I believe, then, that the attempt to justify the use of animals in scientific/medical inquiry must begin by accepting what Western religious traditions have, on the whole, denied. Namely, we must accept that animals are members of the moral community, that they have lives of value, and that they can, on occasion, have lives of higher value than some human lives.

Some may wonder why we cannot accept the premises but avoid the conclusion. That is, why can't we affirm that animals are experiential creatures, that they have a welfare and a quality of life, that such things are relevant to moral standing and the value of human lives, but deny that these things are morally significant in the case of animals? Of course, the British utilitarian Jeremy Bentham thought that the capacity to feel pain was enough to confer moral standing upon animals.[8] Pain is an evil, as much an evil and a blight on the lives of experiential animals as it is on the lives of humans. My view includes Bentham's emphasis upon the capacity to feel pain and suffering, but I go further. I think the moral standing of animals derives from their status as experiential creatures, not just their status as creatures that can experience pain. What gives a creature a welfare and a quality of life are *all* of its experiences, not merely its experiences of pain and suffering, however important these kinds of experiences may be to the animal and however significant they may be in determining the quality of life of any particular animal.

Why not go on, however, to deny that even pain and suffering are morally significant in the cases of animals? That is, why not maintain that, if felt by a human, pain and suffering are morally significant features of one's life that are directly relevant to determining one's quality of life, while denying that such experiences, if felt by an animal, are of any such relevance? It is difficult, however, to make this position seem coherent.

Suppose a child pours kerosene over one of his pet rabbits and sets it alight. It would seem quite extraordinary to say that what is wrong with this act has nothing essentially to do with the pain and suffering that the rabbit feels. Consider how that argument might be made: one could argue that the act was wrong because it might encourage the child to set fire to his friend; or because it might help to induce in the child a character trait that is socially disadvantageous; or because it failed to exemplify some virtue; or because it violated some human duty to be kind to animals; or because it was upsetting to, and disapproved of by, other family members or society generally. Holding any of these views, however, seems nothing short of incredible, if they are taken in any way to imply that the rabbit's pain and suffering are not the central data bearing upon the morality of what was done to it. Pain and suffering are moral-bearing characteristics. Whether one sets a child or a rabbit alight, the morality of the act is determined (at least in part) by the pain and suffering of the creature in question. This does not mean that other people may not be more outraged by a child setting fire to another child than to a rabbit, though it would be interesting to know why they feel this way. Nor does it mean that one cannot also point to other moral-bearing characteristics that one thinks are relevant. It means only that in the rabbit case, one cannot ignore the rabbit's pain and suffering in the moral equation.

Once one accepts that the pain and suffering of animals is morally significant, it is implausible to suggest that the lives of animals do not morally count. Much of what concerns us with respect to suffering, for animals as well as humans, has to do with the way it blights and impairs a life. In both animals and humans, we judge that lives consisting of intense pain and suffering are blighted or impaired, that they are of a lower quality than lives in which such intense suffering is missing. In fact, then, what makes human lives valuable is the same thing that makes animal lives valuable: their content. This content consists in the lived, experienced life—that is, in the experiences, painful or otherwise, which comprise a life. Moreover, just as for humans, what matters for animals is not life per se, but quality of life: it is quality of life that determines the value of a life, and different lives can be of different quality and, hence, have different value. We acknowledge this precept widely today where humans are concerned, especially in medical ethics: some people seek release from their own lives when their quality of life is judged by them to be such as to make their lives no longer worth living. Equally, however, animals have varying degrees of quality of life and, hence, have lives of different value.

In short, there is, I suggest, a similarity between humans and animals that is relevant to the question of how, morally, members of each group are to be treated. This is the fact that humans and animals are both experiential creatures with a welfare and a quality of life. With this being the case, animal life has value. This does not commit us to the view that all animal lives have the same value, or to the view that animal life has the same value as normal adult human life. It does mean that we must begin our justification of animal experimentation by taking into account the fact that animals are morally considerable beings with lives of value. My view does exactly this. It also takes account of the further fact that not all lives are of the same value, and it tracks two of our intuitions about saving and taking life rather closely. These intuitions are that (1) if we have to take life, we should take lives of lesser value, other things being equal; and (2) if we have a choice of which lives to save, we should save lives of greater value, other things being equal. The problem is that I know of nothing that cedes any and all human life greater value than any and all animal life.

XI. Conclusion: Experimentation and the Argument from Benefit

How is my argument a pro-research position? I accept some version of the argument from benefit and hold that the benefits of scientific/medical research are sizable. I accept that animals may be used in such research. I believe that I have deployed arguments that show that normal adult human lives have a higher quality than animal lives. Animals, then, will remain the creatures of preferred use. However, I have not been able to find an argument that ensures always and inevitably that all human lives will exceed all animal lives in value; hence, I have not been able to come up with an argument that ensures that humans can never be used in experiments. When a human life is of lower quality than an animal life, it will not be right to use the animal rather than the human.

Mine is not a position that advocates the use of humans in experiments. Indeed, the adverse side effects of any such use, especially on those humans who are the weakest among us, are likely to be considerable, and my position would be strongly sensitive to these concerns. Yet however sensitive to these side effects we may be, the fact remains that the argument from benefit, if the benefits in question are all that science and medicine would have us believe and are as desired by the public as the media suggests, seems to demand that we proceed with experimentation and obtain the benefits. My doubt about the argument from benefit, then, is precisely this: I want to realize the benefits, just as other people do, but I can see no way of doing so without it coming into plain view that some humans will be put at risk as potential experimental subjects. In other words, I have found nothing to take the place that God played in the traditional argument: nothing to provide the comforting assurance that humans are the preferred creatures on Earth whose lives are the only ones that are morally considerable and valuable.

I am well aware, of course, that most people will find this starting point for the justification of animal experimentation to be very unpalatable. But I know of nothing that enables us to avoid it if we rely upon the argument from benefit. Failing to find some justification for why it is that the preferred class of nonuse includes any and all humans but no animals, my position is ineluctable, however unappealing it might be.

Finding my view extremely distasteful, many may respond by renewing the search for what makes us unique, for what confers on us the preferred status that we enjoyed under the traditional argument. But how, exactly, will they do this? As far as I can see, their only recourse is to generate yet more abstractions in the search for one that gives us the desired result. It remains to be seen whether or not the next generation of abstractions will be any more tenable than their predecessors.

Some will conclude that my position vis-à-vis impaired humans is so objectionable that my argument is tantamount to a rejection of animal experimentation. I don't see it that way. For me, the crucial question is: will we decide to forgo the benefits that scientific and medical research promise? It is hard to imagine that we will. Hence, we are faced with the problem over humans.

Notice another ploy that might be tried to evade my argument, and how it too goes astray. It might be argued that there are not enough anencephalic infants, or enough people in the final throes of devastating illnesses, to provide anything like the total number of research subjects that we can presently find in the animal kingdom. But the issue posed by my position is not about replacement of animals by humans; instead, it is about our need to come to terms with the issue of human use. It is a moral question, not a practical one. If we are going to use animals, the argument that I have raised in this essay seems to require that we at least be prepared to use certain humans as well, depending upon their respective qualities of life. Can we bring ourselves to do this?

One final ploy might be devised. It might be said that if a quality-of-life argument lands us at my unpalatable conclusion, then I have inadvertently discredited quality of life as the determiner of the value of a life. Yet every hospital in the land uses quality-of-life considerations in making all kinds of judgments, including life-or-death judgments. Hospitals use such considerations constantly in human health care, including situations in which they decide who will receive treatment and of what sort, who will be saved, and who left to nature's course. If quality-of-life is ubiquitous in making health care decisions for humans, how can it be sundered from medicine's bedrock—experimentation? Clearly, it cannot.

NOTES

1. I shall not discuss one of the most common permutations of the argument from benefit, namely, that the subject who bears the costs is the subject who benefits (e.g., as when we subject a child to work by a dentist).

2. The 3R approach emerges from the work of William Russell and Rex Burch. See W. M. S. Russell and R. L. Burch, *The Principles of Humane Experimental Technique* (London: Methuen, 1959). The three components of the approach are much discussed in animal research today, and are frequently portrayed among the goals of such research. However, they are not endorsed by all scientists.

3. See, e.g., my *Interests and Rights: The Case against Animals* (Oxford: Clarendon Press, 1980); *Rights, Killing, and Suffering: Moral Vegetarianism and Applied Ethics* (Oxford: Basil Blackwell, 1983); "Vivisection, Medicine, and Morals," in Tom Regan and Peter Singer, eds., *Animal Rights and Human Obligations,* 2d ed. (Englewood Cliffs, NJ: Prentice-Hall, 1989), 223–36; and "Moral Standing, the Value of Lives, and Speciesism," *Between the Species* 4, no. 3 (Summer 1988): 191–201.

4. In what follows, I draw upon my papers "Ethics, Animals, and Scientific Inquiry," forthcoming; and "Moral Standing, Moral Community, and the Value of Human and Animal Life," forthcoming in *Between the Species*.

5. It might be held that the above argument shows only that we may not use animals that have the characteristics selected as the relevant ones—that, in other words, we are free to use animals that lack these characteristics. But the usual experimental animals, such as rodents, seem obviously encompassed by certain characteristics (e.g., sentience) around which the argument can be formulated, whereas those creatures that lack the characteristics are hardly likely to serve as animal models for human treatments.

6. See, e.g., my "The Ethics of the Search for Benefits: Animal Experimentation in Medicine," in Raanon Gillon, ed., *Principles of Health Care Ethics* (New York: John Wiley, 1993); "The Ethics of Using Animals for Human Benefit," in T. B. Mepham, G. A. Tucker, and J. Wiseman, eds., *Issues in Agricultural Bioethics* (Nottingham, UK: University of Nottingham Press, 1995), 335–44; "Medicine, Animal Experimentation, and the Moral Problem of Unfortunate Humans," *Social Philosophy and Policy* 13, no. 2 (Summer 1996): 181–211; "Moral Community and Animal Research in Medicine," *Ethics and Behavior* 7, no. 2 (1997): 123–36; and "Organs for Transplant: Animals, Moral Standing, and One View of the Ethics of Xenotransplantation," in Alan Holland and Andrew Johnson, eds., *Animal Biotechnology and Ethics* (London: Chapman and Hall, 1998), 190–208.

7. See the material referred to in notes 3, 4, and 6.

8. Jeremy Bentham, *The Principles of Morals and Legislation* (London: Methuen, 1982), chap. 17, sec. 1.

Contributors

Ellen Frankel Paul is Deputy Director of the Social Philosophy and Policy Center at Bowling Green State University, and is also Professor of Political Science and Philosophy at Bowling Green State University. She is the editor of *Social Philosophy and Policy* and the book series *The Constitution and Economic Rights,* and is the author of *Moral Revolution and Economic Science* (1979), *Property Rights and Eminent Domain* (1987), and *Equity and Gender: The Comparable Worth Debate* (1988).

Kenneth F. Kiple is Professor of History and a Distinguished University Professor at Bowling Green State University. He has written several books and numerous articles on the biological history of slavery in the New World and on migration to the New World. His books include *The Caribbean Slave: A Biological History* (1984) and *The African Exchange: Toward a Biological History of Black People* (1988). He is also the editor of *The Cambridge World History of Human Diseases* (1993) and the coeditor of *The Cambridge World History of Food* (with Kriemhild Coneè Ornelas, 2000).

Kriemhild Coneè Ornelas is a sociologist and anthropologist who has written essays on the "Columbian Exchange" of plants, animals, and diseases between the Old and New Worlds. She is also the coeditor of *The Cambridge World History of Food* (with Kenneth F. Kiple, 2000).

Adrian R. Morrison is Professor at the School of Veterinary Medicine at the University of Pennsylvania; a Fellow of the Center on Neuroscience, Medical Progress, and Society at George Washington University; and Secretary-General of the World Federation of Sleep Research Societies. He has written numerous articles on the neurological aspects of sleep and on the animal rights movement, and in 1991 he received the Scientific Freedom and Responsibility Award of the American Society for the Advancement of Science.

Stuart Zola is Professor of Neuroscience at the University of California, San Diego. He received his Ph.D. in physiological psychology from Northeastern University in 1973. His research focuses on animal models of human amnesia and addresses how memory is organized in the brain. His recent articles include "Ischemic Brain Damage and Memory Impairment" (with Larry Squire, 1996) and "Structure and Function of Declarative and Nondeclarative Memory Systems" (with Larry Squire, 1996).

Jerrold Tannenbaum is Professor of Veterinary Medicine at the University of California, Davis. He is also a member of the Bioethics Program at the UC-Davis School of Medicine. He is the author of *Veterinary Ethics* (2d ed., 1995), the first major comprehensive study of that field. His research interests include veterinary policy studies, animal ethics and law, animal research ethics, and the study of the bonds between humans and animals. He is also the founder (and past president) of the Society for Veterinary Medical Ethics.

Baruch A. Brody is Leon Jaworski Professor of Biomedical Ethics and the Director of the Center for Medical Ethics and Health Policy at the Baylor College of Medicine; he is also Professor of Philosophy at Rice University. He is the author of numerous articles on medical ethics, and has coedited several books in related areas, including *Surgical Ethics* (with Laurence B. McCollough and James W. Jones, 1999) and *Social and Political Philosophy: Contemporary Readings* (with George Sher, 1999). His most recently authored book, *The Ethics of Biomedical Research: An International Perspective* (1998), compares various nations' official regulations on a wide variety of issues in research ethics.

Charles S. Nicoll is Professor of Integrative Biology at the University of California, Berkeley, where he first began teaching in 1966. His research interests include the regulation of growth and development by hormones and growth factors. In addition to his work in this area, he has also written widely on issues involving animal experimentation; he is a cofounder of the Coalition for Animals and Animal Research.

Sharon M. Russell worked in the Department of Physiology-Anatomy at the University of California, Berkeley from 1973 to 1997, serving as both a lecturer and a research physiologist. She received her Ph.D. in physiology from Stanford University in 1971. She is currently a freelance author and editor, and serves on the boards of directors of both the Incurably Ill for Animal Research and the American Animal Welfare Foundation. She is also a cofounder of the Coalition for Animals and Animal Research.

H. Tristram Engelhardt, Jr., is Professor of Medicine at Baylor College of Medicine, Professor of Philosophy at Rice University, and Member of the Center for Medical Ethics and Health Policy at the Baylor College of Medicine. He is the editor of the *Journal of Medicine and Philosophy* and of the book series *Philosophical Studies in Contemporary Culture*. He is also the coeditor of the journal *Christian Bioethics: Non-Ecumenical Studies in Medical Morality* and the book series *Philosophy and Medicine*. His publications include *Bioethics and Secular Humanism* (1991) and *The Foundations of Bioethics* (2d ed., 1996).

R. G. Frey is Professor of Philosophy at Bowling Green State University and a Senior Research Fellow at the Social Philosophy and Policy Center at Bowling Green State University. He has written numerous articles and books in moral and political philosophy, eighteenth-century British moral philosophy, and applied ethics. Most recently, he is the coauthor of *Euthanasia and Physician-Assisted Suicide* (with Gerald Dworkin and Sissela Bok, 1998); he is also the author of *Interests and Rights: The Case against Animals* (1980).

Index